PROJECT MANAGEMENT, DENIAL, AND THE DEATH ZONE

Lessons from Everest and Antarctica

Grant Avery, MBA, PMP

Foreword by Sir Ranulph Fiennes

Project success rates haven't changed in 20 years.
Learn why, and what you can do to improve them in your organization.

ISBN-13: 978-1-60427-119-5

Printed and bound in the U.S.A. Printed on acid-free paper.

10 9 8 7 6 5 4 3 2 1

Library of Congress Cataloging-in-Publication Data

Avery, Grant, 1958-
  Project management, denial, and the death zone : lessons from Everest and Antarctica / by Grant Avery, MBA, PMP.
    pages cm
  Includes index.
  ISBN 978-1-60427-119-5 (hardcover : alk. paper) 1. Project management. 2. Project management—Case studies. I. Title.
  HD69.P75A954 2015
  658.4'04—dc23

                          2015030043

Direct all inquiries to J. Ross Publishing, Inc., 300 S. Pine Island Rd., Suite 305, Plantation, FL 33324.

Phone: (954) 727-9333
Fax: (561) 892-0700
Web: www.jrosspub.com

Dedication

To my wife Melanie and my children Timothy and Charlotte, for their patience and support while I was writing this book.

To my parents Colin and Yvonne Avery, who encouraged me to ask *why*— and then were so patient with me when I did.

To all those who have died in the Antarctic in the support of science or the pursuit of adventure.

To all the victims of the tragic 2015 Nepal earthquakes.

Contents

Acknowledgments

There are many people whose support I wish to acknowledge in the writing of this book and in my traveling of the journey which led me here.

First, I want to thank everyone at Victoria University who really did teach me to think differently during my MBA studies from 2003 through 2005. I'd especially like to thank Professor Brad Jackson, Dr. Paul McDonald, Professor John Davies, Professor Steve Cummings, and Lawrence Green for conversations during my MBA days, and more recently, for conversations and support concerning this book.

Thanks to Craig Pattison for his mentoring, support, and the many discussions we had about the book over beers on Wednesday afternoons. Thanks to Sarah Packer and Derek LeDayn for our conversations and the many hours you both spent reviewing PDDZ chapters for me. Thanks to Natalie Stevens for her thoughts on the book's proposal and introduction.

Thanks to Lloyd Figgins for the discussions on risk and adventure that we had over lunch that day and by e-mail, and for sending me the copy of *Captain Scott*, a biography of Scott by Sir Ranulph Fiennes. Fiennes' analysis and insights on Scott were spot on.

Special thanks to Sir Ranulph Fiennes, for providing the Foreword for this book, and for writing the biography *Captain Scott*—a thoroughly researched and critically important work that set the history records straight on Scott. Your book's dedication "To the families of the defamed dead"— spot on.

Thanks to Dr. Susan Solomon for supporting my use of the quote from her excellently researched and written book *The Coldest March* which revealed the 1-in-35 year *rogue wave* of cold weather that claimed the life of Scott and his traveling companions on their return from the Pole.

Thanks to Professor Gerald Wilde, the father of modern day risk homeostasis theory (www.riskhomeostasis.org), for the copy of the book you sent me, your e-mailed thoughts, and feedback on my risk homeostasis chapter. Thanks also to Dr. David Hillson for his work on risk appetite and our conversations at conferences and by e-mail.

Thanks to my friend Margot Morrell, the author of the best-selling leadership text *Shackleton's Way* (www.leadershiplives.com), for the many discussions we had on Shackleton and Scott, and for your patience with my questions over the years.

Thanks to Professor Michael Elmes for the insights, over coffee and by e-mail, on your and Daved's paper *Deliverance, Denial, and the Death Zone: A Study of Narcissism and Regression in the May 1996 Everest Climbing Disaster*. And thanks to both Michael and Professor Daved Barry, joint authors of the 1996 tragedy paper, for allowing me to borrow the flavor of that paper's title for the title of PDDZ. Thanks also to Dr. Jeff Simpson in Wellington for our discussion of narcissism in business and in projects.

I'd also like to thank a number of people for their various assistance and conversations including: Rod Sowden and Mike Acaster in the UK for reviewing my Level-3 chapter, Craig Letavec of PMI's (then) PMO CoP in the U.S., and for my conversations with Gina Barlow, Ron Van De Riet, Mel Wallwork, Frank Morris, and Jenny McDonald. Thanks also to Jeff Gardner and the crew of the Upper Hutt Muffin Break (where much of this book was written).

Thanks to my wife Melanie for her encouragement, testing of my ideas, and reviewing of chapters. Thanks to my friend Michelle Rogan-Finnemore of Gateway Antarctica for being so helpful in response to my random e-mails. Thanks also to Dave Lucas, my friend from Antarctica and still today, for our many conversations and shared thoughts on the risks and the beauty of that place.

Thanks to Suze Kelly and Mark Morrison of Adventure Consultants, a high quality Everest guiding company, for the photos and information they kindly provided me, and for the photography by Guy Cotter.

Thanks to my sister, Gaylene, for phoning me up at work that day to tell me the Antarctic Division was recruiting for staff at Scott Base. It initiated a series of amazing experiences for me, which but for that phone call, might never have happened. Thanks to my brothers, Steve and Paul, for our discussions on things Antarctic over the years. Thanks also to David Percy for his insights on business and on life all those years ago, and since—and to Dave Geddes for his support and advice during my time at Scott Base. And thanks to the management of Antarctica New Zealand for conversations on risk in Antarctica that we had some years ago.

Thanks to the Scott Polar Research Institute, University of Cambridge, for their license and permission to include the two photos from Scott's 1910–13 Terra Nova Expedition—being of the motorized sledge (Image 10.1) and the dog teams (Image 10.2), and the photo from Shackleton's 1914–17 Endurance Expedition of the *Endurance* caught in sea ice (Image 2.1).

Thanks to the Royal Geographical Society (with IBG) for their permission to include the 1924 photo of Mallory and Irvine (Image 1.2), and the 1953 photo of the successful Everest team (Image 13.2).

Thanks to the Department of Treasury and Finance (DTF) in Victoria, Australia, for their brilliant development of investment logic mapping (ILM) and the 16 questions checklist, and for their support of my including these in this book.

Thanks to Standards New Zealand for their permission to quote the definition of *risk appetite* from ISO Guide 73 (provided under license 001017).

And most importantly, thanks to all the people I worked with in Antarctica and on my way there—the people at Antarctica New Zealand in Christchurch, McMurdo Station, Scott Base, South Pole Station, Sandia Labs Albuquerque (Kent Anderson and the guys), my winter-over teammates, many summer friends, my friends at McMurdo Station, JASART team members, and the NSF Office of Polar Programs in the U.S. Individual names are too many to mention, but there are some great people out there with whom I shared many experiences, from midwinter man-hauling sledge trips, to watching the stars from Crater Hill and auroras out at the A-frame.

Foreword

During our early planning of the 1979 Transglobe Expedition, the British Antarctic Survey and the Royal Geographical Society told us they believed the expedition was hopelessly ambitious and probably impossible. The Special Air Service, who we were hoping to bring on board (to give us office space in their London HQ building), described the expedition as unbelievably complex. And on the day we set out, Prince Charles described the scope of the journey's requirements as *monumental*.

It was a 52,000 mile (84,000 km) journey—the first circumpolar navigation of the earth using only surface transport, crossing both Antarctica at the bottom of the world and the Arctic Circle at the top—but we didn't believe it was impossible. After seven years of unpaid, full-time planning, we had 1,900 sponsors from 18 countries, £29 million ($60 million) of goods and services support, and a team of 52 unpaid individuals, including myself and my wife.

We set out from England on September 2, 1979, and three years later, almost to the day, after many adventures and even more close calls, the journey was complete.

I learned many lessons from those years—such as, the importance of avoiding last-minute rushes like the plague—phased planning and constant checks on progress were the antidote for these. I also learned that sometimes it is better to err on the side of caution, while at other times it is better to err on the side of risk. Whichever is the case, a leader needs to be able to trust his or her instincts—ideally, based on experience. Good planning, good experience, and good judgment are hard to beat when you are doing the *unbelievably complex* or *hopelessly ambitious*.

My planning and execution of that expedition, and many others since, has given me the greatest respect for the accomplishments of Captain Robert Scott of the Antarctic. Scott was a leader of men and a manager of complex risks from whom we can all learn many lessons.

Shortly after Clements Markham, the President of the Royal Geographical Society, heard of Scott's death, he wrote:

> *"It was a serious responsibility to induce Scott to take up the work of an explorer; yet no man living could be found who was so well-fitted to command a great Antarctic Expedition...*
>
> *"The object of Captain Scott's second expedition was mainly scientific, to complete and extend his former work in all branches of science. It was his ambition that in his ship there should be the most completely equipped expedition for scientific purposes connected with the Polar Regions, both as regards men and material that ever left these shores. In this he succeeded.*
>
> *"The principal aim of this great man, for he rightly has his niche among the polar Dii Majores, was the advancement of knowledge."*

Scott knew the value of planning and experience, and of choosing a good team. He was also a man who trusted his own judgment, and as some of the chapters in this book explore, a man who served those he led and who could make success happen in spite of the constraints and ambiguities that surrounded him. The power of these combined talents can be seen in Scott's achievements.

Scott's first expedition was the British Antarctic Expedition (1901–04), known as the *Discovery* Expedition—after his ship. That expedition's science program was commended for its work in meteorology, geology, geomagnetism, zoology, and biology. Discoveries of major scientific importance were made.

Scott's second expedition was the British Antarctic Expedition (1910–13), known as the *Terra Nova* Expedition—after that expedition's ship. The Terra Nova's scientific program was one of the most comprehensive ever undertaken in Antarctica during the *Heroic Age*. The expedition published over 80 reports on topics as diverse as meteorology, geology, geomagnetism, glaciology, and physiography, botany, zoology, and geographic mapping. Their accomplishments included the finding of fossil evidence that subtropical forests existed on the continent before the polar ice cap formed.

Three of the expedition's men, Wilson, Bowers, and Cherry-Garrard, undertook a five week midwinter sledging journey to Cape Crozier in temperatures colder than −40°C (−40°F). They were caught in a blizzard, had their tent ripped away, and nearly died. The journey's purpose was to collect Emperor penguin eggs which are only laid in winter. They succeeded in that, and in surviving, but it was a horrific experience for them. On their return Cherry-Garrard wrote:

"Antarctic exploration is seldom as bad as you imagine, seldom as bad as it sounds. But this journey had beggared our language: no words could express its horror."

The successful execution of such a complex and risky program as the Terra Nova Expedition was a testimony to Scott's leadership and management abilities.

But I have sometimes asked, what is the relevance of the explorers of the *Heroic Age* for us today? Their ambition, determination, and bravery set an enduring example—and their scientific and geographic discoveries laid an invaluable foundation for those who followed. But what is their relevance for future generations in our increasingly business-focused world?

I think *Project Management, Denial, and the Death Zone* helps answer this question. It opens a chapter of learning for the leaders and managers of complex business projects who are looking for new ways to reduce their risks of failure.

Lessons on success in difficult environments are provided by men such as Scott, and also John Hunt of the 1953 Everest Expedition. They had none of today's management planning tools; they had to find something deeper, something timeless—courage, judgment, and leadership.

This is how we can reduce the risks of what we do—even in unbelievably complex or hopelessly ambitious business situations. Management schools can't always teach us these things, but our heroes of old often can.

Sir Ranulph Fiennes

About the Author

Grant Avery, MBA, PMP, is a leading expert and recognized international speaker on the subject of risk and quality assurance in projects, business cases, and capability maturity models used in project and program management. Mr. Avery has reviewed, overseen, or managed the quality, risk, and success assurance of over $20 billion of high-risk projects and programs in the New Zealand and Australian public and private sectors, including over 100 information and communications technology (ICT)-enabled business change projects. Grant is a Certified Project Management Professional (PMP®), and has undertaken certified registered consultancy reviews in project and program management, and P3M3 capability maturity. He has an MBA with Distinction from Victoria University in New Zealand.

Earlier in his career, Grant developed a unique perspective on the successful management of project and program risk, in part from the knowledge and experience he gained as manager of New Zealand's Scott Base where he was responsible for the success of New Zealand's science program on the ground in Antarctica, and was a team leader for the joint (USA-NZ) Antarctica search and rescue team (JASART). Prior to developing his own business, Grant was Director (Project Advisory) for KPMG in New Zealand.

Grant Avery is now President of Outcome Insights, a specialized consultancy that provides success and quality assurance advice and reviews for large and high-risk projects and programs delivering ICT-enabled business change, and initiatives introducing new organizational capabilities. Mr. Avery, coauthor of the current (2015) edition of the P3M3® maturity model, provides specialist assessment and capability improvement advice on the project, program, and portfolio management practices in organizations. He is an active member of the international Project Management Institute and the New Zealand Risk Society. If you are interested in Grant Avery for a speaking engagement or the services provided by his firm, please visit his organization's website at www.outcomeinsights.com.

At J. Ross Publishing we are committed to providing today's professional with practical, hands-on tools that enhance the learning experience and give readers an opportunity to apply what they have learned. That is why we offer free ancillary materials available for download on this book and all participating Web Added Value™ publications. These online resources may include interactive versions of material that appears in the book or supplemental templates, worksheets, models, plans, case studies, proposals, spreadsheets and assessment tools, among other things. Whenever you see the WAV™ symbol in any of our publications, it means bonus materials accompany the book and are available from the Web Added Value Download Resource Center at www.jrosspub.com.

Downloads for *Project Management, Denial, and the Death Zone: Lessons from Everest and Antarctica* consist of a:

- 10 factor table to test for *death zone* risk factors in a project
- 4 factor table to test for signs of high risk-propensity in a project
- 10 factor table of Level-3 project management maturity success factors
- 10 factor table for estimating a project's relative complexity
- 7 factor table for assessing the potential of leaders to manage complex projects

Author, Antarctica (Mount Erebus in background)

Introduction

Why This Book Was Written

I was driven to write this book because I saw something fundamental missing in the debate on project failure—something that the constant flow of books proposing better and more processes just weren't addressing. For 20 years, businesses have been investing in methodologies, frameworks, practices, training, standards, and many books, and yet our projects are still failing at the same rate that they were 20 years ago (and what an appalling rate it is). We are getting larger outcomes, sure, but still failing at the same rate. And because of the larger outcomes, the failures are growing in size.

Before we can begin to solve our risk and capability problems, we need to understand where they come from. What is it within us that drives the constant gap we see in organizations between galloping complexity and struggling capabilities? The answer is our risk appetites and the inherent forces of risk homeostasis, which hold them constant—in the absence of a changed risk culture that is.

But how do you change a risk culture? What does that look like in terms of capability, maturity, heroism, denial risks, and leadership? This book addresses these questions using Everest/Antarctic analogies and current leading thinking (many academic papers, Project Management Institute (PMI)® *Pulse* reports, multiple surveys, and books) and a couple of high return examples from the aerospace industry.

THE RULE OF THIRDS

Give or take, about a third of projects do well, a third experience a level of noteworthy loss, and a third don't do well at all. It's the rule of thirds. The

1

rule of thirds also applies to the maturity of organizations who manage projects. About a third get it (the value of good project management), a third intend well but struggle, and a third don't get it at all. Actually that last third will probably never get it—not without some major catastrophe or a change of leadership precipitating a change in business culture.

Project Management, Denial, and the Death Zone (*PDDZ*) is a story of hope. If we can understand why project management as a profession hasn't succeeded in 20 years and why project success rates are so poor globally, then we have the power to fix them. As this book reveals, the problems are very fixable.

The first part of this book looks at the constancy of failure that pervades all human endeavors, especially high-risk endeavors. From Scott of the Antarctic in 1902, to the Everest climbers of today, people have felt the need to challenge or improve themselves. Challenge and self-improvement, though, come with risk.

But what can the owners and managers of modern-day projects learn from the early explorers of yesterday? Plenty.

Robert Falcon Scott was one of the greatest managers of risk and complexity of his time. His 1902 and 1910 expeditions to Antarctica made multiple scientific and geographical discoveries, far beyond those of his contemporaries. The environmental, technological, and resourcing ambiguities that Scott had to deal with would challenge project managers even today. Scott's stakeholders were senior and varied, his budgeting and schedule pressures were significant, and his team was large, multidisciplined and came from multiple backgrounds.

As a leader of men, we now know that Scott was one of the best and most respected of his time. We also now know, from the research of respected authors such as Sir Ranulph Fiennes and Dr. Susan Solomon, that Scott's death was not the result of any planning deficit, but of a once-in-35-years weather event that no one could have seen coming.

People such as Scott and Shackleton, and Colonel John Hunt, the leader of the 1953 British Mount Everest Expedition, were good at managing complexity. They had good instincts, good judgment, and were good at leading. They operated in places where the likelihood and price of failure was high, and where stakeholder, scope, and technology ambiguities constantly stalked them. Their challenges were not dissimilar to those of the project managers of complex projects today.

With the experience and methodologies that are available in the modern world, why do we still fail? The short answer (to use a climbing metaphor) is that armed with new capabilities, people don't climb safer, they climb higher.

We call this behavior *outcome-maximizing*—the tendency to do *more* rather than to fail *less*. It is explained by the principles of risk homeostasis and risk appetite, which are driven by our risk personalities. Our risk personalities, and those of our organizations, are driven by our subconscious need to self-heal. Social and organizational psychologists call this *normal narcissism*. A little bit of self-healing on our journeys is okay—it's what drives us to want to be successful in our lives—but too much will increase a project's costs and halve its benefits in almost no time. Normal narcissism in abnormal amounts is our problem.

The solution is simple, but comprises elements and relationships that are poorly understood in business today. As well as describing the nature of the problems that we face, and why it is so, *PDDZ* explains what the core elements of sustainable project success are, and the importance of the relationships between them.

To sustainably succeed, we need to balance three things: (1) the understanding of the *capabilities* that our organization has available to deliver complex change; (2) our understanding of the complexity, size, and risks of the *outcomes* we are seeking to deliver; and, possibly most important of all, (3) our understanding of project *risk appetites* and how to manage them. Together these elements form what *PDDZ* calls *the* **CORA** *triangle*.

This book explains why CORA balance is important, and how to achieve it. What does a risk appetite process for a project look like? How is project risk appetite different from organizational risk appetite? What are the value-added practices that complex projects today should be using, but so often aren't? Why is keeping the size and complexity of projects small so critical? What is a Level-3 organization and how is that level attained? And why is heroism in project management still important today?

Perhaps above all, what are the leadership traits that we should be looking for in the managers and sponsors of complex projects, and what does the emerging field of neuroscience tell us that project leaders should be practicing and thinking if they are to be successful with complex change?

PDDZ is a book for the owners and managers of high-risk projects, the portfolio owners of change in modern business, and for anyone charged with reducing project costs, schedule overruns, and under-delivery of benefits in their organizations.

A CASE STUDY APPROACH

PDDZ makes extensive use of actual cases—sometimes in-depth, sometimes high-level—to explore and communicate complex lessons on risk taking in high-risk environments. These are not just the physically dangerous and cold environments of Everest and Antarctica, but are the high-risk worlds of modern business and complex project management.

The case study approach provides access to complex relationships and behaviors that the bland recitation of rules and processes doesn't provide. You cannot fix complexity by plastering layers of methodology and process over the top of it.

The analogies and case studies used in *PDDZ* are combined with the findings of major studies and academic research to provide readers important new knowledge, and to emphasize critical lessons of old.

The case studies in this book also serve a second purpose—they are a diversion of your thinking processes to a different part of your brain, a distraction from the structured logic of processes and frameworks that this book occasionally dips into. These diversions, neuroscience tells us, are important for learning, and as Chapter 13 (Strong Humble Servants) tells us, are important for managing complexity.

Powerful learning and judgment processes occur in the part of our brain called the amygdala. Multitasking and intensive intellectual thinking are its enemies—quiet time and reflection are its friends. Even if you are not a student of adventure or polar history, I encourage you to read the examples and cases presented in this book for the levering of thinking power that they provide. The case study approach also, frankly, is a more enjoyable way to learn.

ALL THESE THINGS HAPPENED

Unless I have said otherwise in the text, all the events I have recounted and the cases presented in this book actually occurred. I have changed some details and the names of people involved in a number of these (but not in those of historic interest) to protect those parties involved—the innocent and the guilty.

ICT-ENABLED BUSINESS

In this book I make frequent reference to information and communications technology (ICT)-enabled business (ICT-EB) projects because these projects are good examples of complex change initiatives. The lessons in this book though are not restricted to ICT-EB projects; they are just as relevant to the transformation of business models, the development and the roll-out of online services, or the planning and delivery of large civil engineering programs.

THE WORD *PROJECT*

To simplify the text and make things generally more readable I have used the word project to mean both projects *and* programs.

In the technical world of project management the words *project* and *program* have related, but distinctly different meanings. The overlap between these words in actual usage, though, can be large. The purpose of this book is not to explore the finer points of project or program management methodologies, but to advise on the higher-level challenges and risks of complex change. In higher-level discussions, the use of the word *project* to also mean *program* is an accepted approach in the profession and is the approach I have adopted in the writing of this book.

CULTURALLY DIFFERENT

I use the word culture in this book to mean the different business cultures that we see in different business sectors (health, defense, manufacturing, government, etc.) and different organizations (brand-based, price-based, mercenary, or servant).

CURRENCIES, TEMPERATURES, AND LANGUAGE

Because there has been wide international interest in this book, I have settled on the U.S. system of currency and language for the examples and cases I have presented. Apparently (I am informed), the U.S. spelling of words is more internationally recognized in more countries these days than the UK spelling.

Exchange rates vary, of course, but it is the scale of the examples I present that are important, not the precise dollar figures used. One U.S. dollar is not far in value from a Canadian, Australian, or New Zealand dollar, in any case (although they were much closer some years ago), and the English pound and Euro are not far from two U.S. dollars—for the sake of the scale of lessons I am trying to communicate.

I have used degrees Celsius as the primary unit of temperature because of its relevance to ice and snow (water freezes at zero degrees Celsius), but have included the equivalent Fahrenheit temperature in parentheses in nearly all cases because of the frustration that readers from countries that don't use Celsius might otherwise experience, particularly given the number of references to temperature which are made in some parts of the book.

Similarly, I have used kilometers as the primary unit of distance, but again have provided the equivalent unit of miles in nearly all cases.

Heights of mountains are also given in both meters and feet. Even in countries using the metric system, many climbers, for some reason, still think in terms of feet. I know how frustrating it can be when you are used to one system of units and reading a book which uses another.

THE CHAPTER EPIGRAPHS

I thank many people in the acknowledgments section of this book. Without their help, this book would not have been written.

In particular, I want to thank the people who contributed epigraphs for me to place under the relevant chapter headings. Where those epigraphs were personally provided, I have noted the contributors' names and the relevant text they have written and/or the organization they are associated with. These people are thought leaders in their fields and I am indebted for their contributions.

REFERENCING

I have cited many authors, researchers, and other references throughout this book and their details are contained in the bibliography.

This book is not an academic text or a research paper, and I have not included every date and every author in brackets within the text itself. I have, however, sought to make sure the names of all authors and their works appear in the body of the book at the relevant locations, so that their more complete details can be readily located in the bibliography.

I do encourage further reading of the references that have been provided. Many of these are more detailed research works or books which are rich in teachings relevant to the world of modern project management. Many of them, such as the works of Fiennes, or of Allsop and other Everest climbers, are also good reads.

A BOOK TO BE ENJOYED, AS WELL AS LEARNED FROM

I have intended this to be a book as much enjoyed as it is learned from. What is the point of improving ourselves if we are not enjoying ourselves while doing it? Please both enjoy and learn from the chapters that follow.

CHAPTER OVERVIEWS

Chapter 1: The Constancy of Failure

The primary message of this chapter is that when faced with a choice between doing something more safely or doing something more ambitiously, risk takers—in high-risk environments—frequently choose the latter. The loss of a 2013 Antarctic flight is referenced, along with the similar loss of a science support helicopter in 1993, and the rescue of passengers from a science tourism ship in Antarctica in 2014. The question is asked: In this modern world of science, technology, and risk management—why aren't the lessons from our failures sticking?

The chapter then presents the 1922 British Mount Everest Expedition and its tragic conclusion, as well as the death of Mallory and Irvine on the 1924 expedition. Armed with the latest supplementary oxygen breathing equipment, Mallory and Irvine had chosen to climb higher, not safer.

There is an overview of the high death rate of Everest climbers that has occurred since 1924, the tragic loss of 16 professional climbing Sherpas in 2014, and the loss of other top climbers in modern times. A reduction in death rates on Everest (per summit achieved) that has occurred with the growth of commercial climbing is noted, but it is also observed that climbers still outcome-maximize to the extent of their personal comfort levels. Failure and death on Everest are a constant.

Chapter 2: A Risk-Rich Environment

This chapter introduces the *Heroic Age* of Antarctic exploration. Because of Antarctica's remoteness and extreme climate, it has been the subject of many high-risk expeditions. It is an excellent context for the study of risk taking, and of failure and success in high-risk projects.

The achievements and hazards of Captain Scott's 1902 and 1910 expeditions to Antarctica are discussed, and an analysis of the risks that Scott took in 1910 is presented. The significant complexity and high risks that Scott was able to successfully manage are described in this analysis, along with the one risk, the rogue event, that no one of that time saw coming—an event that cost Scott and four of his men their lives.

The chapter then discusses Shackleton's good judgment in stopping 180 km (110 miles) short of the South Pole on his 1907 expedition, and the amazing story of his survival after his failed attempt to walk across Antarctica in 1915. Shackleton, like his peers before him, was very human when it came to trading risk mitigation for greater outcomes.

More recent examples of this behavior are examined, including the 2014 rescue of 52 passengers from a science and tourism ship trapped in ice off the coast of Antarctica, and the author's own experience of surviving a high-risk situation on a particularly cold spring day in Antarctica's Ross Sea region.

This chapter reinforces the message of Chapter 1—rather than consciously reducing the risks of what we are doing, it is in our natures to consciously maximize our outcomes and unconsciously increase our risks. The chapter concludes with the question, what is it that drives this constancy of failure in almost everything we do?

Chapter 3: Risk Homeostasis Theory

This chapter presents risk homeostasis theory and its importance when it comes to understanding the constancy of failure in high-risk situations, including in project management.

Risk homeostasis was first discussed by Professor Gerald Wilde in his book *Target Risk* in 1994 (updated in 2001 and 2014). He states that when a person is feeling comfortable with the amount of risk they are exposed to, they will tend to engage in actions that increase their exposure to risk. Conversely, if a person is feeling uncomfortable with the amount of risk they are exposed to, they will tend to engage in actions that decrease their exposure to risk.

Risk homeostasis theory provides an explanation for outcome-maximizing. This chapter provides examples of this theory at work on Mount Everest. Malcolm Gladwell's article on the role of risk homeostasis in the 1986 space shuttle Challenger disaster (first published in *The New Yorker* in 1996) is also discussed.

The chapter presents a schematic of the cycle of risk homeostasis at work in projects. *Normal narcissism* (discussed in more detail in the chapter entitled *Denial*) is introduced as a key driver of risk taking in high-risk situations. The principle of the *Shadow of the Leader* is described and noted as an important driver of risk homeostasis at the project and organizational level.

The chapter notes that the different levels of comfort with risk that each of us has, personally or organizationally, is risk appetite.

Chapter 4: Risk Appetite

This chapter discusses risk appetite in projects, noting that it is different for different people in different contexts—and is not the same as organizational risk appetite. Important drivers of personal risk appetite are presented.

Official definitions of risk appetite are summarized—provided by the International Standards Organization (ISO) and others—but it is noted that risk appetite is still an emerging area in business today. The issue of different people having different levels of risk appetite is discussed, and case examples from Everest and Antarctica are provided.

Risk appetite in ICT-EB projects is introduced, and an example of corner-cutting in a high-risk ICT-EB project is given. A schematic is provided, showing how personal and organizational risk appetites modify the cycle of risk homeostasis in projects.

Risk personality—which drives our risk appetites, both consciously and unconsciously—is introduced, along with the factors which comprise it.

Chapter 5: The CORA Triangle

This chapter introduces a new model of risk appetite relationships—capabilities, outcomes, and risk appetite (CORA). The model emphasizes the importance of all three elements being managed, if sustainable improvements in project success rates are to be achieved.

The chapter opens with the case of a friend of the author who was the head of Projects Quality Assurance in a major organization. A new projects-review process designed to reduce the failure rate of large and high-risk projects in the organization didn't seem to be working.

It is noted that risk appetite rebalancing in project management is an international issue. Data from a number of global project performance studies are referenced (PMI, PWC, KPMG, Standish). There has been no improvement in project success rates in the last 20 years, in spite of substantial improvements in best practices and methodologies. Management of CORA and a step-change in risk management culture are needed to improve project success rates. Examples of where this has happened are presented.

Chapter 6: Managing Risk Appetite in Projects

This chapter provides advice on how to manage risk appetite in projects. It commences by emphasizing the importance of managers understanding that risk appetite at the corporate level and at the project level are different. Organizations are urged to think *outside the triangle*—to not treat time, cost, and quality (or scope) equally in projects, but to understand what is important or not important to the success of each project individually. Examples from Scott in 1911 and from a modern day information security project are provided.

The chapter presents a risk appetite process for projects, an example of risk appetite statements for a hospital extension project, and advice on how readers can reduce net project risk appetite in their organizations.

Chapter 7: Denial

The more ego that is invested in a project, the more denial of personal limitations, of organizational limitations, and of project risk that we see. This denial is the cause of much added risk in projects and has underpinned many large project failures.

This chapter discusses what social and organizational psychologists call *normal narcissism* in risk taking. Studies suggest that the higher-risk the project, the higher the levels of normal narcissism that can be found in the project. The chapter discusses the reasons for this, the risks it creates, and how we can manage them.

Examples are presented of narcissistically affected decision making in the high profile deaths, and rescues, of climbers on Mount Everest. These include David Sharp (2006), Lincoln Hall (2007), Beck Weathers (1996), and the 1996 Everest tragedy where eight climbers died after being caught in a storm in the death zone.

The chapter goes on to explore *denial risks* in major ICT-EB projects, and the increased risk that can result when services are excessively commoditized in high-risk environments.

An assessment framework is provided for readers to use to test for the presence of narcissism and related structural risks in projects, and the chapter concludes with advice regarding specific denial risks that can arise in projects, along with actions that readers can take to mitigate these.

Chapter 8: The Death Zone

The *death zone* is defined as that region of portfolio risk appetite where the ambitions of projects exceed organizational portfolio, program, and project management (P3M) capabilities by significant amounts. Risks compound, and failure rates are high in the death zone. Advice is provided on how organizations should avoid or mitigate the death zone.

This chapter describes the author's personal experience of rapidly compounding risks on a sea-ice side trip made by inexperienced adventure tourists and their tour guide in Antarctica.

Ten symptoms that projects operating in the death zone frequently display are presented and the risk of *comfort* in high-risk projects is discussed. Six suggestions for mitigating death zone projects are then provided.

The chapter includes a table of the 10 death zone signs, and a shorter table of four high-risk propensity signs that readers can use to assess death zone factors in their projects.

Chapter 9: The Level-3 Organization

This chapter discusses the importance of project management maturity and provides high-return advice and tips on how organizations can achieve it. The chapter references international studies (PwC, PMI) that report the high correlation between project management maturity and project success.

The chapter then describes how, in addition to an inherent ability to manage the scoping and stakeholder ambiguities that characterize complex projects, Robert Scott had a mature understanding of planning structures and processes which the successful delivery of complex projects requires. Scott's maturity in these areas underpinned the success of his scientific and geographic exploration programs in the Antarctic.

The chapter references the two P3M maturity models that are most commonly used in project management today—PMI's OPM3® and Axelos's P3M3®. The five levels of generic P3M maturity are described and Level-3 is proposed as the maturity level that all organizations should be striving for. The chapter provides high-return advice to help organizations achieve Level-3 maturity, and includes a table for readers to use to test for the success factors that achieving Level-3 requires.

Chapter 10: The Heroic Manager

This chapter expresses the importance of *heroism* in complex projects today. More commonly an attribute of Level-1 P3M maturity, heroism is increasingly key to the success of complex programs even in mature organizations.

The chapter commences with a description of what a heroic manager is and notes that Level-3 maturity alone is not enough to ensure success in complex projects today. It presents the Transglobe expedition in 1979–82 of Sir Ranulph Fiennes—the world's greatest living explorer—as an example of heroic leadership, and discusses difficult and high-risk decisions that Fiennes had to make during that expedition.

The chapter references PMI's 2014 report *Navigating Complexity* and its survey findings, which recommend skill sets that we see captured by definitions of heroism and demonstrated in the behaviors of Fiennes. The chapter then assesses Captain Scott's approach to his various program challenges, by using a list of heroic manager skill definitions. The case of absent heroism in a major ICT-EB project is then presented.

The chapter provides a table of 10 complexity factors for readers to use to estimate the complexity of their projects and the consequent importance of heroism to their success.

Chapter 11: Advanced Basics

Many struggling complex projects today are either not aware of or not using important developments in project management practice that have occurred in the last 10 years. This chapter commences with a description of the value that using the latest thinking and technologies provided for Scott and the leaders of the 1922, 1924, and 1953 British Everest expeditions.

Two areas of modern project management (PM) practice noted as particularly high-return are *business cases* and *quality assurance*. The chapter then describes high return techniques and tips (*advanced basics*) within these two and related areas that managers and owners of complex projects should be using.

Chapter 12: The Circle of Project Management Ethos

This chapter presents on the importance of project management ethos—the alignment of a project's purpose, its values, the actions the team takes, and the project's strategy. Stephen Cummings' *Circle of Corporate Ethos* and the Ashbridge Mission Model are referenced.

In particular, when the leader or manager's ethos doesn't match the way a project has been set up, or the way the project's steering committee wants things to happen, high-risk conflicts of ethos can arise. The story of the selection of Colonel John Hunt as the leader of the 1953 British Mount Everest expedition is then presented as an example of the importance of aligned ethos in projects and *leadership fit*.

Examples of broken PM ethos within and external to major ICT-EB projects are discussed.

Chapter 13: Strong Humble Servants

This chapter presents some of the insights that neuroscience provides on the type of leadership skills needed to successfully deliver complex projects. Servant leadership is a focus.

Current thinking on servant leadership is discussed, along with its ability to produce strong outcomes in difficult and complex situations. John Hunt, the leader of the successful 1953 British Mount Everest Expedition, displayed a number of strong servant leader behaviors, and these are reviewed.

An important paper is introduced on Naomi Eisenberger's neuroscientific research on how *social pain* is felt by the brain—and the implications of this for leaders of complex projects are presented. Daniel Goleman's writing on intuition and self-awareness, and a more recent paper by McDonald and Tang on metacognition and mindfulness are also referenced.

The chapter concludes with a seven-point table that lists the behaviors that should be looked for in the leaders and managers of complex projects.

Chapter 14: Epilogue

This chapter presents a schematic summary of the chapters that comprise *PDDZ*, the tools and teachings they provide, and the primary areas of sustainable project performance improvement that they address.

MAP OF ANTARCTICA

Figure I.1 shows the shape and size of Antarctica and identifies the location of many of the events that are described in the case examples provided in the book.

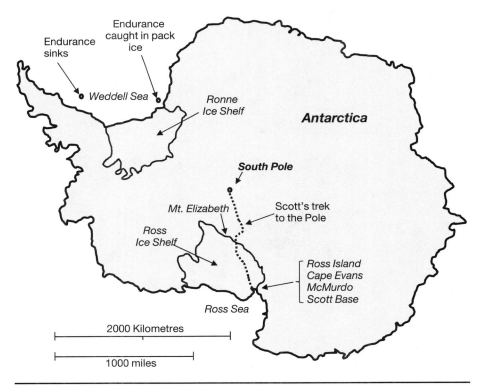

Figure I.1 Map of Antarctica

1

The Constancy of Failure

"Why aren't these numbers moving? What will cause noticeable change?"

(Referring to four years of flat project success-rate data)
From *PMI's Pulse of the Profession*®: "Capturing the Value
of Project Management," February 2015

TRAGEDY ON MOUNT ELIZABETH

At 10 p.m. on Wednesday, January 23, 2013, the emergency locator beacon on a Twin Otter aircraft carrying three Canadians from the South Pole in Antarctica to Terra Nova Bay, 2,200 kilometers (1,400 miles) away on the Antarctic coastline, began transmitting. Both the airline operating the plane and the aircraft's commanding pilot possessed significant experience with Antarctic air operations.

Initially there were hopes that the plane and its crew might be found alive. The plane was equipped with survival equipment, mountain tents, and supplies for five days. Because of heavy cloud cover and high winds in the area, a specially trained Antarctic Search and Rescue (SAR) team was unable to make visual contact with the accident site until the afternoon of Saturday, January 26. Although January in Antarctica is summer, and there is 24-hour daylight, it is also the season when the weather is at its worst. Strong wind, clouds, and blowing snow are common. When visual contact was finally made at the site of the crash, the decision was made that it was not survivable.

In the evening of the following day, a SAR team was able to reach the wreckage and recover the cockpit voice recorder. Unfortunately, bad weather and treacherous terrain prevented the recovery of the bodies of the plane's three-person crew. Temperatures drop quickly at the end of summer in the Antarctic, and Antarctic flying operations shut down in early February. There was no time to put in place the major logistics support that a body and wreckage recovery operation would need. This was not helped by the crash site being nearly 700 km (450 miles) from the nearest base that had a permanent search and rescue presence. Antarctica is a big place—nearly 50% larger in area than the United States.

Later, in October of 2013, it was reported that due to the remote and dangerous location of the crash site, there were no plans to launch any further effort to recover the bodies. Preliminary investigations reported by the Aviation Safety Network suggested the accident was what is called a *controlled flight into terrain*. The aircraft had impacted, while being flown under control, just a few hundred feet from the top of the 14,700 foot high (4,480 meters), steep, snow- and ice-covered Mount Elizabeth—about halfway from the South Pole to the aircraft's destination at Terra Nova Bay. It is believed that the mountain would have been in cloud cover at the time of the crash.

The accident was a tragic example of how, regardless of the level of experience that we have in a high-risk activity or the preparations that we might make for performing that activity, failures still happen. This is the inherent meaning of risk. Whether it's high or low, there is always some likelihood that an undesirable event might occur. We cannot remove risk completely.

We hope that the probability of failure is low, of course. In fact, we don't just *hope* that it's low; in professional risk management we use a formal process to identify, assess, and manage all the risks we can think of. But, failures still happen, and sometimes they're really bad.

In the mid-1990s, two friends whom I was working with in Antarctica were killed in a helicopter crash, in circumstances not dissimilar to those of the 2013 Twin Otter crash. Nearly 20 years separated these accidents, but both involved highly trained pilots striking terrain in bad visibility.

Three people died in the helicopter crash, but two, amazingly, survived. The helicopter, a bright orange U.S. Navy Bell UH01 Iroquois, or *Huey* as they were called, was flying at a low level down the coastline of Ross Island on its return to McMurdo station, after picking up two workers from Cape Bird. Ten minutes after taking off, the pilots lost visibility out the right side of the aircraft, toward the sea, due to light snow which had begun to fall. The pilot shifted the aircraft closer to the shoreline to maintain visible contact with rocks he could see below him on his left side. Keeping in touch with features and maintaining a horizon is important in helicopter flying.

What the pilot couldn't see above the rocks, due to the flat light and growing white-out conditions, was a 30 meter (100 foot) glacier face.

The helicopter struck the snow slope just above the face, rolled over, and tumbled back down the face to the rocky ice-slope below. The tail of the aircraft and the roof were torn from the cabin. The crewman and the two passengers in the back were killed instantly. Somehow the pilots survived, still strapped in their seats as the wreck rolled to an upright position. The winds were steadily strengthening and the visibility steadily reducing. One of the pilots tried to find something to use to protect his injured friend from the wind.

The search and eventual rescue of those pilots was a testimony to the skills and training of the SAR team and U.S. Navy helicopter crew who found them five hours later. As the rescue helicopter hovered above the crash site, unable to land, its wind-speed indicator read 50 knots—over 90 km per hour (60 miles per hour) of wind was blowing—a blizzard. After rescuing the pilots, the SAR team members were unable to be lifted off the site until the weather improved 24 hours later.

Image 1.1   The wrecked helicopter in which the two pilots survived a horrific crash and then five hours of blizzard (Photo: Grant Avery).

In the early 2000s I was traveling in Antarctica with a small ice-strengthened tourism ship, the *Akademik Shokalskiy*, when it became stuck in heavy sea ice. After a number of hours charging the ice, backing up, and charging the ice again, and with the weather helping, the ship was able to break itself free. Major cost and risk were narrowly avoided. Then in 2014 the *Shokalskiy* became stuck in sea ice again. This time it was stuck fast and a major rescue operation was needed. Three icebreakers came to the rescue and 52 of the *Shokalskiy's* passengers were airlifted to another ship.

I've spent a lot of time working, living, and playing in Antarctica. It's a place of great beauty, but also a place of great risk. In spite of the significant experience and training of most who go there, accidents and incidents still happen. Major incidents may be separated by many years, but the failures are strikingly similar as to the risks they involve.

Risk and failure goes in cycles in all environments. Immediately after an airplane crash is the safest time to fly. People's personal tolerance of risk, their risk appetite, is reduced, thus, everyone takes extra care. But then time heals the fears, and the memories become less real, comfort returns, and with it, failure.

In this modern world of science, experience, and risk management, why don't the lessons from our failures stick?

EVEREST 1922—LEARNING AND LOSS

The first mountaineering expedition to seriously attempt to reach the summit of Everest was the 1922 British Mount Everest expedition, led by General Charles Bruce. The expedition didn't succeed, but the climbers did learn a lot about high-altitude climbing, altitude sickness, the use of supplemental oxygen, and the all-important Everest weather patterns—any one of which will kill you, if you aren't prepared.

At 29,035 feet (8,850 meters), Everest is the world's highest mountain—and it's the most deadly. The top 3,000 feet are known by climbers as the *death zone*. It's so named because there is not enough oxygen in the air at that height to sustain life. The atmospheric pressure at 29,000 feet is about one third of what it is at sea level, so you're only able to breathe in one third of the oxygen with each breath. The human body actually begins to die at those pressures, and staying in the death zone for an extended length of time is fatal. Stories of people surviving in the death zone for more than 24 hours are rare.

Without the use of supplemental oxygen delivered through a heavy breathing apparatus, the 1922 climbers' rate of ascent dropped to below

100 vertical meters (330 feet) per hour. This is very slow, when one considers that casual alpine hikers at lower altitudes climb at around 300 meters (1,000 feet) per hour. Although supplemental oxygen technology in 1922 was in its infancy, by using it on higher parts of the mountain, the 1922 climbers were able to climb at rates similar to those of casual hikers at lower altitudes.

Supplemental oxygen also provides climbers the ability to think straight. This is critical for high-altitude climbing survival. When an Everest climber is just 250 meters from the top, and the prearranged, supposedly irrevocable turn-around time of 2 p.m. has been reached, it is the poorly oxygenated brain that will make the decision to press on for one more hour. That *one more hour* has probably killed more people on Everest than any other single factor.

Slippage in a climber's ascent schedule, like slippage in a business or information and communications technology (ICT) project schedule, is a sign that something is wrong. Whether it's poor snow conditions, a bottleneck of too many people in the same place on the mountain (common on Everest), or the climber's fitness or skills not being up to the job (also common on Everest), slippage in a schedule on the way up means greater problems coming down. On Everest, that can mean risk levels being pushed dangerously high.

In the 1922 expedition's first two attempts to reach the summit, their risk levels were very high. Luck was playing too great a part. There were near-fatal stumbles, and life-saving breaks in the weather. When safety in climbing, or in anything, depends on good luck, it's only a matter of time before failure occurs. That's the nature of probability—roll a dice often enough and you'll eventually get a six. On the 1922 expedition's third attempt to summit, that's what happened.

Early in the afternoon of June 7, three climbers and 24 porters, with climber George Mallory leading, was ascending to their North Col camp at 23,000 feet—relatively low on Everest. The plan was to set another camp at 26,000 feet and to launch a final summit attempt from there. The large group was split into three smaller groups, with members of the groups roped together for safety. The theory was that if a climber fell, the others in his group would be able to arrest his fall. As three long strings of climbers, one following the other, climbed a perilously steep slope, they noticed heavy snow had recently fallen in the area where they were climbing.

With just 600 feet to go until reaching the safety of their camp, there was what Mallory described as *an ominous sound, like an explosion of untamped gunpowder*. It was an avalanche. Mallory was quickly engulfed in snow. He swung his arms wildly in a swimming motion to break free. As the sliding wall of snow came to rest, he found himself near the surface, and was able to struggle out without help. He looked around and found the rope tied to his waist pulled tight to a porter buried in the snow. This porter was lucky as he was buried near the surface and also broke himself free. Nine others, tied together on a different rope, were swept down the slope and over a 15 meter (50 foot) bluff. Snow from the avalanche buried them in a crevasse at its base. The climbers from the first two ropes rushed to dig them out but only two of the nine could be saved. The avalanche was a tragic end to the expedition.

Much of what had been attempted on the expedition was dangerous. They were constantly operating on the edge of the *risk envelope*—the boundary that separates risks that are being managed in control, from risks that aren't. The expedition's use of technology, together with their climbing skills and experience, had reduced some of their risks, but it had also enabled them to climb higher, exposing them to new risks with which they had less experience.

The 1922 expedition ended in tragedy, but their failures provided the climbing world with valuable knowledge and skills of high-altitude climbing. Mallory had not been put off by his near-death experience in the avalanche. After he returned home, he quickly became involved in preparations for an expedition to be undertaken in 1924.

CLIMBING HIGHER, NOT SAFER

The 1924 British Everest Expedition was also led by General Bruce, but he became ill with malaria before the expedition reached Everest however, and had to return home. Leadership of the expedition passed to Major Edward Norton, who then appointed Mallory, a survivor of the 1922 avalanche, as second-in-charge of the 1924 expedition. Mallory was also given responsibility for planning the climbing program.

The first deaths on the 1924 expedition occurred early in May during the establishment of the two staging camps sited above Base Camp. Cerebral edema (excessive fluid on the brain) is a classic high-altitude condition, caused by a lack of oxygen in the air. Some people are more susceptible to it than others, and anyone can get it at high altitudes if they have not allowed themselves sufficient time to acclimatize. Cerebral edema claimed the first victim of the 1924 expedition and severe frost bite claimed the second. Both victims were buried at Base Camp.

After further camp establishment work, Norton, the expedition's leader, and Melville, another highly experienced climber on the team, made the team's first attempt on the summit. There were many close calls, both on their attempt to reach the top and on their way back down. Norton made it to within 900 feet (300 meters) of the top before making the courageous decision to turn back. His high point was 28,126 feet (8,572 meters).

At that altitude, Norton was exhausted, and had experienced several close calls. He was also not using supplemental oxygen. Although his thinking would not have been sharp under those conditions, he had still been able to mentally reason that he would not be able to reach the summit and still return safely in the time he had left. This was good judgment at that altitude, and it probably saved his life. It is judgment that most of those who die on Everest get wrong.

Norton's attainment of 28,126 feet was a great achievement, and set a record that lasted 30 years. What Norton had learned from his attempt and was able to pass onto the climbers making the next assault 24 hours later, should have put that attempt (to be led by Mallory) in a good position to succeed.

If a climber could benefit from Norton telling them about the route to the top, what he saw as the key risks, and how he managed them—and in particular, why and how he made the decision to turn around before reaching the top—and if that climber could also benefit from the use of supplemental oxygen, which Norton hadn't used, then you might reasonably think that climber's risks would be much reduced and their chance of success much increased.

But human nature doesn't work that way. Making ourselves safer is the last thing we do when we are provided new knowledge, experience, and technology—collectively *new capabilities*. What we *do* is try to increase our outcomes—i.e., to achieve more. As a result, whether it is on the side of a mountain, or on a complex ICT-enabled business (ICT-EB) change project, people's risk levels often increase.

Risk levels go up because when people make a choice to do more, rather than to be safer, the *doing of more* takes them into new territory. Starting from a complex and risky position, the decision to move into new territory adds complexity to an already complex situation. A fresh set of *unknowns* mix with existing unknowns—risks combine with each other like different alcohols in a cocktail. Because people have chosen to do *more* instead of being *safer*, the value at stake is also larger, and often, so are the failures.

Armed with new capabilities, people don't climb safer, they climb higher.

MALLORY AND IRVINE'S SUMMIT ATTEMPT

And so it was with the 1924 expedition's second attempt on the summit led by Mallory. After his record-breaking climb, Norton had descended to

Camp 4 and, resting to regain his strength, told Mallory about what he'd seen and experienced. Mallory listened to Norton intently. Mallory figured that if Norton went as high as he did without the use of supplemental oxygen, then surely he, Mallory, could go a lot higher with it—maybe even to the top.

Mallory advised Norton of his decision to make his attempt using supplemental oxygen. Norton wasn't enthusiastic, but he didn't feel in a fit state to argue. He was suffering from exhaustion after his own summit bid, and had developed severe snow-blindness—an extremely painful condition described by climbers as being like having powdered glass beneath your eyelids. Norton had to be assisted down to Base Camp by the expedition doctor. Mallory proceeded to organize his summit attempt.

From the climbers available, Mallory chose Andrew Irvine to accompany him. Irvine was young but had a reputation for proficiency with the new oxygen equipment. This could be useful, given that the oxygen sets they were using had not been trouble free. With his climbing partner chosen, Mallory announced the plan. They would climb to Camp 6, spend the night there, and early the next morning, June 8, 1924, make their bid for the summit.

The last person to see Mallory and Irvine alive was Noel Odell, another of the expedition's senior climbers. Odell was making his way up to Camp 6 late on June 8, to leave supplies for Mallory and Irvine to use on their

Image 1.2   The last known picture of Mallory and Irvine on Everest, adjusting their oxygen sets before commencing their fatal summit assault (Photo: Royal Geographical Society).

return, when he noticed the two climbers high above him. He described them as two black dots making their way slowly up the mountain, and estimated their height to be somewhere around 28,000 feet—only 1,000 feet from the summit. Clouds closed in around the dots while Odell watched. It would be 75 years before Mallory's body was found, and Irvine's is still missing today.

There has been much debate among climbers and historians about whether Mallory and Irvine reached the summit. Since the finding of Mallory's body in May 1999, and the extra information this provided—his body had been in a fall, and he wasn't wearing his oxygen set—there is a growing consensus that the chance of either of the climbers summiting was very low. Factors counting against them included the limited amount of oxygen that they took on the morning of their summit bid, the late start they made that morning, the technical difficulties of the climb which lay ahead of them, and the deteriorating weather.

Whether they made it to the top or not, the tragic fact is that they didn't make it back down. The experience and knowledge of Norton's ascent, which Mallory and Irvine had added to their own, and the use of the oxygen sets which Norton hadn't used, had not kept them alive.

What these strengthened capabilities did do for Mallory and Irvine was to enable them to go higher on the mountain than they would otherwise have gone. This new territory, which involved more difficult climbing and dependency on a fragile new oxygen technology, had added complexity and risk to their already highly complex and risky venture.

New knowledge and new technology had not reduced their risks, but instead, increased them. It had done this because they had, consciously or unconsciously, chosen to climb higher, not safer.

Safety versus altitude trade-offs are a recurring theme on Everest.

OUTCOME-MAXIMIZING

Throughout the years, significant improvements in climbing knowledge and experience, improvements in supplemental oxygen technology, and increased understanding of Everest's weather, have failed to make Everest a safer place to climb.

In 1999, an expedition entitled the *Mallory and Irvine Research Expedition* searched the upper slopes of Everest looking for the bodies of Mallory and Irvine. In a shallow depression which served as a natural collection zone for anyone falling from the mountain higher up, they found what they described as *a virtual graveyard of mangled, frozen bodies*. Over 200 people have died climbing on Everest, and most of their bodies are still there. All of the bodies the 1999 expedition found in the hollow depression were wearing modern clothing, except one—this was George Mallory's.

Everest is littered with examples of climbers translating risk-reduction opportunities into outcome-maximizing opportunities, and the increased risk (and failure) that this creates. The 1920s to the 1950s were the learning years for Everest climbing (the mountain wasn't successfully summited until 1953). But the knowledge learned made little difference in the death rates. Most of the fatalities on the mountain have occurred after the summit was conquered. It has been nearly 40 years since there was a fatality-free season on Everest (the last reported year of no fatalities was 1977). Interestingly, the last reported year of no one being successful on the summit was around the same time—1975.

Particularly bad years for Everest fatalities have been:

1970: 8 climbers

1974: 6 climbers

1982: 11 climbers

1985: 7 climbers

1988: 10 climbers

1989: 8 climbers

1993: 8 climbers

1996: 15 climbers

2006: 11 climbers

2012: 10 climbers

2014: 16 climbers (season canceled due to loss of life in ice fall)

2015: (season canceled due to high loss of life and damage to the mountain caused by the Nepal earthquake on April 25)

EVEREST 2014

The risks that climbing Everest presents for even the most experienced climbers were demonstrated tragically in April of 2014. It was the deadliest climbing accident to occur on the mountain—16 professional climbers were lost.

The 16 were all Sherpas—highly skilled and well-equipped climbing guides from the Everest region of Nepal. Large numbers of them are employed on Everest by commercial climbing companies. Sherpas are sometimes misunderstood, usually by people not familiar with Everest or Nepal, as being porters employed to cart heavy loads up and down the mountain. Sherpas do carry heavy loads and are extremely fit, but they are much more than porters. They are regarded as some of the best climbers in the world and they are certainly, on average, the fittest.

Early on the morning of April 18, 2014, several groups of Sherpas were making their way up through the Khumbu Icefall—a technically challenging, glacial section of the mountain that starts just above Base Camp at 5,400 meters (18,000 feet). It climbs to 6,000 meters (19,500 feet), finishing just below Camp 1.

All climbers who ascend Everest via the Khumbu glacier (and that includes most of them) have to climb the Khumbu Icefall. The route traverses 600 vertical meters (2,000 feet) of jumbled, house-sized blocks of ice and deep crevasses, all of which are on a slow-motion journey down the mountain.

Climbing the icefall is like a game of Russian roulette, or a deadly game of musical chairs. The name of the game is not to be in the icefall when the blocks of ice move or when crevasses suddenly open or close. The movements of ice are slow enough that most climbers make it through without getting caught. It takes from six to ten hours for the average climber to complete the journey (a few, mostly Sherpas, do it in much less). But there are many close calls, and every now and then someone dies.

On the morning of April 14, the Sherpas had headed into the icefall early, as Everest climbers have to do, before the sun has a chance to warm the ice too much. The sun's warmth causes the massive blocks of ice to loosen and sometimes fall. This is the time when avalanches are most likely. Some accounts of that day said that although the Sherpas had departed Base Camp early, it was still about an hour later than they had planned.

Just below the halfway point in the icefall is an area known as the Popcorn Field. The Sherpas were climbing through this area when a house-sized block of ice broke free, some distance above them. The first block of ice crashed into other blocks, breaking them free, and creating a deadly avalanche in seconds. Roped together in groups for safety, the Sherpas had no chance of escape. Twenty-five climbers were caught—sixteen of them were killed and nine were injured, several seriously.

The loss of the Sherpas was tragic for their families and their villages. Such was the scale of the loss, that all climbing on the mountain for the 2014 season was immediately canceled.

Too often Sherpas are the victims on Everest. They do some of the most dangerous climbing, and they do a lot of it. If you do something dangerous often enough, then statistically, you're going to be more involved in incidents. Unfortunately, on Everest, this means more deaths.

These deaths can happen to even the most experienced. In 2001, one of the world's most experienced and capable Sherpas was killed from a fall into a crevasse. His name was Babu Chiri. He had summited Everest ten times and held the record for the mountain's fastest climb (16 hours and 56 minutes from Base Camp to the Summit).

Some of the world's best Western climbers have also been killed. One of these was the New Zealander, Rob Hall. Hall was the first non-Sherpa to summit the mountain five times. He owned a commercial climbing company called Adventure Consultants, and between 1990 and 1995 successfully guided 39 clients to the mountain's summit. Each of these clients paid as much as $60,000 to be on one of Hall's expeditions.

In 1996 Hall died when he was caught in a bad storm at the summit while assisting a struggling client. In addition to the loss of Hall and his client, six others died that day. Two of these were also experienced guides: Andy Harris, a New Zealand (and ex-Antarctic) guide who was working for Rob Hall, and Scott Fischer, owner of an Everest guiding company called Mountain Madness. Four fee-paying clients died in the same storm.

Strong climbing experience, an in-depth knowledge of Everest, and the latest climbing and supplemental oxygen technologies do not make people safe there—it seems as though they should, but they don't. What we see too often is climbers translating increased capabilities, not into lower risks, but into maximizing their outcomes—more climbs, higher climbs, and climbs in more challenging conditions.

COMMERCIAL CLIMBING ON EVEREST

Until the mid-1990s the death rate on Everest was one death for every four climbers who summited. In the late-1990s the advent of commercial climbing began to change this. One death for every four summits wasn't sustainable for a commercial operation. The fee for being guided to the top of Everest in the '90s was around $50,000 (in recent years it has climbed to as much as $75,000). No one wants to pay that kind of money if it comes with a 1 in 4 chance of dying. To succeed commercially, the guiding companies had to reduce the risks—and they did.

Commercial climbing on Everest is now highly commoditized. Climbing routes and safety ropes are prepared in advance of the arrival of the fee-paying clients on the mountain; climbing safety rules are strictly enforced by leading companies, and guiding ratios are high (the ratio of professional guides to fee-paying clients is sometimes one-to-one). As a result, commercial climbing on Everest has grown significantly. In the 2007 season there were a record 633 successful summits. In 2012, there were 176 successful summits—in one day alone.

Anyone with sufficient funds and sufficient determination, is now able to attempt Everest. Large numbers of people, climbers and nonclimbers alike, try it every year. Many are successful and many are not.

The move to climbing as a commodity has created a significant cultural shift on Everest. Death rates have dropped from one fatality per four summits to one fatality per 50 summits. Some would say this is still too high a price to pay, for professional and nonprofessional climbers alike, to achieve their dream of summiting the world's highest mountain.

The lower Everest death rates are an improvement, but they are also now the new constant. The climbers who go there today know these odds, and accept them.

The message from Everest is that, regardless of the year, the motive, the experience level, or the equipment, many climbers outcome-maximize. When provided with the capabilities or support that allows them to do so, they will climb higher, rather than be consistently safer.

Without culture change (such as commercialization), failure tends to be a constant. But as we read in the first part of the chapter, these recurring failures are far from just an Everest thing.

2

A Risk-Rich Environment

"We took risks, we knew we took them."

(Reflecting on his impending death, on the return from the Pole—
his final letter)
Captain Scott, March 29, 1912

THE HEROIC AGE

Everest is not the only place where people fail to reduce their risks in spite
of improving their experience and capabilities; during the *Heroic Age*, Antarctic explorers did it a lot. The Heroic Age was the 25-year period from the
late 1800s to the early 1920s, when the exploration of Antarctica occurred
in earnest. In this time period, a number of difficult and dangerous expeditions were led by explorers, such as Robert Scott and Ernest Shackleton.

Many explorers made repeated visits to the continent with no reduction in their risk levels. The number of accidents and fatalities they experienced was pretty much a constant, in spite of the significant experience they
gained from earlier trips and their explorer-peers. What they did achieve,
as their experience grew, was *more*. They traveled further from their bases,
discovered and explored new areas, and added to the world's knowledge of
Antarctica's geography, weather, and science. They achieved greater things
each time they traveled to Antarctica, but they were never noticeably safer.

Antarctica is a large, cold, and inhospitable place. To walk from one side
to the other is a journey of 2,900 km (1,800 miles), at its narrowest point.
By area, Antarctica is nearly 50% larger than the U.S. and nearly twice the
size of Australia. The coldest temperature on earth was recorded there:

−89.2°C (−129°F) at the Russian base of Vostok Station in July, 1983. The strongest wind gust on earth was recorded in Antarctica—327 kph (203 mph) at the French base of Dumont d'Urville in July, 1972. For comparison, hurricane force winds are anything over 120 kph (75 mph).

Antarctica is also the driest place on earth. There is almost no water in Antarctica and this is critical for a number of reasons. Water is not the same thing as ice—any moisture that forms in the air, if it doesn't fall as snow around the fringes of the continent, it falls to the ground as ice dust in the interior. You can't drink that dust and you can't put out fires with it. The dry air causes building materials to dry out so completely that they become extreme fire risks. There has been some spectacular destruction of bases in Antarctica by fire.

In these very cold, windy, and dry conditions, it's not just bases and machinery that are affected—the performance of humans, too, can become variable. There can be long periods of time when people are unable to go outdoors, and when they do, what they are able to achieve is limited and dangerous. In the cold, colorless extremes of Antarctica the morale of individuals can drop, and team performances can be affected.

The extremes of the weather and the variable performance of people and teams intersect in Antarctica to increase complexity, uncertainty, and risk. There are lots of ways people can get it wrong—and the price of failure can be high in dollars, uncompleted science, and lives.

Antarctica is a *risk-rich* environment. It is also a *learning-rich* environment.

A PLACE OF FIRSTS

Antarctica is a place where people have competed fiercely to be the first to accomplish things.

The first confirmed landing on continental Antarctica was January 24, 1895. The identity of the first person to actually step ashore that day has been in dispute ever since. The expedition that claimed credit for the first landing started out as a search for whales by an Old Norwegian steam whaler named *Antarctic*. When the crew sighted land in the Antarctic region they sent a boat ashore.

Three of the seven people in the boat each claimed to have been the first ashore. They were Leonard Kristensen (the *Antarctic's* Captain); Carsten Borchgrevink (a deckhand and part-time scientist); and Alexander von Tunzelmann (a crewman). Borchgrevink later went on to lead the first expedition to winter-over in Antarctica at Cape Adare in 1899—and the first to experience a death.

The 1895 landing, regardless of whose boot it was that contacted the shore, or the seabed first, was the beginning of the Heroic Age of Antarctic exploration. Firsts that were attempted in that age included:

- **The first to spend a winter on the Antarctic mainland:** This comes, courtesy of Antarctica's extreme southern latitudes, with three or four months of 24-hour nighttime, during which the sun never rises. Winter, of course, is also the continent's coldest time.
- **The first to reach the geographic South Pole (the imaginary point on which the earth spins):** This requires a return walk totaling nearly 2,700 km (1,700 miles) in freezing and desolate conditions.
- **The first to reach the *magnetic* South Pole (the point which magnetic compasses point to):** This is quite different from the *geographic* South Pole. The magnetic South Pole is in the sea, near to, but *north* of the coast of Antarctica. It is nearly 2,700 km (1,700 miles) from the geographic South Pole.
- **The first to walk from one side of Antarctica to the other:** This is a journey of around 2,900 km (1,800 miles) at its narrowest point, and is not that dissimilar in distance to walking across the continental U.S. (but a little colder).

The pursuit of all these firsts resulted in many failures, a number of them the subject of incredible stories of bravery and heroism, death, and near-death.

Robert Scott, the leader of the first British expedition to reach the South Pole (though he did not survive the journey back) is one of the most famous of these. Earnest Shackleton, the first person to attempt to walk from one side of the continent to the other would have to be a close second (he didn't succeed but he didn't die either).

In Scott and Shackleton we see demonstrated the recurring theme of the explorers of that age translating their increased experience and knowledge, not into reducing their risks, but into the pursuit of more ambitious goals—i.e., outcome-maximizing.

CAPTAIN SCOTT—NEW TERRITORY, NEW RISKS

When we look to maximize our outcomes, the complexity of what we take on climbs. We enter new risk territory, and a consequence of this is increased risk. Scott was a brilliant leader, but when enough risks go against you in Antarctica all the leadership in the world can't help.

Scott's trek to the South Pole in 1911 was undone by a single risk that no one, at that time, could have predicted. It was a once-in-35-years climate event that Scott's meteorologist commented on as it occurred, but the severity of which would not be fully understood until the Antarctic scientist Dr. Susan Solomon published her 2001 book *The Coldest March: Scott's Fatal Antarctic Expedition*.

Scott was a Royal Navy officer who, at age 32, was chosen to lead the 1901–1904 British National Antarctic Expedition, called the Discovery Expedition (after the expedition's ship). The expedition was given two primary goals: to explore as far south on the Antarctic continent as they could possibly go, and to undertake scientific studies of the Ross Sea area of Antarctica in which they were based.

Early in 1902, during the Antarctic summer, the expedition built a hut on the coast of Antarctica in the Ross Sea region. They spent the following winter making preparations for a major exploration program in the summer. This was to include a major sledging trip towards the Pole.

Tragically, before their winter-over had even commenced, one of the team members—George Vince—was killed when he slipped over a cliff during a blizzard.

Early in the summer of 1902 (November) Scott led Edward Wilson and Ernest Shackleton on a sledging trip to explore the terrain toward the South Pole. They managed to get about a third of the way to the Pole (400 km, 250 miles) before hunger, exhaustion, and the cold forced them back.

The 1902 expedition spent two winters in Antarctica and learned much about Antarctic weather, traveling, safety, and scientific and geographical exploration. On Scott's return home, he was promoted from the rank of Commander to Captain, a relatively senior rank in the Navy.

In 1910, armed with the knowledge and experiences of his 1902 trip, as well as lessons shared with him by explorers who had led their own expeditions there in the intervening years (including a failed attempt on the Pole by Shackleton in 1907), Scott returned as leader of the British Antarctic Terra Nova Expedition. He based himself at Cape Evans, not far from the site of his 1902 hut.

In the middle of the winter of 1911, three of Scott's top men—Wilson, Bowers, and Cherry-Garrard—embarked on a side expedition to Cape Crozier, 100 km (60 miles) to the east of Cape Evans. The purpose of their trip was to obtain Emperor penguin eggs for scientific study. Emperors only lay these eggs in the winter so they could only be collected during the winter time. This made the trip very risky. It was pitch dark 24 hours a day and dangerously cold. On the coldest day of the trip, Wilson's thermometer recorded –61°C (–78°F).

When they reached the penguin rookery (a colony of nesting penguins), Wilson and his colleagues were struck by a blizzard and their tent ripped away. Cherry-Garrard tells the story of their fight for survival in his book (appropriately entitled) *The Worst Journey in the World*. The three men got the eggs they were after, and made it back to Cape Evans, but just barely in time to escape death.

Six other members of the Terra Nova expedition also narrowly escaped death. They were Scott's Northern Party, and in 1912, were transferred by ship to an area called Evans Coves, some 320 km (200 miles) northwest of Cape Evans. In mid-February the Northern Party's ship was scheduled to return to pick the group up, but it couldn't get through the thick sea ice to reach them.

The Northern Party was left marooned for the winter of 1912—surviving by living in a snow cave and eating fish and seal meat. It wasn't until September 1912, with the arrival of the Antarctic spring, that they were able to attempt the long (five weeks), dangerous walk across the frozen sea back to the Cape Evans hut. They made it, but just barely.

SCOTT'S FATAL TREK

The ultimate tragedy of the Terra Nova expedition was the death in March 1912, of Scott, together with four of his best men—Wilson, Bowers, Oats, and Evans. Wilson and Bowers had been on the earlier winter trip to obtain the penguin eggs. All five died on the return from the 2,762 km (1,700 miles) round-trip polar trek.

They reached the Pole but were not the first men to arrive there. The Norwegian Roald Amundsen beat them by 34 days. At the Pole, Scott's team found a tent that Amundsen had left for them, along with a letter. This depressing find, after trekking for nearly 1,400 km (860 miles) did not help the morale of Scott's men for their return journey.

A large part of the tragedy of the death of Scott and his men was that they were so very close to making it. They succumbed to cold and starvation only 18 km (11 miles) from a large depot of food and fuel which they had been prevented from reaching by four days of bad weather. The food depot was just 294 km (155 miles) from the safety and warmth of the Cape Evans hut.

Scott's polar team had endured for 149 days, walking 2,468 km (1,534 miles), and had completed 90% of the journey—but it wasn't enough.

COMPLEXITY EQUALS RISK

On Scott's polar journey, outcome-maximizing created high levels of complexity and risk. This wasn't unusual for explorers of the time—stretch-goals were common. Where Scott's expedition differed from those of others was that if just one of the risks which turned out against Scott had instead gone in his favor, he would have survived.

There are many distortions, actually myths, written about Scott's expeditions. Most of these are put to rest in the best-selling biography *Captain Scott* written by the polar adventurer Sir Ranulph Fiennes in 2003. Fiennes is one of the few Scott biographers to have actually visited Antarctica, and the only one to have man-hauled a sledge across it, using techniques similar to those of Scott. Fiennes knew what he was talking about when he wrote about Scott's planning and leadership style. Fiennes also understood how diaries—an important source of the accounts of the Heroic Age explorers—work in that part of the world, unlike some of the earlier Scott biographers.

Like many explorers of that time, Scott traded his steadily growing experience and capabilities for increased outcomes, not reduced risk. Scott was able to succeed in this high-risk zone because of his exceptional planning skills (Chapter 9), his intrinsic managerial heroism (Chapter 10), and his team leadership skills (Chapter 13). All three of these are critical for the management of complex projects, then and today.

SCOTT'S RISK REGISTER 1910

The extent of the complexity and risk that Scott took can be seen in the risk register entries that follow. The register also shows the extraordinary fall of the dice against Scott on his polar journey, and the once-in-35-years climate event which was the primary cause of his death. The information contained in the register below is factual, only its form is hypothetical. Risk registers of this form were not in common use in the Heroic Age.

The risk register approach used here is a simple 3x3 matrix, where the risks are rated using three levels of *likelihood*—low, medium, or high; and the *consequences* of a risk happening are rated using three levels of *severity*—low, medium, or high. The *final* rating of low, medium, or high given for each risk is a product of the likelihood and consequence ratings combined.

1.	Risk	*That the polar sledging team members don't function as a high-performance team, causing the daily mileage targets to be insufficient and compromising safe return (injury or death).*		
Likelihood: *Medium*		**Consequence:** *High*	**Overall:** *High*	**Did it occur?** *No*

2.	Risk	*That just one of the cached supply depots cannot be found by the polar team on their return from the Pole, causing starvation and failure (death).*
Likelihood: *Medium*	**Consequence:** *High*	**Overall:** *High*	**Did it occur?** *No*

3.	Risk	*That the ponies don't perform as planned in hauling the supplies part-way to the Pole, causing failure to reach the Pole, or failure to survive (death).*
Likelihood: *Medium*	**Consequence:** *High*	**Overall:** *High*	**Did it occur?** *No*

Risk 3 Notes: It is a common misconception that Scott made a mistake choosing to use ponies combined with man-hauling, instead of dogs, to pull his sledges (a proposition of some early biographers). Dogs were the higher-risk choice for the type of journey Scott planned. His use of ponies on the polar journey combined with man-hauling (four or five men harnessed to a sledge to pull tent and supplies) worked to plan.

4.	Risk	*That one of the polar team becomes injured or incapacitated, causing the safe return of the team to be slowed down or compromised (risk of death).*
Likelihood: *Medium*	**Consequence:** *High*	**Overall:** *High*	**Did it occur?** *Partly*

Risk 4 Notes: Two of the five members of the polar team were injured or incapacitated on the return journey, causing the team to lose several valuable days on the return journey.

5.	Risk	*That an extreme **warm**-weather event occurs which results in the sledging surface becoming soft, causing the sledges to bog down, delaying progress (possible death).*
Likelihood: *Low*	**Consequence:** *High*	**Overall:** *Med.*	**Did it occur?** *Partly*

Risk 5 Notes: Halfway to the Pole, a four-day blizzard associated with unusually high temperatures delayed them and created a thick blanket of wet, soft snow which slowed the team's advance on the Beardmore Glacier. This was an unusual event in that area, at that time.

6.	Risk	*That a sustained extreme **cold**-weather event occurs which results in the sledging surface becoming dry and sand-like, causing the sledges to not slide properly and adding significant delays to progress (and possible death).*
Likelihood: *Low*	**Consequence:** *High*	**Overall:** *Med*	**Did it occur?** *Yes*

Risk 6 Notes: Halfway into the team's return from the Pole, they experienced a sustained drop in temperatures of 10 to 20 degrees Celsius colder than the average temperature for that location at that time of year (the temperatures they experienced at night on the Barrier were regularly −47ºC), and which lasted for three weeks. Dr. Susan Solomon's book , *The Coldest March*, and Ranulph Fiennes' biography, *Captain Scott*, both reference this event as a major contributor to Scott's death.

7.	Risk	*That a sustained extreme **cold**-weather event occurs, causing the polar sledging team's performance to drop (separate from the changed snow conditions) and increasing the risk of hypothermia (possible death).*
Likelihood: *Low*	**Consequence:** *High*	**Overall:** *Med*	**Did it occur?** *Yes*

Risk 7 Notes: Refer to earlier risk. The temperatures they experienced were in the mid-late minus 40 degrees Celsius. Average temperatures in the low minus 30 degrees was what they had been expecting—and correctly so, based on averages both then and today. The sustained cold weather event they experienced was a once-in-35-years event.

8.	Risk	*That environmental (terrain, weather, sea ice, etc.) or people factors cause a failure (or partial failure) of the expedition's science or geographical exploration programs.*
Likelihood: *Low*	**Consequence:** *High*	**Overall:** *Med*	**Did it occur?** *No*

Risk 8 Notes: Scott and the other members of the polar sledging team lost their lives, but the expedition's broader scientific and geographic exploration programs, including the data collected by the polar sledging team, were acclaimed as being among the most successful of their time.

9.	Risk	*That the stored body fat and muscle reserves of the polar sledging team will be insufficient for the duration of the polar journey, causing individuals to weaken to the point of failure (death).*
Likelihood: *Low*	**Consequence:** *High*	**Overall:** *Med*	**Did it occur?** *Partly*

Risk 9 Notes: The daily energy-burn rate of Scott and his polar team is estimated in Fiennes' biography of Scott to have been around 7,000 calories per day while the team was sledging. This may have been as high as 11,000 calories per day during their many-more-than-expected harder days. The calories provided by their diet for the polar journey, however, are estimated to have been only 4,500 per day, and even less for the days that they were not at the higher altitudes of the polar plateau (for which they had a different diet). Due to the extreme weather events which they experienced, some of their hardest days were experienced off the polar plateau, when they were on their lower-calorie diet. The severe weather conditions also increased the number of high-calorie-burning days which they experienced.

A calorie deficit of the above order is not uncommon among polar explorers, but its impact on the human body is no less severe. Fiennes' calorie figures were developed from a scientific study undertaken by Dr. Mike Stroud, a physician and Fiennes' sledging partner during their Trans-Antarctic trek of 1992/93. In a 68-day period during the Fiennes-Stroud polar trek, Fiennes and Stroud lost forty-four pounds of body weight. Scott's polar journey went for 149 days before he and his men finally succumbed.

This is where the duration of Scott's polar sledging journey—and delays to it—was critical. Every day of dragging the sledges was a day that the bodies of Scott and his men were burning fat, and then muscle, and losing weight, heat, and strength, to compensate for their daily calorie deficits. Most of those days were spent dragging their sledges in more difficult conditions than they ever expected (and statistically, based on meteorological studies of that time undertaken by modern-day scientists, more than they should ever have expected).

The consequences of the delays to Scott's polar schedule caused by this *rogue-wave*, cold-weather event were ultimately fatal.

10.	Risk	*That the last supply depot which the polar sledging team will need to reach on the return journey (known as* One Ton Depot*), placed 57 km (36 miles) further north than the original plan, will be too far north from the second-to-last depot for them to reach in a weakened state, causes failure (death).*
Likelihood: *Low*	**Consequence:** *High*	**Overall:** *Med*	**Did it occur?** *Partly*

Risk 10 Notes: Scott and his men were only 18 km (11 miles) south of One Ton Depot when they died. They were unable to make the last day's walk to the depot, as a blizzard trapped them in their tent for four days, during which time their food, fuel, and water ran out.

11.	Risk	*That the Polar sledging team's fuel containers might be poor quality, allowing leakage and/or evaporation of fuel, causing fuel for cooking food and melting water to run out before the final supply depot can be reached (risk of death).*
Likelihood: *Low*	**Consequence:** *High*	**Overall:** *Med*	**Did it occur?** *Partly*

Risk 11 Notes: The loss of cooking fuel from the storage tins, through leakage from poor quality seals and seams on the tins, was significant, and coupled with delays caused by the poor snow and weather conditions, contributed to the team's death.

12.	Risk	*That the team's contingency rescue/support plan (to have a relief team from the main expedition hut come out and meet the polar sledging team during their journey back from the Pole) might not happen for whatever reason, causing a failure of rescue if it is needed (risk of death).*
Likelihood: *Low*	**Consequence:** *High*	**Overall:** *Med*	**Did it occur?** *Yes*

Risk 12 Notes: For various reasons, including poor prioritization of tasking and poor decision making by non-Polar team members left at the main expedition hut, the relief team sent to help Scott's team return from the Pole was not strong enough, and/or were unclear on their orders, and traveled only as far as One Ton Depot. If they had been stronger, or traveled further south for three more days (the location Scott was at when the relief team stopped at One Ton Depot), they might have found and rescued the struggling polar sledging team.

We'll never really know how Scott and his team might have rated these risks themselves, had they been using a risk work-shopping technique like those we use in high-risk projects today. The risk assessments in the table above are based on information contained in the various diaries of those involved at the time, as well as the biographical review of these by more recent researchers.

Scott understood the extraordinary fall of the dice against him. In one of the last letters he wrote, as he lay dying in his tent, trapped by the blizzard that prevented him from reaching One Ton Depot, he wrote "*... our journey has been the biggest on record, and nothing but the most exceptional hard luck would have caused us to fail to return.*"

Ultimately, risk is a numbers game. If you take enough risks—either a few *high*-rated ones, or a few more *medium*-rated ones—some are going to occur. Scott took on huge complexity and a number of his risks occurred. It was the rogue cold-wave that so tragically killed him, but he might well have survived had any one of those lesser risks also not occurred.

This is the sort of bad luck that high complexity triggers. Whether a Heroic Age explorer or the owner of a modern day information and communications technology-enabled business (ICT-EB) project, complexity and risks can interact, and if you're having a bad day, the consequences can be severe.

You are constantly working in a zone that is unpredictable. The risk of failure in this zone is higher than what most are used to.

Scott—caught out by extreme temperatures on his return from the Pole—was not the only Antarctic explorer to suffer this problem.

EARNEST SHACKLETON—RISK, FAILURE, AND LUCK

Ernest Shackleton was an exceptional leader of men, but his planned attempt to walk from one side of Antarctica to the other via the South Pole in 1915 was, like Scott's return from the Pole, going to take more than just good leadership. Shackleton's plan was very outcome-maximized.

Shackleton had learned much about operating in the Antarctic during his journey with Scott in 1902. Shackleton had become very ill during that trip's exploration of the route to the Pole in 1903, but he wasn't put off by this. In 1907 he returned to Antarctica as the leader of the British Antarctic (*Nimrod*) Expedition.

During that expedition, Shackleton led his own attempt on the Pole. He set off with three men, Adams, Wild, and Marshall, and got to within 180 km (112 miles) of his goal. They were forced to turn back because of a lack of food, and their safe return was a very closely run event. Marshall collapsed when they were just a couple of days from the safety of the main hut at Cape Royds.

Shackleton made a decision to leave Adams to care for Marshall while he and Wild went ahead for help. Shackleton was also anxious to stop their ship departing from Antarctica for New Zealand, scheduled for the next day. He didn't want to spend another winter in Antarctica if he could avoid it. Shackleton and Wild reached the hut just in time to stop the ship, and Marshall and Adams were successfully rescued. The expedition packed-up and left Antarctica several days later.

Shackleton's decision to turn back from his South Pole trek with just 180 km to go to reach the Pole displayed both good judgment and courage. With a powerful goal in sight, the judgment of many leaders can be affected by a *sunk ego*—the ego that people subconsciously invest in achieving major goals. Sunk egos, and its parallels to *sunk costs*, are discussed in more detail in Chapter 7.

THE 1914–17 TRANS-ANTARCTIC EXPEDITION

Three years later, Shackleton received the news that the Norwegian Roald Amundsen had beaten Scott to the Pole by four weeks and that Scott had died trying to return. Shackleton was devastated by the loss of Scott, but also looked to his own next challenge.

With the Pole conquered, Shackleton needed a new goal. Armed with his 1902 and 1907 experiences, and his knowledge from Amundsen's and Scott's expeditions, he announced he was going to trek across the continent—2,900 km (1,800 miles). Most of the trek was to be across unexplored territory.

This was a very outcome-maximized plan. There had been four attempts on the Pole at the time, two of them involving Shackleton, and only Amundsen's had been successful. Even today, adventurers of various types attempt to walk or ski to the Pole, with the occasional one looking to cross the entire continent. Few of these succeed and deaths still occur.

Shackleton's planning was necessarily complex. He and his Trans-Antarctic team would be landed on the Weddell Sea side of the continent, the opposite side from the Ross Sea where most previous expeditions had started.

While Shackleton's Weddell Sea team trekked their way toward the Pole, a Ross Sea support group would lay supply depots for Shackleton to use on their outward trek from the Pole. Shackleton would be dependent on finding these supplies, not just to be successful, but to survive. The expedition was to become Shackleton's greatest failure. It was also to become one of the greatest survival stories of all time.

Before the Trans-Antarctic team could set a foot on shore, their ship became trapped in sea ice. Shackleton and his men were forced to spend the following winter in the ship, hoping they would be able to break the ship free in spring. As spring approached, the pressure on the ice became worse. Slowly the ship was crushed by the pack ice, and in early spring (October) the order was given to abandon ship. Shackleton's team camped beside the ship for the next few weeks—until she sank on November 21, 1915.

The expedition and the crew of the ship, 28 in total, were left on the floating ice with three small lifeboats and a few supplies. The story of how Shackleton kept his men alive after the sinking, and until the last of them was rescued 283 days later, is told in Alfred Lansing's book, *Endurance*. A best-selling discussion of the leadership skills that Shackleton displayed during this time is also contained in Margot Morrell's 2001 book, *Shackleton's Way*.

Had Shackleton's 1914 Trans-Antarctic party landed on the continent as planned, there was every chance they might never have been heard from again. The technical challenges of the unexplored side of the continent were significant. Crevasse fields abounded. To overcome these and successfully reach the Pole, and then to traverse the second half of the continent to the

Image 2.1   Shackleton's ship *Endurance* slowly being crushed by the Antarctic sea ice (Photo provided under license from the Scott Polar Research Institute, University of Cambridge).

Ross Sea, finding the critical supply depots laid by the Ross Sea party along the way, would have been challenging, to say the least.

Shackleton's survival from the sinking of his ship involved good leadership, but it also involved good luck. His team had to drag their lifeboats across unsafe sea ice to find open sea, and they weathered ocean storms and blizzards with little shelter.

Shackleton's sea captain, Frank Worsley, navigated their tiny lifeboat, the *James Caird*, across hundreds of kilometers of open southern ocean to seek help at South Georgia—a relative dot in the great southern ocean. After reaching South Georgia, Shackleton, Worsley, and Crean had to trek across a mountain range without climbing equipment to reach the whaling station at Stromness. So many things could have gone wrong for them, and if just one of them had, it is likely Shackleton would never have been heard from again.

Like his peers before him, Shackleton often traded risk mitigation opportunities for greater outcomes.

ANTARCTICA TODAY

Nearly 100 years after Shackleton's ship sank, in a more modern time and with better weather and sea ice information, people still outcome-maximize at the expense of safety in the Antarctic.

On January 2, 2014, 52 passengers were evacuated by helicopter from a small science and tourism ship traveling off the coast of Antarctica. The ship, the *Akademik Shokalskiy*, had become trapped in sea ice on Christmas Eve. On Christmas day the captain sent out a call for help. Two icebreakers in the area went to the ship's assistance, but were unable to free her. On January 2, the decision was made to evacuate the passengers.

The risks to the *Shokalskiy*—and those aboard her—were real. I had been traveling with the *Shokalskiy* when she became trapped in a sea ice channel in Antarctica's McMurdo Sound in 2001. I saw how she struggled against the power of the wind and currents that caused ice to build up around her. Although she is *ice-strengthened*, the *Shokalskiy* is not an icebreaker and is not able to free herself if trapped in ice. When a ship is caught like this, as well as the crushing forces of the ice, there is a risk of collision with icebergs. Sea ice is typically only a meter or two thick, but icebergs can be the size of houses or office blocks, and the ice which comprises them, although it floats, is as hard as concrete.

The risk is greater than many realize because icebergs, being so large, are affected by wind and currents differently than sea ice and can move in different directions as a result. When a ship trapped in ice is held fast, icebergs that are nearby can continue to move, crunching through the sea ice as they travel. If this movement is in the direction of the ship, issues can arise. Several icebergs were reported to have been in the area of the *Shokalskiy* when the decision to evacuate her passengers was made.

The effect of wanting to go further and do more, and so to push the boundaries of achievement rather than reduce the levels of risk, were likely to have contributed to the *Shokalskiy* becoming trapped. The ship had been operating in an area known for ice build-up, and strengthening winds had been forecast. It was reported that some of the passengers wanted to see more of an area that they had been exploring some distance from the ship. These passengers had reportedly been slow to return to the ship after being called by the captain, when he became concerned about the changing weather.

A week after the passengers were airlifted off of the *Shokalskiy*, the sea ice pressure eased and the remaining crew were able to break the ship free. Everyone was safe—but the cost of the rescue was high. Three icebreakers had been diverted to the rescue, and they are not cheap to run. The Chinese and Australian icebreakers worked for days trying to free the *Shokalskiy* before a helicopter from the Chinese *Xue Long* was used to transfer the passengers to the *Aurora Australis* for transport back to Australia. Expensive international science programs had been disrupted. The reported cost to the Australian government alone was over two million dollars.

In the newspaper reports that followed, people blamed the incident on the power of nature and *unexpected circumstances*. But this is the nature of complexity that outcome-maximizing creates. One ends up in territory, physical or virtual, with which one is not familiar. Failure then happens in ways which one does not see coming (noting the *Shokalskiy's* reference to unexpected circumstances). Those aboard the *Shokalskiy* said they did not feel they were in any danger, but the occurrence of a second unexpected circumstance could have changed that dramatically—perhaps a nearby iceberg moving their way?

The lesson here is that outcome-maximizing in high-risk environments can create new risks, which are difficult to see coming until they have occurred.

THE ICEBERG TRIP

I experienced this issue myself in Antarctica, some years ago. The issue of people translating increased capabilities into greater outcomes, instead of reducing risks, is not exclusive to Everest climbers or Antarctic explorers from the Heroic Age.

I'd been well-trained by the New Zealand Government's Antarctic research institute before traveling to Antarctica, and received more advanced training on subsequent trips. By the time the incident that I'm about to describe happened, I had accumulated some two and a half years of experience working in Antarctica—experience which included field work, along with Search and Rescue (SAR).

For adventure, and the opportunity to escape from the confines of our base, I became a part-time member of the Joint USA-NZ Antarctic Search and Research Team (JASART). Most of our call-outs were for national program workers who were overdue on hiking or skiing trips off-base. Falls and frostbite were common, and occasionally *adventure tourists* got into trouble, as well. Sadly, our SAR call-outs included several fatalities.

In spite of my training and experience—actually, likely *because* of it—the complexity of the risks that the Antarctic cold can create caught me out badly one afternoon. It was a classic case of outcome-maximizing.

After lunch one Saturday, at the end of a busy week, I decided I would throw a small tent and a sleeping bag onto a light sledge and ski out to an iceberg not far from our base. I had found, during my time working and living on the ice, that trips like this are great for resetting a tired brain and recharging the spirit.

There are strict safety rules in place for people who are working with most national Antarctic programs. These include bans on people traveling away from bases alone. Although, if individuals are field-qualified, they stick to known routes, and carry radios, then solo travel is permitted—in some instances. On this particular day, I decided I needed the extra challenge of doing something on my own.

The month was September—early spring in the Antarctic. It's one of the coldest times of the year, but it is also the calmest wind-wise. That Saturday afternoon as I set off, the temperature was −43°C (−55°F), but it was sunny, and there was no wind. My plan was to ski about 10 km from the base, across frozen sea ice (about two meters thick—no problems there), and set up my tent next to a gigantic iceberg which had become trapped in the frozen sea late the previous summer. Towing a small sledge containing my tent, sleeping bag, cooking box, and extra cold weather gear, the ski to the iceberg should take me about three hours. I was looking forward to getting my lungs working and, metaphorically, blowing out the cobwebs that come from being indoors for too long.

After I set off, I began to find the skiing harder than I'd expected. About an inch of light snow had fallen earlier in the week. Because it's so cold in the Antarctic at that time of year, fallen snow is dry and powdery. It doesn't melt or mush together like it might in milder climates or at ski resorts. Pulling a sledge across that type of snow is like pulling a sledge along a sandy beach—it's hard work.

To avoid over-heating and my clothes becoming damp from perspiration, I was lightly dressed. Underneath a nylon wind-proof shell I had on a set of polypropylene underclothes, a pair of shorts, and a vest. It's amazing how little one can wear in subzero temperatures as long as one keeps moving. A balaclava covered my head, and a neck gator was pulled up over my mouth and nose. I was also wearing sunglasses to reduce the glare from the sun. To protect my fingers from frostbite, I had on three layers of gloves—light polypropylene gloves against the skin, a pair of woolen gloves over the top of those, and a pair of bulky, heavy mittens over them both.

The mittens were identical in design to those worn by polar explorers from the Heroic Age of the early 1900s. The design of polar clothing in those days was relatively effective. My mittens were made of leather, with a warm wool lining on the inside, and a piece of sheepskin, affectionately known as a nose-wiper, sewn onto the outside at the back of the hand. The exterior surface of the palms of the gloves was soft leather—soft at room temperature anyhow. The leather palms of these mittens were the start of my problems.

I reached the iceberg feeling a little tired. It had taken me four hours of hard hauling to get the sledge across the sand-like snow, instead of the easy three I'd planned. Now that I was no longer moving, I needed to get the tent up quickly, change out of perspiration-damp clothes, and cook up a hot, reenergizing orange juice.

During my ski across the ice, a light breeze had come up, maybe only 5 knots (10 kph or 6 mph), and now that I was away from the land the temperature had dropped several more degrees. The cold temperature combined with the breeze created a wind-chill effect on my body of around −60°C (−76°F). I wasn't particularly worried about this for the moment, as I'd been out in colder weather before, but I knew that I didn't want to be standing around lightly dressed for too long.

I pulled my heavy winter jacket off the sledge and put it on over the top of my wind-shell to give me some extra protection while I put the tent up. I got the small nylon tent off the sledge, assembled the poles, and began to slide them into the nylon sleeves of the tent. This was the first step, and pretty much the only step required to get the tent up. But that's where there was a major problem.

The light-weight, skinny aluminum poles wouldn't slide through the nylon sleeves. The low temperature had caused the normally flexible sleeves to become rigid after being folded flat on the sledge. They wouldn't open up. This shouldn't have been such a problem—I should have been able to force the poles through the sleeves with a bit of wiggling. What prevented me from doing this was that the leather lining on the palms of my heavy mittens had lost their softness in the cold weather and had become shiny and hard. This was causing my hands to slip along the skinny poles as I tried to push them into the sleeves. I needed to be able to get more grip on the poles. I didn't want to take my mittens off because, even though I would still have my woolen gloves on and my lighter polypro gloves on underneath those, there was a risk my fingers would become frost-bitten in the cold wind-chill.

I'd been stopped for about ten minutes by then and could feel myself starting to cool down. My underclothes, damp from perspiration, were wicking away my body heat.

I thought about quitting and simply returning to base but I didn't want to risk the four-hour ski back feeling as tired and cold as I was if I could avoid it. When your core begins to feel cold in that sort of climate, you are already in some potential trouble. It's a bit like an astronaut finding a leak in his or her space suit. You have to take action very quickly to avoid a serious problem. The feeling of cold can quickly advance to shivering, then heavy shivering, and then no shivering. This is hypothermia. The next stages are mental confusion, loss of consciousness, and death. All this can happen in a couple of hours, or quicker, depending on what one is wearing. The process is accelerated when tiredness or exhaustion are factors. This was me. I decided to go for the *mittens-off* option.

In the freezing temperatures the soft wool of my under-glove was as slippery as the mitten. The pole moved just a few millimeters further into the sleeve. I tried some different sleeves but they were all the same.

I decided I'd better radio the base and let them know I'd arrived at the iceberg, and maybe let them know I was experiencing a small problem. It was fifteen minutes since I'd stopped and I was starting to get cold. The small VHF radios we carry in the field are usually slung around our necks and tucked under our arms, under our jackets, to keep the batteries warm. A cold battery at those temperatures is a flat battery. Because I was putting up the tent though, I'd taken my radio off and put it in my pack on the sledge. I thought I could always warm it up again and recover its charge if needed.

I pulled the freezing radio off the sledge, clicked the volume dial to *on*, and keyed the transmit button. The transmit button, a long piece of spring-loaded plastic attached to something important inside the radio, broke off, and fell onto the snow. The cold had contracted the plastic, making it loose in its mount, to the point that it no longer fit as designed. I picked up the plastic button and looked at it. I couldn't reattach it. Now I had no radio.

I needed to get the tent up. If I tried to ski back to base, but got into difficulties on the way, then I wouldn't be able to call for assistance. That was too high risk in this environment. If I twisted an ankle it could become serious. I wasn't sure, in any case, that my rapidly cooling body would be able to make the four hours back to base. But I couldn't get properly warm where I was unless I was inside the tent with my cooker running.

I stripped off the woolen glove from my right hand in the hope that the thin polypro glove would give me a better grip than the fluffy wool. The palm of my hand was toasty warm from a warming pad I'd put in the glove, but the fingers themselves were becoming numb from the cold since I'd taken the mitten off. Gloves are not nearly as good as mittens at keeping fingers warm.

I pushed on the pole. The polypro gloves gripped brilliantly. The pole finally started to move through the tent sleeve. In five minutes the tent was up

Image 2.2   The author's campsite at the iceberg—a cold day in spring (Photo: Grant Avery).

and I quickly put my gloves back on. In that short time, the middle fingers on my right hand, from the middle joints to the tips, had turned a gray color and frozen solid. I decided I would worry about that later and for now was just pleased to be able to get out of the breeze and into the tent. Soon I was toasty warm and enjoying a hot meal and drink. My fingers painfully thawed as I clutched my plastic cup. I had had a close call and had a fitful sleep as the tent cracked in the wind. I got up early to make the trip back to base. The dry snow had not become any easier to drag a sledge across and it was a long ski back.

I was amazed at how exhausted I was when I got back to base. Scott had talked in his diaries about the unusually cold temperatures he experienced on his return from the Pole and how hard it was to drag a heavy sledge across snow at those temperatures. Now I understood first-hand how much those temperatures would have slowed Scott's return, ultimately causing his demise. My sledge weighed just a fraction of what his did.

The tips of my thawed-out fingers blistered from the frostbite but nothing dropped off. I was very lucky. Those fingers are still prone to cold temperatures today.

The lesson for me from that incident was that although I'd been well trained in the risks of the environment, and had accumulated quite a bit of experience working there, I had taken on complex extra risk without realizing it. Individually, the extra risks were small, but their combined effect was high. I'd traded risk mitigation for outcome-maximizing. My extra outcomes included the increased satisfaction of traveling alone, the lighter weight of my sledge carrying a lighter design of tent (but one known for being difficult to put up in cold temperatures), and traveling outdoors on a much colder day than is usual. My alternative was not to go at all, but I really wanted to get out for a break at the iceberg. In an already high-risk environment, stretching to these extras was a dangerous thing to do.

And this is the issue that the Everest climbers, the Heroic Age Antarctic explorers, and the modern-day adventure tourists on the *Shokalskiy* suffered from. It is the same issue that affects the managers and leaders of high-risk initiatives anywhere. Rather than consciously reducing the risks of what we are doing, we consciously maximize our outcomes and unconsciously increase our risks.

Culture change can reduce failure rates, but in the absence of culture change, failure in human endeavor, and in projects, is largely a constant.

What is it that drives this constancy of failure in almost everything we do?

3

Risk Homeostasis Theory

"Take risk in your life like salt in your soup: not too much, nor too little."

Professor Gerald Wilde (Emeritus professor of psychology,
Queen's University, Kingston, Ontario, Canada)

ONE STEP FORWARD, ONE STEP BACK

The tendency for humans to maximize their outcomes instead of reducing their risks is explained by a concept called *risk homeostasis theory*.

Risk homeostasis, also known as *risk compensation*, was researched and written about by the Canadian psychologist, Professor Gerald Wilde, in his 1994 book *Target Risk* (updated in 2014 as *Target Risk 3: Risk Homeostasis in Everyday Life*).

Wilde wrote:

> *"In any ongoing activity, people continuously check the amount of risk they feel they are exposed to. They compare this with the amount of risk they are willing to accept, and try to reduce any difference between the two to zero. Thus, if the level of subjectively experienced risk is lower than is felt acceptable, people tend to engage in actions that increase their exposure to risk. If, however, the level of subjectively experienced risk is higher than is acceptable, they make an attempt to exercise greater caution."*

In Wilde's view, the risks people are willing to accept (also known as *target risk*) depends on four utility factors: (1) the expected benefits of risky behavior, (2) the expected costs of risky behavior, (3) the expected benefits of safe behavior, and (4) the expected costs of safe behavior.

Thus, the higher the values of factors 1 and 4, and the lower the values of factors 2 and 3, the more risk will be taken.

Wilde has written a number of papers and books on risk homeostasis. Examples of its application can be found in many areas of society. One example that Wilde gives is advanced driver training courses. These have also been found to be effective in increasing the skills of drivers, but they have been found to increase the *confidence* of drivers. The result is that graduates from these courses have been found to have higher accident rates than drivers who haven't taken the courses. Better skills offer people the feeling that the expected cost of risky behavior will be lessened (a *we-can-handle-it* attitude) and thus, the willingness to engage in risky behavior is enhanced.

Another of Wilde's examples is the introduction of child-proof medicine containers. Although these containers make it harder for children to get the lids off, their introduction has been associated with increasing rates of accidental poisonings. One of the causes is believed to be that parents become less careful in the handling and storage of the safer bottles.

Wilde notes that while the theory of risk homeostasis was primarily developed from research on road safety, supporting data comes from many different domains. A basic principle of risk homeostasis is the idea that the outcome of a person's behavior—one's own or another's—may alter a person's perception of the value of the four utility factors previously mentioned, and so alter their subsequent behavior. People learn from their own accidents, and the accidents of others.

INCREASING COMFORT CREATES INCREASING RISK

2006 was a bad year on Everest—twelve climbers died. Most of them died not because the weather was bad that year, but because it was good. Three climbers were killed in an avalanche low down in the ice fall early in the season, but the other victims were lured, one at a time, to levels of altitude and risk taking which they would never have reached but for the good weather. The good weather lessened the perceived level of risk, and so climbers' willingness to take on other risks increased.

When the weather is bad on Everest—windy, cold, or snowing—it acts as a filter. Weak and inexperienced climbers are turned back before they have a chance to get close to the summit or even to get too far from the safety of their tents. As one experienced climber put it, "climbing Everest is a bit like swimming as far out to sea as you can go, and then turning around and hoping you can make it back to shore."

When people reach the summit of Everest most of them are physically and mentally drained. It is the long climb down which then kills people.

Even some of those who turn around before the summit—defeated early by a lack of fitness, skill, or tolerance of extreme altitude—make their turn-around decision too late.

And so in the same way that a stormy or choppy sea will prevent weak swimmers from getting too far out to sea, bad weather on Everest reduces the number of weak climbers who are able to reach the exposed summit ridge. As risk homeostasis theory predicts, bad weather causes climbers to become less comfortable with the situation around them, so they compensate by taking less risks in other areas. They are inclined to turn around and head back down more quickly than they would on a calm day.

On a calm day, Everest allows climbers to stretch themselves, including the weak ones. Their comfort increases and so does their risk taking. And then, when the altitude and the exhaustion catch up with them or the weather changes for the worse, high risk becomes critical risk.

Good weather on Everest creates an outcome-maximizing opportunity for climbers in the same way in which supplemental oxygen did for Mallory in 1924. People treat the good weather, not as an opportunity to extend their safety margins, but as an opportunity to climb higher, putting themselves into new risk territory, and increasing their chances of catastrophic failure.

DEXAMETHASONE

Dexamethasone, or *dex* as it is more commonly known, is a high potency steroid that can work miracles on climbers suffering from severe altitude sickness. Commonly carried by climbers and guides, dex is supposed to be used only in emergencies.

The problem today is that dex is increasingly being used by climbers on Everest—not as a medicine to treat altitude illness, but as a performance enhancer to boost energy levels and reduce the negative effects of altitude before they occur.

When used as a performance enhancer, dex triples a climber's risks in these three ways:

1. It increases the comfort of climbers, encouraging them to climb higher and take greater risks than they would otherwise be capable of.
2. A well-known side effect of its use is medically induced euphoria. Climbers who use it actually feel more capable, fitter, and stronger than they really are.
3. In the event that a climber who has already taken dex as a preventative measure suddenly finds the need to use it to treat a real emergency, it can't be used for fear of an overdose—thus the options for saving the

climber become greatly reduced. Dex has saved countless lives on Everest, but not often in those who have already been taking it.

Dex is a good example of risk homeostasis at work. It increases comfort, and puts climbers into a more complex zone of risk than they otherwise would find themselves.

THE SPACE SHUTTLE

In 1996, Malcolm Gladwell, in his article for *The New Yorker* entitled *Blowup*, discussed the role that risk homeostasis played in the 1986 loss of the space shuttle *Challenger*. The Challenger shuttle exploded 73 seconds after lift-off, killing all seven astronauts on board.

In his article Gladwell referenced Richard Feynman, the Nobel Prize-winning physicist who served on the Challenger accident investigation commission. Feynman had said that decision making at NASA, at that time, had turned into a kind of *Russian roulette*. Rubber O-rings on the shuttle's solid fuel booster rockets had been found to be the cause of the Challenger accident—they had failed to seal properly on the very cold morning of the launch. But the O-rings had exhibited problems on earlier launches—they just hadn't failed to the extent that they did on the day of the tragic explosion. NASA had been aware of these earlier problems, but because there had been no catastrophe, they had talked themselves into believing that the risk for subsequent flights was lower than it was—hence the game of Russian roulette.

With each subsequent launch, NASA's comfort with the O-rings increased. This growing comfort resulted in NASA—just as risk homeostasis theory predicts—increasing their risks in other areas. One of these areas was their tolerance to the temperature at which launches could occur. NASA became more comfortable launching shuttles on colder and colder days. Eventually, the temperature on one of the launches—the shuttle Challenger's—became so cold that the O-rings failed completely. They no longer sealed, and burning hot gases were able to escape and cause the main fuel tank to explode when the shuttle was 15 km (48,000 feet) above the ground.

We also see risk homeostasis in major information and communications technology-enabled business (ICT-EB) change programs. People become comfortable with the risks of what they have done in previous years, or with the assurances that eager vendors provide them, and they take on more risk as a result. The resulting risks combine in unpredictable and complex ways.

Near the end of the space shuttle article Gladwell wrote:

> *"What accidents like Challenger should teach us is that we have constructed a world in which the potential for high-tech catastrophe*

is embedded in the fabric of day-to-day life. At some point in the future—for the most mundane of reasons, and with the very best of intentions—a NASA spacecraft will again go down in flames."

These 1996 words were to prove prophetic. Seven years after Gladwell's article, on February 1, 2003, the space shuttle *Columbia* disintegrated while re-entering the earth's atmosphere over Texas. Seven more astronauts lost their lives.

Risk homeostasis drives outcome-maximizing (up to the level of the person's risk comfort levels). When our capabilities in something increase—when we get good at doing that specific thing—our comfort with the risks that we have been taking increases, and we take on more risk in subconscious compensation as a result. These risks are new, and they combine with the old risks in ways we haven't experienced before. The result can be a net and dangerous increase in risk, often without us realizing.

This cycle of capability improvement, comfort, outcome-maximizing, increasing risk, and failure which characterizes risk homeostasis in projects of all types is shown in Figure 3.1.

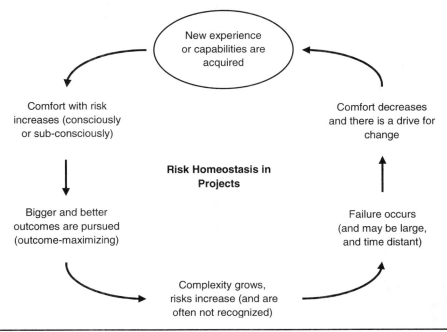

Figure 3.1 The cycle of risk homeostasis in projects

NORMAL NARCISSISM A DRIVER

Risk homeostasis originates in the subconscious, from a person or organization's *risk personality*. It is a function of the individual's (using Wilde's words) *subjective experience of risk*. We all experience risk differently. It is driven by our genetic makeup, our upbringing, our personality, the culture we live in, and the attitudes of the people—and the businesses—that surround us. Some people are comfortable with high levels of risk and others aren't.

Normal narcissism (something we all have a little bit of—some more than others) is a personality variable that has been found to be positively correlated with risk taking. The more normal narcissism you have, the more risks you tend to take.

One of the more common tests used to assess an individual's level of normal narcissism is Raskin and Terry's 1998 *Narcissistic Personality Inventory* (NPI). The NPI is a relatively straight-forward, 40-item, forced-choice questionnaire that is used by social psychology researchers. The higher one's score—the higher one's level of normal narcissism. In extreme forms, normal narcissism moves from being an everyday personality trait to becoming a distinct mental disorder where clinical support is often recommended. Fortunately, the disorder narcissism personality disorder (NPD), is much less common than normal narcissism, the trait.

In their 2004 paper, *Narcissism, Confidence, and Risk Attitude*, Campbell et al., noted two pitfalls of narcissists (who they define as people scoring *higher* on the NPI) when it comes to their decision making. The first of these is that narcissists might be expected to display elevated degrees of overconfidence, and the second is their willingness to take risks. In projects that are already risky, high levels of narcissism are a dangerous attribute to add to the mix.

Another way to view narcissism is the amount of ego that we invest in the things that we do. The more ego that we have invested in something (e.g., a high-risk project), the more likely it is we will take risks to protect that ego.

More detail and examples of normal narcissism, and its role in the failure of high-risk projects, are provided in Chapter 7.

ORGANIZATIONS OUTCOME-MAXIMIZE

If we are to improve the success rates of our projects, it is important for us to be aware that organizations are affected by risk homeostasis just like people are—and to understand why this is so and who drives it.

When organizational leaders become uncomfortable with their levels of risk, they seek to reduce them. They might do this by taking on less-risky projects, or by strengthening their project management capabilities. Sometimes they will make these risk adjustments as conscious, step decisions—for example in response to a major failure, or after observing a major failure in a related organization. At other times these risk adjustments are more incremental.

A problem for organizations is that the opposite also applies. When leaders are feeling more comfortable with organizational capabilities, or less challenged by organizational ambitions, they take on more risk in response. A commonly heard call to arms from new executives arriving in a new organization, or at times of commercial pressure, is: *if we're going to succeed more, we have to take more risks!* The implications of that cry are not always understood by those who make it. Any call for more risk taking, without understanding what one wants from it, and in what areas—and what one *doesn't* want from it—is a call for more failure.

Another trigger for unknowingly adding risk can be the employment of an experienced and qualified senior project manager or business change executive. Such moves can leave an organization feeling empowered to increase the complexity of their projects or the quantity that they are managing.

So, as it is for *Heroic Age* explorers and modern project managers, movements to increase outcomes in organizations, if not carefully managed, can shift the organization into a more complex and higher risk place.

Just as a personal level of normal narcissism is a driver of personal risk taking, organizational narcissism is a driver of organizational risk taking. Social psychologists tell us that businesses have corporate egos (their cultures), just like people have personal egos, and when these are strong, risk taking can be high.

Professor Manfred Kets de Vries in a work entitled *Organizations on the Couch*, described how unconscious psychodynamics can have a significant impact on the life and behavior of organizations. He noted that organizations can exhibit personalities and behaviors not dissimilar to those of individual people, narcissism included.

THE SHADOW OF THE LEADER

So—if the organization behaves like a person, which person does it most behave like?

The *Shadow of the Leader* is a concept referenced in some leadership books to describe how organizations take on the personalities of their leaders, whether those personalities are good for the business or bad for the business.

The concept goes beyond the direct influence that leaders have over their followers' actions. It describes how followers actually begin to take on the behaviors and values of the people leading them. One driver of this is the type of person that the leader recruits, and another is the self-selection of new staff who applies for jobs.

A larger driver is the actual evolution of followers' behaviors and values over a period of time under the new leader—the changing of the culture of the business itself. Followers begin to adopt values and behaviors similar to those of the leader. These values may include the way the organization deals with its staff (harshly or collaboratively?), the way it views its customers and partner businesses (supportively or mercenary?) and, in particular, its approach to risk taking.

Aggressive, risk-taking leaders can quickly create a culture where aggression and high risk taking are a core value. Conversely, *servant leader* CEOs can quickly create high levels of team collaboration and interpersonal trust. Sometimes the personality of the CEO will itself be the result of a stronger shadow, for example cast by the organization's owners or its governing board.

Risk homeostasis and outcome-maximizing in an organization, at both the personal and organizational level, can be mitigated, but only through active and constant management. A vague call such as *we mustn't fail* will do little for reducing risk where it counts, and may even increase it.

A key to managing risk homeostasis is having awareness of the different types of risk that each of us, and our organizations, are comfortable with—and then assessing those risks against what it is that we are trying to achieve. Specifically, what must happen, what must not happen, and what can we experiment with that might pay high returns, but that won't matter too much if it doesn't succeed.

So how do we begin to understand our comfort levels with different types of risk, and how do we change them—particularly in an organizational context? The different levels of comfort with risk that each of us has for different types of risk, personal or organizational, is called *risk appetite*. It's a formal term and appears in a number of risk standards and international guidance notes. Unfortunately, too many managers and organizations are not aware of risk appetite as a concept, and particularly not of how to manage it in projects.

The following chapter explores risk appetite in projects, and ways that it can be managed.

4

Risk Appetite

"I'd say this to myself ... 'This is Everest and you've got to take a few risks.'"

Edmund Hillary, as he neared the summit of Everest, May 29, 1953
(From his autobiography, *Nothing Venture, Nothing Win*)

"Time, Cost, Quality (or Scope)—pick two," as the saying goes, but which two? The saying *pick two* is a humorous reference to the essential difficulty of project management—the successful delivery of the three components which define any project. In the classic project management Iron Triangle, shown in Figure 4.1, sometimes called "the triple constraint", more than two thirds of projects fail to deliver on all three of their scope, time, and cost promises. About a third of projects fail to deliver on any of them.

The problem is that the choice of which two sides of the triangle should be prioritized for success frequently occurs in an uncontrolled way.

Figure 4.1 The Iron Triangle

When the pressure comes on in your high-risk project, do you choose for your project to be a little bit late, to go a few percent over budget, or to under-deliver some of the benefits it promised? Risk appetite provides the answer to this question.

A HUNGER FOR FAILURE

The term used in business and academia to describe a person or organization's comfort with certain levels of risk in certain situations is *risk appetite*.

Risk appetite is a measure of our comfort with the gap that exists between our abilities and our ambitions. It is the difference between what we *can* do and what we *want* to do, our comfort with a level of risk, and our tolerance to a level of uncertainty regarding our success.

When two people are confronted with the same risky situation they will each experience the situation with different levels of comfort. Sometimes these levels of comfort will be similar, and sometimes different.

The key thing about risk appetite is that it is different for each of us, for our different organizations, and for the different types of risk that we face. For a common situation, some of us are risk averse and others of us are risk hungry, but we are never solely risk hungry or solely risk averse for all the risks we encounter.

The International Organization for Standardization (ISO) defines risk appetite in ISO Guide 73 as: *The amount and type of risk that an organization is willing to pursue or retain.*

David Hillson and Ruth Murray-Webster, in their more detailed 2011 white paper, "Shedding Light on Risk Appetite," define it as *the tendency of an individual or group to take risk in a given situation.*

Our risk appetites are driven by our comfort with the risks in front of us as well as our comfort with what we don't know. If I don't know what the risks are of a situation that is new to me, but I am prepared to proceed regardless, then my risk appetite is higher than someone who is concerned at proceeding in the same situation.

The metaphor *risk hungry* is sometimes used to describe a risk appetite where there is comfort with high levels of risk. The Institute of Risk Management (IRM), in their 2011 "Risk Appetite & Tolerance Guidance Paper," prefers to think of risk appetite more in terms of *fight or flight responses to perceived risk.* Unfortunately, in many organizations—and especially in project management—risk appetite is not thought about at all.

DIFFERENT RISK APPETITES—EXAMPLES FROM EVEREST AND ANTARCTICA

In 2007, Mike Allsop, a modern-day adventurer and author of the 2013 best seller *High Altitude*, was at Camp 2 on Mt. Everest when members of his group proposed they do a short acclimatization hike up to the Lhotse Face.

The Lhotse Face is a 1,125 meter (3,700 feet) wall of ice that people climbing Everest via the South Col must ascend to reach Everest's summit. Because it was early in the climbing season, no ropes had been put in place and no crevasses had been marked in the area in which the group proposed to hike. Critically, Allsop's group had no spare rope for tying themselves together for safety, and had not planned to go further than Camp 2 for this acclimatization hike.

Safe travel in crevasse fields requires climbers to link themselves together with 7 to 10 meters (20 to 30 feet) of rope. Most crevasses are hidden under thin blankets of snow and if a climber accidentally steps into one unroped, there is a good chance of injury or death. Crevasses are very scary things to look into—an evil infinite blackness is what one often sees. To fall into a crevasse unroped is a climber's worst nightmare.

The process of death, if the victim doesn't break their neck in the fall, is often for the victim to fall until they are jammed in a narrow point between the crevasse walls. The victim's body heat then melts the ice a little, causing the victim to slip further. Their body then cools down, the melted layer re-freezes, and the victim is stuck fast. The victim then dies from hypothermia as the crevasse walls pressing in on either side of them wicks their body heat away. It's not necessarily painful, but if you're a claustrophobic like me, it holds little appeal.

Allsop questioned his group on the wisdom of making the one-hour trip, given the risks that they would not be roped together and that there were crevasses ahead of them which had not been mapped. He felt it wasn't a smart thing to do, especially since the route would be marked and would be more accessible, making it safer, in just another day or two. After a short discussion the group decided they still wanted to do the hike. Allsop wisely elected not to join them.

Allsop's Camp 2 story is a good example of different risk appetites at work. The risks of the situation were largely the same for both parties—one party was comfortable with them, one was not.

The drivers of risk appetite can be complex, but in Allsop's book there is a clue as to why his risk appetite differed, at least in part, from that of his fellow climbers. Allsop writes that although he was an experienced climber (to the point of being able to climb Everest unguided), this was his first trip to the mountain. Most of the guys in his group had climbed on Everest before. Risk homeostasis theory suggests that the climbers who had been on the mountain before, and who had taken risks that they were comfortable with then—and which they had gotten away with—were likely to have been comfortable taking similar or greater risks again later. In fact, it is likely they would add risk to what they were doing without realizing it—taking on new risks to compensate for their increased comfort, just as NASA did with the *Challenger* launch in 1986.

A short time after Allsop's teammates departed for their walk, he noticed a group of British Special Forces climbers traveling across the same glacier—roped together. Forty-five minutes later, one of these men stepped into a crevasse but was saved by his rope and was able to be extracted by his team. That group then terminated their climb and headed back down. Even if you are roped up, falling into a crevasse can result in injury—chunks of ice can fall with you or on you, limbs can be broken, and concussions can occur. It's to be avoided, if at all possible.

Ten minutes after the soldiers had headed back down, Allsop's own team returned. They had experienced a couple of close calls themselves, and decided it was indeed too dangerous to continue without ropes. They were lucky to have learned the lesson without losing someone down a crevasse in the process. The smart thing they did was learning from their close calls.

Close calls are often a sign of a bigger failure to come. We see this in the failure of major information and communications technology-enabled business (ICT-EB) projects. The projects most likely to fail catastrophically are the ones which keep over-running their budgets and schedules, or have trouble getting their business cases approved.

Sometimes, it is not familiarity with an environment that causes risk appetite to increase, but the lack of it. Familiarity can generate the comfort that causes risk levels to grow, but so also can an absence of experience altogether.

Some years ago we ran a major search and rescue exercise (SAREX) in Antarctica in the middle of winter. Large midwinter SAREXs in Antarctica are not common because they are risky—there is 24-hour darkness and temperatures are very cold.

This particular exercise was run early in the afternoon, which is still pitch black in the Antarctic winter time, and the temperature was around −40°C (−40°F). The moon that we had been counting on to help us see was obscured by a layer of thick cloud. We couldn't see anything beyond the 20 meters or so of vague shadows cast by the headlights we wore on our heavily balaclava'd heads. It was quite eerie—everything around us was blackness. There was no sound, apart from the crunch of the snow beneath our boots and the occasional clunk of our equipment.

The crevassed terrain we would have to cross with no marked trail made the exercise more dangerous. There is a point at which the benefits of doing something outweigh the risks. This exercise should never have started but there was a classic case of group-think at work. No one felt brave enough to put their hand up to say we shouldn't do it. Partly, we were hoping our head-lamps would show us more than what they did, and partly, no one wanted to appear unconfident. The SAR coordinator was an army officer with little mountaineering or SAR experience, but he was the boss. We joked that he was thinking an absence of moonlight would provide us a tactical advantage like it does for some military situations.

The SAR coordinator was also running the exercise via radio, from the well-lit warmth of the map room in the SAR command center back at base. In risk homeostasis terms, he had a high comfort level with the risks of the operation originating from both his low experience and low situational awareness. It was likely he would add risk to his decisions without realizing he was doing it. His risk appetite was high in a situation where it needed to be low.

The SAREX was being executed in a large icefall some distance from the main bases. The icefall was several square kilometers of crevassed glacier, house-sized blocks of ice, and deceptively peaceful snowfields hiding many crevasses. We had trained a lot in this icefall during the summer and knew it well—when we could see it. In the dark, with only a few meters visible to us at any one time, it was very different. My team of four hiked up into the fall, roped together for safety, heading toward a rendezvous point where another team, having taken a different route, was waiting for us. The rendezvous was marked by a ragged black hole in the snow, the only sign that is left when someone steps through a snow bridge into a hidden crevasse. When we reached the rendezvous it would be our team's job to rescue the *victim*—a dummy planted in the hole several weeks earlier when there had been more light.

We worked our way up through the icefall, making changes to our course based only on guestimates of how far we had traveled and our rough recollections from the summer of what angles we needed to turn to find the rendezvous. The other team was using headlights, but we could not see them because of the jumbled features of the icefall that lay between us and them. As we reached the top of the icefall, we hiked across an area of gently upward-sloping snow which I knew hid crevasses—large ones. I was sweating, not from the effort of lugging a pack full of rope and ice rescue equipment up a hill, but from the fear of knowing what lay beneath us. A sickening feeling of weightlessness could occur at any moment as the snow we trudged across collapsed into one of the hidden monsters. We were probing with our ice axes for crevasses as we went, but in the cold conditions the snow was hard and there were no guarantees we would find them, especially the bigger ones that were hidden by thicker snow coverings.

A mantra in my head kept asking, *what are we doing up here?* The bizarre worry added to this was that we represented half of the SAR team in that part of Antarctica at that time of the year. Other than our cold and tired colleagues further up the hill, there would be little rescue available if our role suddenly changed to that of victim. No planes or helicopters operated in Antarctica during the winter months.

We knew that the other team was waiting, and that the SAR coordinator was following our progress by radio. The pressure that we all felt not to turn back, not to put a hand up and cancel the exercise for safety reasons, was interesting. A couple of us stepped into smaller cracks hidden under the snow at different times but we kept going. Through shear good luck we made it to the rendezvous without any major collapse of the snow beneath us.

The other team were stomping their feet to stay warm, standing next to the hole in the snow which signaled the crevasse with a dummy anchored three or four meters (12 feet) below. One member of our team bravely volunteered to go down the crevasse to rescue the dummy. The plan was that we would set up a system of ice and snow anchors, connected with ropes and pulleys, to recover the victim.

As the team leader, with a dummy stuck down the hole rather than a real victim, and given the risks we'd taken simply walking to where we were, I had to ask myself if the risks of doing this outweighed the training benefits we would receive. We knew how to extract people out of crevasses. It was the bread-and-butter of the exercises we performed all the time in summer. We also exercised in springtime, when temperatures were just as cold, but there was more light. Hikers are forbidden in the icefall area at any time of the year, and in winter time, even hiking the trails on flat areas nearby is forbidden. I decided I wasn't prepared to take the risk of sending someone down a black hole into a bottomless crevasse, in very poor light and low temperatures, just to pull up a dummy.

With the dummy considered *rescued* we followed our tracks back down to the vehicles and returned to base. I called the SAR coordinator after we got back and told him the exercise had been a daft thing to run in that light. He suggested we discuss it in more detail at a SAREX debrief that was scheduled for the next day.

A number of senior managers from the local bases attended the debriefing. I outlined my concerns that such an exercise shouldn't be run again in the winter. The risks were too high and the back-up cover that we had was too light. One of the senior base managers chipped in, "But you guys are trained to get yourselves out of crevasses if you fall into them, aren't you?" He was showing his comfort—and hence his higher risk appetite—for risks that he also wasn't experienced with. The answer to the question was, "Sure, we can get ourselves out of crevasses, but only if we haven't broken a leg or our neck in the process."

During that particular SAREX there was also the risk that, being roped together, we might take our fellow climbers into the crevasse with us. This can happen when you can't see in which direction the crevasses run. Sometimes a team traveling in bad visibility can find itself walking parallel with crevasses instead of at right angles to them. If a roped-up team had fallen into a crevasse during our exercise, it would have been a very serious situation.

The meeting concluded with the agreement that a SAREX wouldn't be performed in the icefall during winter months again.

On that SAREX, as with Allsop's team on Everest, there were different risk appetites at work. Some of these were higher than they needed to be on an exercise. In environments where the results of poor risk judgment can be severe injury or death, the effect of high risk appetite can be very visible.

The photo in Image 4.1 shows the frozen face of a SAR team member after a midwinter SAREX in Antarctic darkness during temperatures of −45°C (−45°F).

The impact of poorly judged risk appetite in high-risk business projects, although not usually measured in lives lost or limbs broken, can still be life or death for the project or the sponsoring business.

RISK APPETITE IN ICT-EB PROJECTS

Risk appetite is present in all decision making. The greater the risks in a decision, the greater the risk appetite present, even if risk appetite as a concept isn't understood. ICT-EB projects have high failure rates globally and risk appetite is present in all of them. Very few ICT-EB projects achieve all their goals.

A high-risk $160 million ICT-EB project that I was advising on recently, called the Transformation X Project (TXP), was under some pressure to get its business case to the company's board for approval. As is not uncommon in these situations, a slippage in the business case writing schedule created

Image 4.1   Frozen face of a SAR team member.

extra pressure for the quality assurance reviewers who sat at the end of the decision-making chain.

The quality assurance review of a major ICT-EB investment is critical. Because of their high failure rates, ICT-EB project boards and chief executives depend on independent quality assurance reviews to provide them with confidence that the risks of such uncertain investments are manageable. They also depend on these reviews for advice on how to reduce losses and maximize the delivery of promised benefits.

The ICT-EB projects that have the highest failure rate are those that are large and transforming some or all of the business. Nearly one in five of these projects fails outright globally, and two thirds of them suffer heavy losses.

The project sponsor of TXP was insisting that there was no time for the independent quality assurance (IQA) review to occur before the final business case was due for presentation to the company's board. They had already had a major review six months ago. That review had been sched-uled to occur when the draft business case was completed, but the project schedule had slipped, delaying the business case, and the assurance manager hadn't wanted to cancel the expensive reviewers contracted to undertake the review.

So the review had proceeded with no business case for the reviewers to look at. Christmas was now approaching and if the scheduled board meeting was missed, there would be a three-month delay until the next board presen-tation opportunity. Such a delay would mean that project heads could roll.

The reason the project was suffering timeline pressures was that it had struggled to obtain support from stakeholders for the proposed solution in its earlier indicative business case (the organization was sensibly using a two-stage business case approval process). Some stakeholders from within the organization did not believe the project should proceed in its current state at all. The project was troubled and the risks of proceeding to board approval without a robust, independent review were high.

Sometimes I use the metaphor of an airplane with a troubled mainte-nance history to help businesses understand the risks of this type of situa-tion. Let's say that you have an airplane that has been suffering from some maintenance issues and is running late against its schedule of flights. When it is about to fly a load of important people to a conference—the plane's last flight of the day—you are told that the only way the plane will get there on time is if its preflight checks are skipped. Do you allow the plane to fly? The answer, of course, is *no*.

TXP was a good example of different risk appetites at work in an ICT-EB project. The sponsor had a high risk appetite, coming from having no previ-ous experience of a major ICT-EB project failure and from career pressure to deliver an important business change investment.

External observers on the other hand, myself included (being the con-sulting quality assurance advisor, but not the IQA reviewer), were more nervous. The cost of a delay might be high, especially to the project spon-sor's career, but the cost to the organization of a poorly scoped project being approved would be much higher. We advised against a decision to proceed without a more robust technical review of the business case occurring.

The business case didn't proceed to the board meeting and at the time of writing this, the sponsoring business department is still trying to broker an agreement on a solution that everyone supports. The project sponsor has also reduced their engagement with external advisors. They were not happy with the advice to delay the project, and potentially their careers.

Understanding the drivers of risk appetite is important in decision making, be it climbing a mountain, or managing or sponsoring a major ICT-EB project.

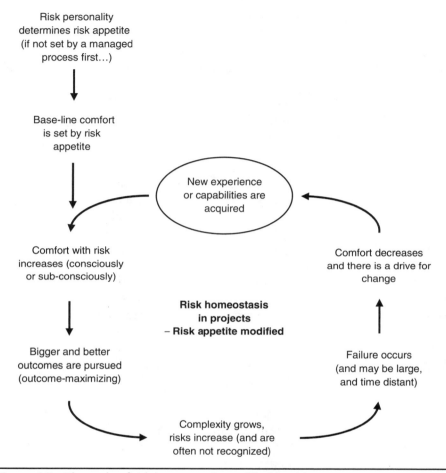

Figure 4.2   The cycle of risk homeostasis modified by risk appetite

While risk homeostasis explains the tendency in human behavior and project management for risk levels to return to a baseline after a failure or an improvement in capabilities has occurred, risk appetite explains how that baseline is determined. The relevant relationships are shown in Figure 4.2.

PERSONAL RISK APPETITES

Some of us are risk hungry and some of us are risk averse. And where we may be risk averse in one area, we may be risk hungry in others. For example, in matters of my personal finances and the management of the security of my home, I am risk averse. I'm also risk averse when it comes to the safety of my children. A good example of this occurred during our family vacation last summer.

My son Timothy was 13 years old at the time and my daughter Charlotte was 11. We had been traveling on holiday around New Zealand's beautiful South Island when we stopped at one of the wild and spectacular beaches on the West Coast. The surf was rolling in and crashing with great booms against the steeply sloping shoreline of polished stones and pebbles. It was a beautiful scene and the children wanted to go down to the water's edge where the water from the waves was making the pebbles jangle against each other as it ran back out to sea.

I knew that these beaches were infamous for big waves taking people by surprise. Too often, people, frequently children, had lost their lives on beaches like this. I wouldn't let the children go near the water's edge. They protested, "You're too conservative Dad!" but I wasn't giving in. The kids had a good time in spite of me, as they usually do. They even found some pieces of naturally occurring jade hidden among the surf-polished pebbles higher up the beach.

A couple of weeks after we got back from our vacation, our local news station showed footage of attempts by the public to rescue a boy caught by a big wave on a beach in another part of the country. Fortunately the rescue was successful, and the news footage was dramatic (Google: *Napier beach rescue human chain*). The footage shows people rushing from all directions and forming a human chain to reach the boy being tumbled over in the surf. My children watched the news footage, fixated by what they saw unfolding. Being played out on the television in front of them was just the risk that I'd warned them about on our vacation.

After the news story, Timothy and Charlotte's comfort with the risks of playing on steep surf beaches reduced. They had less appetite for that type of risk. Hopefully they'll be safer as a result, and at some point in the future, might even think Dad's advice isn't always so boring.

In other parts of my life, I enjoy risks. I've sky-dived, bungee-jumped, and jumped through snow bridges into crevasses in Antarctica—all, mostly, for the fun of it. In all of these situations, I've been confident that I had a back-up system covering me if something went wrong. Back-up systems are great for increasing risk appetite. Failure of the goal is allowed to occur in these situations, but loss of life is never an option.

RISK PERSONALITIES

What drives our comfort, or discomfort, with different risks? These factors are important in projects because they are the main drivers of the type and amount of risk we are prepared to accept—and therefore of the level of failure that we should expect to experience. There are many academic and business papers written about what it is within our personalities that drives us to take risks (or not to take risks) in different situations. Some of the key factors that are recognized contributors to our risk personalities are listed in Figure 4.3.

The variable nature of these factors is the reason it is important that an organization's board should formally define risk appetite for different aspects of the business's operation. In the absence of formal risk statements, the personal risk appetites of the CEO and senior leaders (led by their risk personalities) will dominate. Do we want organizational risk taking to default to a set of personal risk characteristics? The resulting risk culture may not be in the best interests of the organization.

And so it is with projects and programs. Risk appetite in a project or program should be set by the project or program board—not by an individual and not by the organization's corporate board. This is because although a project's risk appetite statements should be informed by the organization's risk appetite statements, they will not be the same.

SET PROJECT RISK APPETITE SEPARATELY

The goals that a project must achieve, the things that mustn't go wrong with it, and the things that it can experiment with for high return (without fear of too much damage occurring if they don't work out) may not be the

Figure 4.3   Key factors contributing to our risk personalities

same as for the strategic level of the organization. There should be a specific exercise to develop these risk appetite statements.

If the project board does not actively consider and set the risk appetite for the project, the risk appetite of the strongest personality will dominate. That might be the project sponsor, or it might be a project director or manager. The result either way will be risk taking and risk aversion in the project, which will be based on the risk personality of an individual, and not on the considered reflection of the project's outcome and risk needs.

Is it time, cost, or quality that should dominate? Or should it be the customers' needs, security of commercial information, or the success of a new business idea? Where should the trade-offs be made? In what areas can slippage be allowed to occur so that something critical doesn't *slip* in another area?

RISK APPETITE REBALANCING

Risk appetite rebalancing is risk homeostasis at work in projects. When we get too comfortable with the risks of what we're doing, we take on more risk—and as a result, we put our risk appetite back into balance. We most often do this by increasing the level of ambition for the projects in our organizations' portfolios. We take on projects that are bigger or more complex, or both; we outcome-maximize, just like the climbers on Everest. When we're feeling comfortable with where we're at, we don't translate our comfort into climbing safer (safer projects), we climb higher.

The extra risks that organizations take when they increase their capabilities, and choose to do more with them (i.e., outcome-maximizing) almost always results in a more complex environment. The result is an increase in portfolio risk that frequently goes unnoticed until a major failure or cluster of failures occurs.

As with the 2013 Twin Otter flight, the *Shokalskiy's* 2014 capture by the sea ice, Mt. Everest (yesterday and today), and the 2003 Columbia shuttle disaster, this is the nature of complexity and our appetites for risk—we solve or learn from a risk, and then we take on more risk, because it's in our nature. The new territory we then find ourselves in is more complex, with more ways to fail than before. It contains interconnections and combinations of risk that we haven't experienced before.

WE DO THIS IN OUR EVERYDAY LIVES

We see the effects of risk appetite, risk homeostasis, risk appetite rebalancing, and risk overshoot in our everyday lives. It's a very human thing.

In our careers, when we start a new job, we're looking for a level of challenge to keep us interested. More challenge means more risk. For some of us, the level of challenge we seek might be relatively low. For some of the readers of this book, I suspect, it may be high, at least in some areas. When we have mastered a new level of challenge, our risks reduce, we become comfortable, and we begin the search for our next challenge. It might be a request for promotion, a bigger project, a transfer to a new area, or a shift to a new company altogether. Hopefully we get the move right and can master the increased challenges and risks, along with the growing complexity that we will create for ourselves.

Kids climb trees in much the same way. They start with something small, fall out, learn to climb it better (assuming they didn't fall too far), climb higher, and then fall again—and the cycle continues until they need a bigger tree. Some kids fall a long way during their learning cycles (high-risk appetite) and some not so far (low-risk appetite); but the cycle is usually the same—climbing higher, not safer.

KEY LEARNINGS ON RISK APPETITE

1. Risk appetite is effectively the difference between a project's abilities and its ambitions.
2. Risk appetite is set (in the absence of a more formal process) by personal or organizational *comfort.*
3. Without active management or some type of crisis, risk appetite in different contexts is largely a constant.
4. ICT-EB projects have high failure rates. The risk appetite associated with them is not formally defined in most organizations.
5. If one party is comfortable with a specific risk, but another party is nervous about it, that risk should be questioned. This is especially so if the party who is nervous has relevant previous experience that the party who is comfortable doesn't.
6. Comfort with risk should also be discussed if the party who is comfortable has been successful with similar risks in the past (success increases comfort, which increases risk appetite).
7. A one-in-five chance of outright failure in a $100 million (or a $1 millon) high-risk ICT-EB project is unacceptable for most organizations (it means 8 out of every 40 projects that are running in the business are going to fail outright). Yet this is the default risk appetite level for the average ICT-EB project.

8. Successful delivery of a $100 million (or a $1 million) high-risk ICT-EB project (average outright failure rate of one-in-five) does not mean (on its own) that the risk of failure of the next project in the same organization will be less than one-in-five.
9. To improve risk appetite in a project requires active management.
10. Project risk appetite is not the same as organizational risk appetite, because the goals are often not the same. Context is the key. Each level of outcome needs its own risk appetite discussion.
11. The project sponsor, supported by the project board, should lead the risk appetite setting process for the project.
12. Risk appetite rebalancing is risk homeostasis at work in projects.

5

The CORA Triangle

"Investments, if they are to be made, should have modest aims and use proven technology."

From Robin Gauld & Shaun Goldfinch's 2006 *Dangerous Enthusiasms*

Risk appetite, consciously or unconsciously and usually both, drives risk in projects and programs. If risk appetite isn't determined by a managed process first, it will be determined by the risk personality of the project's leaders and the culture of the surrounding organization.

When we move to reduce the failure rate of projects in organizations, those failure rates can rebound, or even become worse, if our risk appetite is not in control. This rebounding is the rebalancing of our risk appetite caused by the risk homeostasis that is inherent in human behavior. Personal and organizational risk taking tend to be a constant, in spite of steps we may take to strengthen our capabilities.

TOO MUCH RED

Recently I visited my friend Ken, who was the head of the Projects Quality Assurance group for a large global organization. The annual budget for projects in Ken's organization was over 4 billion dollars. Ken was responsible for the quality assurance management of all projects.

When I entered Ken's office, he was scratching his head. Seven years prior to my visit he had introduced a major projects-review process into the company. At key points in the life cycle of projects (initiation, business case approval, go-live, etc.), a hand-picked and very experienced team of reviewers would interview the project team and key stakeholders. The review team would make high-value, but confidential suggestions to the project's sponsor on how he or she might reduce the project's risks and improve its chances of success.

The process was world-leading and variations of it are now used in private and public sector organizations globally. It was not an audit process that looked to judge whether processes had been correctly followed, nor was it a quality assessment process looking to make a judgment on whether the project was of good or bad quality. Audit and quality assurance (QA) assessments of those types have an important role to play, but they can set up defensiveness in the people being interviewed, and encourage *strategic misrepresentations* by those who have a personal performance interest in the project.

Ken's process was about getting high-value *advice* to the sponsors of the organization's most challenging projects, so that they could use that advice to improve their decision making, reduce their levels of *cognitive bias*, and give them confidence in the *sometimes* bold actions that all projects occasionally need to take.

Ken's review process included the reviewers recommending actions needed to ensure that opportunities were not missed along the way. They would also recommend actions needed to avoid risks that sponsors might have missed due to them being too close to the project, or more commonly, not being experienced enough with the scale and complexity of the project. Sponsors and the steering committees who advise them don't always have prior experience with large program governance.

It was an important part of the new review process that suggestions made by the review team would be provided to the sponsor *in confidence*. They would not form part of a human resources (HR) or management performance monitoring process. The organization had plenty of project review and audit processes that already served that function.

Ken's process, with its in-confidence interviews and feedback sessions, seemed to be working well. The review teams were finding high-value opportunities and risks that sponsors were benefiting from hearing about in a nonthreatening way. The reviewers also found that the people they interviewed were much more open when they heard the projects would not be stopped as a result of the review process, or managers sanctioned as a result of anything they might say. The *inside information*, on where the risks were, started to flow.

Ken would personally sit in on debriefing sessions that occurred between his review teams and the project sponsors on the last day of each review. He was pleased by the quality of advice that was being provided to the sponsors and by how open the sponsors were to acting on the advice they were being offered.

As a part of Ken's own quality monitoring process, so that he, and more importantly his boss, could see the money they were spending on the new reviews was paying dividends (the high-powered review teams they were using did not come cheap), Ken would ask his review teams to confidentially rate the level of risk they felt they were seeing in the projects they reviewed. To preserve the confidentiality of the rating process, the ratings were provided (in addition to the project sponsor) only to Ken.

When Ken wrote reports for his boss (reports that might well go higher up the tree, even to the global CEO), it had been agreed that the risk ratings would not be labeled with project names or the names of the sponsors. The CEO and his deputies had agreed to this arrangement—they just wanted to know that their project sponsors were receiving the best advice possible, and that they were acting on it. There were separate processes in place that provided more detailed risk reporting to the organization's portfolio investment committee.

Ken wanted to keep the rating process simple, and asked the review teams to score each project red, amber, or green. A green rating would mean everything was on track and going well, an amber rating would mean that there was a level of risk that needed to be watched, and red would mean there were some serious issues that the sponsor needed to deal with right away. Red could also mean there was an important opportunity that the project sponsor wasn't aware of—and that needed quick action, if it was to be harvested.

Ken kept track of the review teams' ratings for all the reviewed projects, as he received them. As he had expected in the first couple of years of running the new review process, there was a fairly even spread of green, amber, and red ratings being assigned to projects. Ken had graphed these using red, amber, and green colored spheres to represent the ratings that each project was given, plotting them in groups for each year. In the first couple of years there were maybe a few more reds than Ken would have liked, but he felt, on reflection, this was probably a result of the very open, in-confidence process they were running.

Ken had hoped that in years three or four he might see the ratings of projects that were being reviewed for a second or third time, starting to move from reds and ambers, to ambers and greens. This was because he thought that, surely, with the high quality advice he was seeing provided by the review teams, and how receptive the project sponsors seemed to be to the advice, the risks of the projects would be reducing. He had hoped that, by the end of years four or five, he would be seeing more green ratings start-ing to come through, and certainly less reds.

Unfortunately, although in years two and three there did seem to be a slight increase in green ratings (more at the expense of ambers than of reds), by the time the ratings for the sixth and seventh years had been completed, Ken could not see any statistically useful improvement in the risk ratings being assigned by his review teams. Years one and two showed just as many reds being issued as years six and seven.

And, to make things worse, there had been a couple of major project failures in the last year. No one had been expecting these, and Ken's bosses were concerned. Why hadn't the new review process prevented them?

Ken was worried, and couldn't figure out why the red ratings weren't reducing. Recommendations that were being made by the reviewers were making some good saves on projects, and the reviewers were frequently finding the *elephants standing in the rooms* of some of the more troubled projects.

There was the case of the return on investment (ROI) of the expensive new enterprise resource planning system in Europe not stacking up. The reviewers identified this problem and the project didn't proceed. This was classed as a *save* and not a *fail*.

There was also the case of the new customer relationship management (CRM) system that the organization was going to adopt for the global busi-ness. The reviewers had raised a risk that the preferred vendor's system might not be able to cope with a global-scale roll-out—it had only been used at a national level by any business previously. When the program man-ager had investigated this risk more deeply, he had discovered implemen-tations of the system in other companies which had struggled to make the grade at even a multiple-state level.

With these saves and all the wisdom from the reviewers, why were some projects still coming up red? And why had the recent big project failures oc-curred at all? Ken started to look more closely at some of the reports on the big saves that the review teams had made. He found what was happening on those projects was that the sponsors were heeding the advice of the review teams, but then different issues were cropping up on the same projects at the next review, some nine to 12 months (or more) later.

For a new contact center, there had been a high-return review recom-mendation that the scope of the program should be extended to include the use of *real person* contacts on the first phone call, to strengthen customer relations. Astonishingly, the ensuing problem was that the project team did not consider the increased demand for the call center services that would result from providing customers with such a helpful service. This was identified as a red-rated risk at the next review.

The CRM program, in response to a reviewer's recommendation, had halted its engagement with the preferred bidder, and had retendered the CRM system to the market. Unfortunately the first preferred bidder, upset at seeing a major contract slip from their grasp, was now issuing legal proceedings. Ken shook his head. Then he looked again at the pattern of reds and ambers for each of the last six years, and saw something else. The size of the spheres, which indicated the approved whole of lifecycle cost (WOLC) for each project, was increasing for new projects each year. Bigger spheres meant bigger project budgets, and smaller spheres meant smaller project budgets. The average size of new projects as determined by the budgets at business case sign-off, were getting larger every year.

The ownership of projects was also becoming more complex. Ken could see this from the *owner* tags labeled against each project's cost sphere. Dual or multiple owners listed in the project's name tag indicated a joint, interdepartmental, or divisional business case. There were only a handful of these in 2007, but in 2013 over a half of the projects on Ken's graph involved collaboration of two or more business groups.

What Ken's company was experiencing was risk appetite rebalancing. The company had strengthened its project management capabilities, increasing its comfort levels, and then taken on more risk—putting its risk appetite back into homeostatic balance—without realizing it. As well as the new review process that Ken had introduced, his company had created a successful portfolio management office, instituted a talent-management system for project managers that required all senior project managers to be at the international Project Management Institute's (PMI's) Project Management Professional (PMP®) level, and enforced mandatory use of the complex-programs management practice known as MSP (Managing Successful Programmes) in all designated complex business-change programs.

In spite of these initiatives, which should have been making Ken's company's projects more successful, the rate of failure of projects in the organization had stayed the same and the number of troubled projects had actually increased.

On the other hand, the size of projects had grown significantly and their complexity (as determined by the number of business groups involved in the projects and the nature of the technologies they were using) had increased. A summary of the ratings data from Year 1 and Year 7 of Ken's new review process is shown in Table 5.1.

Table 5.1   Ken's quality assurance results

Ken's Assurance Reviews – Ratings Summary Year 1 and Year 7		
Project overall rating (Red, Amber, or Green)	**2007**	**2013**
Percentage of "Reds" (serious risks or issues are present)	24%	26%
Percentage of "Ambers" (moderate risks or issues are present)	44%	53%
Percentage of "Greens" (the project is on track)	32%	21%
Number of projects with WOLC costs larger than $10 million	23	71
Percentage of annual project spend involving more than one business division or group	24%	62%

To use the Everest metaphor, Ken's company had embraced supplemental oxygen technology and had chosen, unconsciously it appeared, not to reduce failure rates, but to climb higher. In climbing higher, not safer, Ken's organization is in good company.

A GLOBAL ISSUE

For all the improvements in project management as a profession over the last 20 years, including the development of sophisticated project and portfolio management tools, international standards, new methodologies, professional advocacy groups, and experience—lots of experience—project success rates have changed little, globally.

The world is delivering bigger and better outcomes using these new and improved capabilities, but the projects themselves are failing at pretty much the same rate that they were 20 years ago. The waste and lost opportunities are significant.

In February of 2015, PMI—the world's largest project management advocacy group with over 450,000 members worldwide and nearly five million copies of its *PMBOK® Guide* in circulation—published a report summarizing its annual survey of global project management performance and practices. The report was entitled *PMI's Pulse of the Profession®: Capturing the Value of Project Management*.

The 2015 report found that the number of organizations capturing the value that project management delivers is unchanged since 2012 at 55%, as is the percentage of projects failing to achieve their original goals and business intent at 36%.

PMI's 2014 report—entitled *PMI's Pulse of the Profession™: The High Cost of Low Performance 2014*—found that nearly a half (44%) of all strategic initiatives worldwide were reported as *unsuccessful*.

In the 2013 *Pulse* report, PMI reported only 62% of projects had met their original goals and strategic intent. The 2013 results represented a *decline* in global performance over the previous five years—as 72% of initiatives had achieved goals and strategic intent in 2008. Furthermore, in 2013, PMI reported over a third of all projects failed to deliver their specified benefits to some degree, and 17% of all projects failed outright. This complete-failure statistic of nearly one in five of all projects has also been found in other studies (PMI noted the high level of consistency between their research and the global research of others).

The Pricewaterhouse Coopers (PwC) 2012 report, *Insights and Trends: Current Portfolio, Program, and Project Management Practices*, stated that only 60% of organizations who used a formal project management methodology were successful at delivering all of their business benefits. The PwC survey also reported only 28% of organizations using established project management methodologies were successful delivering projects on time, and only 38% on budget.

The PMI and PwC surveys were global and covered a variety of sectors such as, information technology (IT), construction, and transportation.

When we look at the performance of information and communications technology-related business (ICT-EB) projects, we find a high degree of consistency between ICT-EB project failure rates and the failure rates of other project types. KPMG's 2005 *Global IT Project Management Survey* found that half of the ICT-EB projects in the average organization were delivering only 51 to 75% of their specified benefits—and this is for the organizations who are *tracking* benefits delivery—many don't.

As PMI reported, the failure statistics are surprisingly consistent between surveys. PwC's first global survey of this type was performed in 2004. That survey found only 2.5% of companies delivered 100% of their projects on time, within budget, and as specified. KPMG's 2005 global survey reported a similar result with only 2% of companies achieving all their targeted benefits, all of the time.

The Standish Group, an organization formed in 1985 with the vision to collect case information on real-life IT failures and environments, regularly publishes a widely-referenced survey of IT project management performance known as *The CHAOS Report*. In 1995 *The CHAOS Report* found that well over half of surveyed projects were challenged or impaired to some extent, and that less than 20% were completely successful. The *CHAOS Reports* in recent years (using different requirements for analysis since 2002), although indicating a small improvement in success rates, continue to classify more than a half of the surveyed projects as either *challenged* or *failed*.

The science of project failure is not a precise one, but the surveyed, average failure rate of projects globally, as found in a variety of surveys, is highly consistent—between *20 and 50%*, with the data centering around the *30%* mark.

This doesn't mean that a third of all projects fail outright, but it does mean that a third of all projects have failed to such an extent that their owners feel comfortable reporting them as having under-delivered in some significant way.

Globally, and within our organizations, this represents huge wastage. If the average project wastage is *30%* in the average organization, what is it in lower-performing organizations?

The problem is worse for organizations undertaking large ICT-EB projects. In some studies *large* is defined as projects greater than $1 million in cost, and in others greater than $10 million in cost. Regardless of the absolute size, the message in the studies is the same—larger projects fail at much higher rates than smaller projects. Projects that are a factor of 10 larger than others in the same organization (e.g., $10 million versus $1 million), can be at a *50* to *100%* greater risk of failure. And when the big ones fail of course, their losses are 10 times those of the small ones.

The relationship between project failure rates and time over the past 20 years is shown in Figure 5.1.

Why, with all the improvements in project management capabilities that have been developed in the last 20 years, are projects still failing at such a high rate?

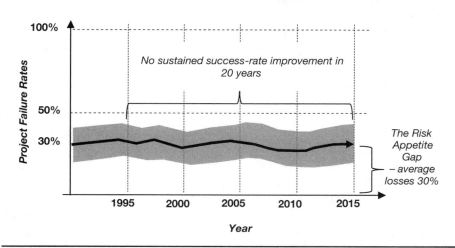

Figure 5.1   The relationship between project failure rates and time over 20 years

The answer is to be found in risk homeostasis (risk appetite rebalancing in projects), and the growth in size and complexity of projects which has occurred over the same period.

COMPLEXITY IS INCREASING

Definitions of complexity vary but there are some common themes. It is multidimensional—a function of the variety and newness of technology being used, the variety and seniority of stakeholders, the number of business groups or organizations involved, the uncertainty of scope, the number of disciplines involved, and the extent of cultural change. It is also increasing globally.

In PMI's September 2013 *Pulse* in-depth report *Navigating Complexity*, PMI found that organizational strategies are becoming increasingly complex as a result of expanding globalization, a rapid pace of change, intense competition, and continual innovation in a *do more with less* market environment.

In IBM's 2010 paper, *Capitalizing on Complexity: Insights from the Global Chief Executive Officer Study*, 78% of CEOs reported that they expected high or very high levels of complexity over the next five years.

Increasing complexity has always been the case. In KPMG's 2005 *Global IT Project Management Survey*, 88% of respondents reported an increase in the complexity of their projects over the preceding two years; 81% of organizations reported an increase in the number of new projects; and 79% of organizations reported an increase in total project budgets.

While project failure rates are a constant, and project management tools and techniques are steadily evolving, the size and complexity of projects have been growing, and continue to grow. The relationship between project failure and complexity over the last 20 years is shown in Figure 5.2.

Of course, as the size and complexity of what we attempt increases, so does our risk of failure, and just as the value of a network is proportional to the square of the number of nodes connected to the network (Metcalfe's Law), so the *damage* caused by our potential failures increases exponentially as the size and complexity of our projects grow.

The Helmsman Institute actually presents this exponential complexity-failure relationship using a scale similar to that of the exponential Richter earthquake scale. In their 2012 paper, *Why Project Complexity Matters*, projects which have Levels 4–5 complexity are described as *small* and typically performed within the business units of large organizations (examples given include product maintenance and competitive enhancements to ongoing

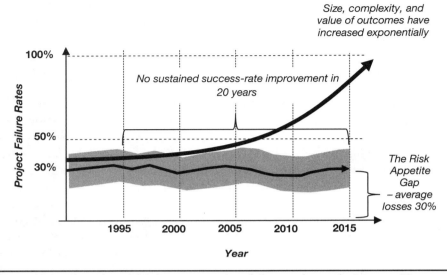

Figure 5.2 The relationship between project failure and complexity over 20 years

business operations); projects which have Levels 8–9 complexity are described as nationally significant, highly complex, and creating potentially significant impacts on a national economy (examples of these include hosting the Olympics and major defense projects).

THE A380 AND THE 787

The airline industry is a good example of the dramatic growth in the size and complexity of projects which the world has been experiencing in recent times. The scale of the airbus A380-800 is large. It is a double-decker passenger aircraft that has seating for up to 853 passengers in its all economy class configuration. With 478 square meters of floor space (5,145 square feet) it has nearly 50% more floor area than its next largest rival, the 747 jumbo jets. The aircraft's cruising speed is 900 kmph (560 mph) and its maximum speed is Mach 0.96, almost the speed of sound.

One of the safety requirements for the A380, before it could be approved to fly, was that it must pass a passenger evacuation test. Incredibly with eight of the plane's 16 exits blocked, and the cabin darkened, 853 volunteer passengers and 20 crew members were able to evacuate the plane in 78 seconds. It passed the test. The development costs of the aircraft are reported to have been over $14 billion. Individual aircraft sell for around U.S. $300 million depending on their configuration.

The project to develop the A380 was big, but so were its problems. Delays in the delivery of the aircraft in 2006 and 2007, together with a reduction in delivery numbers, are reported to have caused (at that time) a 26% drop in the share price of Airbus's parent EADS. In 2012, a serious engine failure in one of the new planes' Rolls Royce Trent 900 engines was reported to have caused a 10% fall in Rolls Royce shares.

Most of the development problems were attributed to the aircraft's complexity and the high degree of customization required for each aircraft. The bigger the project, the bigger the damage when failure occurs.

One of the A380's competitors is the Boeing 787 Dreamliner. With a passenger capacity of 290 people, it holds less people than the A380, but at around $230 million per aircraft (depending on the variant), is much cheaper. Boeing states that the 787 is the first major airliner to use composite materials (such as carbon-fiber reinforced plastic) as its primary construction material. The plane's development costs were reported to have been over $20 billion.

As with the A380 there were a number of schedule overruns experienced in the 787's development. The delays were reportedly caused by the complexity of the aircraft's design and the new materials and technologies that it used. In 2010 it was reported that Boeing expected to write off $2.5 billion dollars due to the first three aircraft being suitable only for test flights, and in 2011 it was reported that Boeing was facing compensation claims from airlines affected by delays to the delivery of their orders.

In January 2013 the entire Dreamliner fleet was grounded after over-heating of batteries occurred in two aircraft. In April 2013 the Federal Aviation Administration gave formal approval for a new lithium-ion battery system, clearing the airlines to fly the plane with passengers again. The three-month grounding of the new planes is reported to have cost Boeing an estimated $600 million.

The 787 and A380 aircraft are representative of the high, and growing, levels of complexity that as humans, we constantly strive for. Multibillion-dollar projects are now common. The following is a small selection from the last ten years.

- **$38.4 billion:** The Australian National Broadband Network—NBN (due to be completed in 2021)
- **$20 billion:** Boeing 787 Dreamliner development
- **$14 billion:** Airbus A380 development
- **$9 billion:** Large Hadron collider—the world's largest and highest-energy particle accelerator (2010)

- **$8.8 billion:** Chicago's O'Hare International Airport modernization project (due for completion in 2016)
- **$3.9 billion:** One World Trade Center (Freedom Tower) in New York—the tallest building in the western hemisphere at 541 meters (1,776 feet) tall
- **$3 billion:** The Human Genome Project (2003)
- **$2.5 billion:** Mars Science Laboratory; the robotic space probe mission to Mars that successfully landed the Mars rover, *Curiosity*, in Gale Crater in 2012

The sizes of projects and programs in the current decade are as never seen before. But while project size and complexity grow ever larger, project failure rates remain steady at 30–40%—including undelivered benefits and cost overruns. How can we harvest this waste as cash in our back packets without slowing down the value opportunities that growth in complexity and size offer?

THE CORA TRIANGLE

Risk homeostasis theory tells us that the risk appetite for an individual or an organization tends to be a constant—or certainly that it doesn't change quickly. When risk appetite does change, it is often the result of an event creating a change in our comfort levels—often an increase in someone's discomfort with their chances of success. This might be triggered by an increase in competitive pressures, a major project failure, or the arrival of a new CEO who has a lower risk appetite.

By proactively assessing and managing risk appetite in projects, we can reduce the gap between our abilities and our ambitions (where they matter) from which risk and failure arise. Managed risk appetite presents an effective and sustainable way to improve project performance in the portfolio. It is underutilized for projects in most organizations.

How risk appetite relates to organizational capabilities, and the ambition of outcomes, is shown in the CORA triangle (capabilities, outcomes, risk appetite) in Figure 5.3.

One side of the CORA triangle cannot change without affecting one or both of the others—similar to the closed-relationships of the Iron Triangle (time, cost, and quality). Increasing risk appetite (for example from a new leader, or external competitive pressures) will increase comfort with taking more risk (for instance, to compete) as greater outcomes are sought. Increasing portfolio, program, and project management (P3M) capabilities will similarly increase comfort with the taking of more risks and trigger a

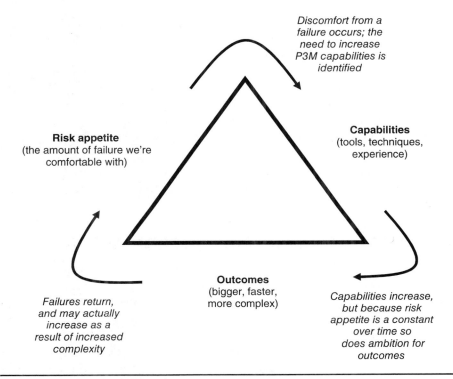

Discomfort from a failure occurs; the need to increase P3M capabilities is identified

Risk appetite
(the amount of failure we're comfortable with)

Capabilities
(tools, techniques, experience)

Outcomes
(bigger, faster, more complex)

Failures return, and may actually increase as a result of increased complexity

Capabilities increase, but because risk appetite is a constant over time so does ambition for outcomes

Figure 5.3 The CORA Triangle

shift toward greater outcomes (e.g., more projects, or faster delivery). Increasing the complexity or size of outcomes will *decrease* comfort, triggering a reduction of risk appetite, and a drive to increase capabilities.

Take the case of a large project failure which damages the organization's reputation (and the discomfort that results). Risk homeostasis theory tells us that risk appetite rebalancing is then likely. That is, the organization will take actions to return to its comfort level—its comfort with the risks as they are experiencing them—to what it was before the project failure occurred. This may mean strengthening the organization's capabilities, perhaps its project reporting and governance, its risk management, or its project quality assurance—and sometimes, all three.

With an increase in the organization's project management capabilities, the risk of further failure is reduced, and comfort with performance begins to return. Over a period of time, confidence in the organization's capabilities strengthens, ambitions grow, and so does the size and complexity of projects that the organization starts to take on. As individuals and as organizations, improved project management capabilities, in the long run, are almost always translated into increased outcomes.

And as we've seen on the slopes of Everest, on the ice of Antarctica, and in the broader large-projects world of today, outcome-maximizing adds complexity on top of complexity, causing failure rates to often increase rather than reduce, and for the resulting failures to be on a much larger scale.

This was the issue for Mallory and Irvine on Everest in 1924. They made the decision to use their new supplemental oxygen equipment after Norton, their leader, had failed to summit earlier without it. Mallory and Irvine died, while Norton set a climbing record that would stand for 30 years and, more importantly, he lived to tell the tale.

A PORTFOLIO VIEW OF PROJECT RISK APPETITE

A plot of the typical organization's capabilities (Y axis) versus a sample of the organization's different ambition levels (X axis) for the complexity and size of their projects, before organizational capabilities have been lifted, is shown in Figure 5.4.

Most organizations have some projects that are outside the full range of their capabilities. The extent to which projects lie outside an organization's capabilities is the extent of their risk appetite. It is their acceptance, consciously or unconsciously, of a level of uncertainty of their success. Figure 5.5 shows how, when an organization strengthens its project management capabilities, the size, difficulty, or complexity of the organization's projects grow with time to compensate for the increased comfort that strengthened capabilities provide.

The curved, semi-S-shaped line plotted on the graph shows how an organization's capabilities tend to relate to the size and complexity of the projects in their portfolio. When the complexity of a project is low—for example, in an initiative that the organization has done many times before—then the organization's capabilities are usually adequate. Replacing all the photocopiers at a company's head office might be an example of this. Even though you can spend a lot of money on photocopiers, projects to install them usually finish close to budget, close to the planned time frame, and with the intended outcomes (hopefully working photocopiers) achieved.

Underpinned by their risk appetite, most organizations have a few projects on their books where on-time, on-budget delivery of outcomes is not always achieved. No one sets out thinking their projects are going to be failures, but in higher risk appetite organizations some of them will be. There

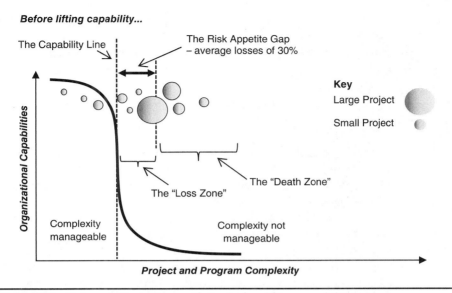

Figure 5.4 Risk appetite in the portfolio, *before* lifting capability

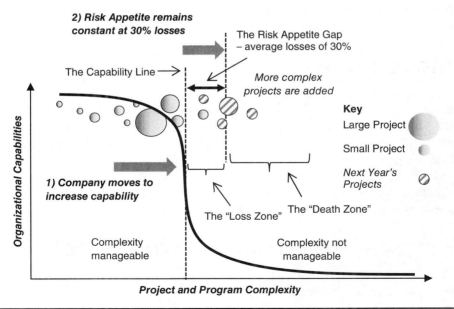

Figure 5.5 Risk appetite in the portfolio, *after* lifting capability

are few companies who don't experience at least some under-delivery of benefits, or overrun of budget or schedule in some of their projects.

As noted earlier, the global research tells us that 30% or more of projects experience a significant degree of failure in schedule, cost, or benefits delivered.

THE LOSS ZONE

The risk appetite gap is shown on the graph as being where the capability-complexity curve begins to drop away. We call this the *capability line*. The space on the graph where risk appetite exceeds the organization's capabilities is called the *loss zone*. The projects in this zone are always, to some degree, outside the capabilities of the organization. This is where most of the budget overruns and failures to deliver all the benefits occur.

An example of a loss-zone project might be an upgrade of an organization's desktop computers, made more complex by a refresh of the operating system, which jumps a generation of software, scoped to run on some economically priced hardware.

Climbing-wise, this zone is Mount Everest territory. Not everyone who goes there is going to be successful with their climb. Some who go there will feel they have experienced a degree of success even if they don't summit. Some who go there will experience frostbite, or altitude sickness, or both. In some cases these issues will be serious.

THE DEATH ZONE

The death zone is the name given to that portion of Mount Everest where the air is so thin that if people stay there for too long they begin to die. It's the top 3,000 feet of the 29,000 foot mountain. The death zone is a metaphor for the zone of high-ambition in which the projects of some organizations sit (it is discussed in more detail in Chapter 8).

Decisions to operate in the death zone of project management are not usually made consciously. These decisions sit at the intersection of unconscious risk appetite and low organizational capabilities.

A STEP-CHANGE IN RISK MANAGEMENT CULTURE

We lose our appetite for risk when the price of that appetite becomes too high. Catastrophic failure of something big, or a series of failures, can trigger a drive for change. A step-change in the way risks are managed—a step-change in people's comfort-point—is required to achieve sustainable improvement in success rates for businesses or projects.

A step-change in risk management culture requires:

- From leadership—new attitudes and behaviors;
- From risk management—increased profile of risk management activities, increased resources, and increased assurance;
- From control frameworks—mandatory processes that prevent personal risk appetites from coming into play (e.g., minimum business case standards, mandatory stage-gate reviews); and
- From governance—discussion and oversight of risk appetite management.

Risk management culture-change is most effective when all of the above occur. As risk homeostasis and the CORA relationships suggest, increasing P3M capabilities on their own won't result in a sustainable reduction of failure without a step-change in risk management culture also occurring.

A formal process of considering the business or operation's risk appetite is usually included in an organization's efforts to make a step-change in risk management culture.

Leaders may not recognize this as *risk appetite* at the time, but when the senior leaders in an organization sit down and have hard discussions about goals and failure, and methodically work through what must happen, what must not happen, and what can be experimented with in the future, this is risk appetite management in action. Action being the operative element— some permanent step-change in the risk management approach has to occur.

Step-changes in an organization's risk management culture can make impressive differences to success and failure.

REDUCING RISK APPETITE IN THE AIRLINE INDUSTRY

Airline fatalities, per year, have been dropping steadily since 1995. In the mid-90s, global airline deaths were averaging 1,400 a year; by 2011 that figure was down to 600. When using the measures of deaths per kilometer, or deaths per hours spent in travel, these figures are safer than automobile travel.

Before 1995 the annual fatality figures were higher. In spite of improvements in airplane reliability, safety technology, and air traffic control, airplane fatalities were climbing. In 1972 fatalities reached an all-time high; 2,375 people died in airplane accidents that year.

It was only when factors affecting the airline sector's *tolerance* of risk were addressed—their risk appetite as a sector—that annual deaths began to consistently decline. The changes created in that sector included increased regulations that made adherence to safety standards non-optional. Powerful safety committees were also established.

One of these was the Commercial Aviation Safety Team (CAST), established in 1998 with the goal of reducing commercial aviation fatalities in the United States by 80 percent. It was acknowledged at the time that this was a very ambitious goal. CAST responded by developing a *Safety Enhancement Plan*, comprised of nearly 200 initiatives. These included:

- Making Directors of Safety roles more visible;
- Providing guidance for air carriers to establish *comprehensive and effective safety departments*;
- Increasing the use of technology to reduce the possibility of high risks inadvertently occurring;
- Increasing the use of standard operating procedures; and
- Increasing training in many risk-related areas.

By 2007, CAST was able to report the fatality rate of commercial air travel in the United States had been reduced by 83 percent. A new goal of reducing fatality risks by a further 50 percent by 2025 was then set.

The effect of CAST and related initiatives was to create a step-change in the risk management culture of the aviation sector. Major, sustainable reductions in fatalities resulted (Europe established similar committees).

REDUCING RISK APPETITE ON MOUNT EVEREST

Until the mid-1990s the reported death rate for climbers on Everest was one death for every four climbers who reached the summit. In the mid-90s things began to change.

The mountain opened up to climbers with variable and sometimes poor climbing skills. Commercial climbing began to dominate the mountain. The majority of Everest climbers, then and today, are not regular high-altitude climbers. The more professional Everest guiding companies insist their clients have or obtain some high-altitude experience before they climb Everest, but some companies require none at all. Climbers have been seen on Everest not knowing the fundamentals of how to use crampons and ice axes.

In spite of the low performers, the top-end guiding companies have been able to reduce Everest death rates significantly in the last 20 years. They enforce strict safety rules, set minimum levels of experience, and tightly manage climb planning and execution.

Commoditization is the standardization of a product or service for commercial sale, and the reduction of differences between the services offered by different providers. This description is applicable to much of the climbing on Everest today. Pre-1990, Everest climbing was mostly nonprofit and expedition-based—today it is mostly commercial. With the strengthening commoditization of climbing, the ability of high risk appetite individuals to behave in high-risk ways is greatly reduced. Death rates on Everest are now down to one or two per hundred summits.

The dramatic effect of the change in safety culture on Everest is shown in Figure 5.6.

Although many lament commercial climbing on Everest and the loss of some of the mountain's spirit that has resulted, from a safety perspective—from a *risk* perspective—Everest is a safer mountain than it has ever been.

REDUCING RISK APPETITE IN ANTARCTICA

What Antarctica lacks in high altitude risks, it makes up for in almost every other risk category. It is colder, vaster, windier, and more riddled with constantly evolving crevasse conditions than Everest. It is a place where adventurers travel to admire the continent's frozen beauty and to experience a challenge, but by dollars spent there, science is by far the biggest activity performed in Antarctica.

In fact some of the world's most important science occurs there. Mankind's understanding of the ozone hole, and its threat to our planet's

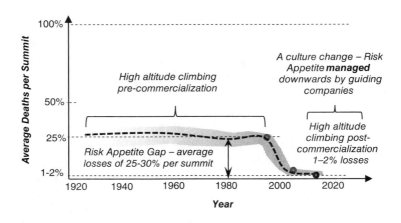

Figure 5.6 Risk appetite change on Mount Everest—culture change

atmospheric chemistry and surface life forms, along with global warming and its threat to the planet as a whole, have both depended heavily on Antarctic research programs.

In Antarctica, climate and atmospheric records are locked into pristine ice and rock formations that are millions of years old. The Antarctic ecosystem includes primitive, rare lichens and unique ocean species that are extremely fragile. Anything living there has evolved under the harshest of conditions and is hanging on to existence by the skin of its teeth. Such a fragile ecosystem creates the perfect early-warning system for the rest of the planet. When earth catches a cold, whole species in the Antarctic begin to die.

Because Antarctic science is so important, risks to the successful completion of research there are taken very seriously by scientists and their national program managers. The contribution that science makes is important, but it is also expensive. The money used to fund it has been hard-won from competitive science funding programs around the world. If an experiment or science investigation fails because of bad planning or execution in Antarctica, it is very likely not to be funded for a second chance.

For these reasons the risk appetite of national Antarctic programs—the government operations which manage science bases, resources, and logistics—is very low when it comes to the support of science. The science must happen.

Antarctic programs have low risk appetite in two other areas:

- Safety of national program personnel and assets, and
- Protection of the environment (which is both fragile, and very high-profile internationally).

Deaths due to the severity of the environment are rare. Occupational accidents are a greater risk because of the extreme cold and the complexities that the weather creates, but these risks are tightly managed. The disciplines applied to logistics planning and research management are also strong. Operations are run with military precision, frequently using military aircraft and logistics support. Management of costs and schedules is important, but management of successful science is more important.

With so many personnel, environmental and high-profile science risks, Antarctica is a risk-rich environment. The United States alone deploys over 3,000 people to Antarctica every year to undertake and support scientific research. Although New Zealand is a much smaller country than the United States (having a population of less than five million compared with 300 million plus in the U.S.), it nonetheless maintains a world-leading research presence on the continent and sends over 350 science and support personnel there annually.

To manage risk and to maintain a tight success culture, national Antarctic program managers invest heavily in processes and protocols targeting safety, protection of the environment, and the assurance of research outcomes.

The approaches used provide Antarctic program managers a level of practice commoditization which ensures risk appetite is kept low in key areas.

Low risk appetite is not just about investment in documentation and training, it's about creating a risk-aware culture. In Antarctica this occurs at multiple levels, from the heads of national programs, to the leaders of science and support teams, to the men and women who operate the bases and assist in the field.

STEP-CHANGING THE RISK MANAGEMENT CULTURE OF PROJECTS

Before step-changing risk management culture, businesses should have a clear understanding of what it is that *must, mustn't*, and *may* be allowed to happen in their various operations. We call this understanding, when it is written down, a *risk appetite statement*. The owners of projects have to repeat this process for every project.

What must, mustn't, and may happen in a project is not the same as what must, mustn't, and may happen in the business, or in other projects. These will be informed by the organization's corporate risk appetite statements, but they will not (necessarily) be the same. It will depend on what the goals of the project are. So at the level of the corporation, risk appetite is usually documented once, for the business as a whole. For projects, risk appetite should be documented as a separate exercise for each project.

CORA BALANCE

For sustainable performance improvement, all three sides of the CORA triangle need to be addressed:

* Risk appetite management
* P3M capabilities improvement
* Outcome ambitions—complexity, size, risk

A balance of focus across all three is needed as shown in Figure 5.7.

When risk appetite is not addressed alongside project and program capability building, and growing outcome ambitions, the triangle becomes unbalanced and a capabilities-outcomes race can develop. Larger or more complex change is requested by senior management, or offered by technology

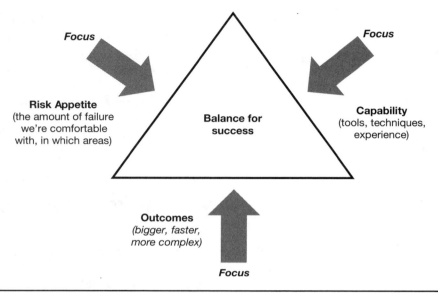

Figure 5.7   CORA focus must be balanced

leaders, a degree of failure occurs—sometimes major; more processes, tools, and experienced people are brought on board in response; a further increase in outcomes is expected or promised; and then further, often larger failures occur.

The cycle can span many years, driven by risk homeostasis and personal and organizational risk appetite. Levels of risk and comfort are different for each of us, and different for the organizations we work in, but they tend, without intervention, to be constant. To avoid this, risk appetite needs to be included in risk management of projects as a formal process.

Risk appetite management works by determining which outcomes are important for a project and which are not, which capabilities are consequently important or not for the project, and closing the risk appetite gap where opportunities arise.

A good risk appetite process should reduce overall risk appetite, create innovation opportunities where they are known to be low-risk, and cause discomfort where there is undesirable opportunity for failure. Practical approaches for achieving this are discussed in Chapter 6.

KEY LEARNINGS ON CORA

1. Risk appetite, consciously or unconsciously (usually both), drives risk in projects and programs.
2. Project failure is a global issue and there has been no sustained improvement in project success rates globally in 20 years. About a third of all projects suffer a significant loss, a third suffers some loss, and less than a third is classified by their owners as fully successful.
3. Although project failure rates are unchanged in 20 years, the size, complexity, and value of projects have been growing steadily.
4. Capabilities, outcomes (size, speed, complexity), and risk appetite form the three sides of the CORA triangle.
5. One side of the CORA triangle cannot be changed without affecting one or both of the remaining two.
6. Driven by risk homeostasis, project failure rates tend to be a constant, unless there is a step-change in risk management culture.
7. Step-change in risk-management culture requires:
   - From leadership—new attitudes and behaviors;
   - From risk management—increased profile, resources, and assurance;
   - From control frameworks—mandatory processes that prevent personal risk appetites from coming into play (e.g., business cases and stage-gate reviews); and
   - From governance—consideration and reduction of risk appetite.
8. For sustainable performance improvement, all three sides of the CORA triangle need to be addressed:
   - Risk appetite management
   - P3M capabilities improvement
   - Outcome ambitions—complexity, size, risk
9. Risk appetite needs to be considered separately for each project.

6

Managing Risk Appetite in Projects

"All organisations have to take some risks and they have to avoid others. The big question that organisations have to ask themselves is: just what does successful performance look like?"

Institute of Risk Management website, www.theirm.org

The three sides of the Iron Triangle are sometimes presented as *cost, time,* and *scope*, with *scope* being defined as the outputs or functionality of the project. Cost, time, and scope, together, are sometimes called *project effi-ciency*.

There is a growing view that the definition of project success that these three dimensions provide is limited. It can be argued that the definition of success for a project should include the achievement of the project's stra-tegic goals, not just the delivery of outputs or functionality to schedule and budget.

Serrador and Turner, in their 2015 paper *The Relationship between Project Success and Project Efficiency*, define project *success* as the project meeting its wider business and enterprise goals as defined by its key stakeholders.

In their study, Serrador and Turner reviewed 1,386 projects, finding that project *efficiency* (cost, time, and scope) is only 60% correlated with project *success* (the meeting of wider business and enterprise goals). The correlation is useful, but the 40% difference shows the limitations of time, cost, and *scope* as a project success definition.

These findings provide support for the Iron Triangle as it is sometimes alternatively drawn, substituting *quality* in the place of *scope*. Quality can be defined simply as *fitness for purpose*—in other words, what the project delivers satisfies the needs of its customers. Needs should be defined in business terms, not information and communications technology (ICT)-output or some other functional-output terms. The Iron Triangle with quality as the project outcome dimension, noting the three sides are not equal, is shown in Figure 6.1.

Often, the three dimensions of the Iron Triangle are given equal weight in project reporting. Portfolio dashboards report a schedule slippage using the same shade of red that they use to report a budget overrun or a benefit under-delivery. Project managers are often admonished in equal amounts for failing any of the three dimensions. A consequence of this is that management effort is frequently spent on making sure that all projects deliver to within the same tolerance of budget (e.g., +/–5%) and to within the same tolerance of schedule (say two days), and that progress toward business benefits delivery (quality) is too hard to report on until the project has closed, or sometimes not at all.

The problem with this approach is that the importance of on-time and on-schedule delivery is not the same for any two projects. For some projects those parameters may not be important at all. The question of the importance of successful benefits delivery is similar. Some benefits are critical and some are not. Sometimes business improvement key performance indicators (KPIs) for projects are not even specified (even if there is a wide range of acceptable delivery of a specified benefit, a KPI or range of KPIs should *always* be specified for benefits).

Without there being a clear and common view of what is important in a project and what is not, efficient and effective delivery of success can't happen. If you don't know what constitutes success, or what the priorities are within those definitions when they have been defined, how can you make the critical prioritization decisions that project management requires?

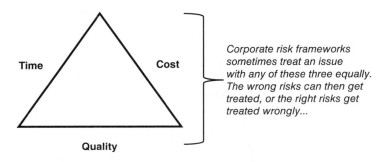

Figure 6.1   The problem with the Iron Triangle

THINK OUTSIDE THE TRIANGLE

What we have to do is turn the Iron Triangle on its side, as shown in Figure 6.2. We need to treat on-schedule and under-budget delivery as being simply two more benefits that may or may not be important, alongside the business outcomes the project has been tasked to deliver.

Remember, in 80% of projects (and you won't know which 80% they are until the project is finished), its *time, cost, quality—pick two*. Eighty percent of projects won't be successful with all three, and a third of projects won't be successful with any of them. So which dimensions are important, and how much more important than others are they? Which dimensions can you take chances with and which ones can't you take chances with? In other words, which ones can you have a high risk appetite for and which ones must you have a low risk appetite for?

On Scott's 1910 expedition the one thing that had to happen was the expedition's science and exploration program. This was the strategic outcome most important for Scott. It was the outcome for which he and his team had to have the lowest risk appetite. If there was a trade-off to be made, the science program must come first.

Scott's focus on this goal did not waiver, even during his desperate trek back from the Pole. On that journey, dragging 250 kg (520 lb) sledges by hand, exhausted, cold, hungry, and in pain, Scott and his four teammates continued to collect rock samples and scientific data, and to document their

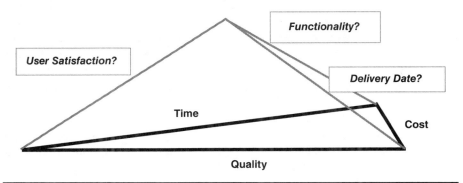

Turn the Iron Triangle on its side
- *Understand the benefits*
- *Then manage the program's risk appetite to deliver these*
- *Work on what's important...*

Figure 6.2 Think outside the triangle

reflections and lessons learned. They did this until, literally, they could no longer hold the pencils they were writing with.

For the 1910 expedition, schedule and budget were only important to a point. There were deadlines to be met and budgets to be worked within, but these were not outcomes to be maintained at the expense of science.

RISK APPETITE FOR A PROJECT IS NOT THE SAME AS FOR THE BUSINESS

The role of a project that is a part of a higher-level portfolio is to support the strategic goals of the portfolio. As such, each project will be focused on delivering, or supporting the delivery of, only a small subset of the higher-level portfolio's strategic objectives. If that strategic subset is not one of the portfolio's priority areas (it might, for example, be an investment in maintenance, or in the development and trial of a limited new service), then the priorities of the project will be different to the priorities of the organization's higher-level strategy.

This is, in part, the reason why the overall risk ratings that are given to projects (red, amber, or green) should always be with respect to the success or failure of the project, and not the success or failure of the overall organization. Project risk rating is not the same at the project level as corporate risk rating. The assessment of the impact of the failure of a project on the higher-level organization is a different process.

If differentiation of risk-rating categories for projects doesn't occur, then a project that might be at high risk of not delivering its goals may not show up as *red* in project portfolio reporting. This might be the case, for example, where the failure of a project, although possibly catastrophic for the business unit sponsoring it, won't significantly damage the organization itself.

The caveat here is that relevant business owners must then translate *project* risk ratings (which appear in project portfolio reporting) into *organizational* (or divisional) risk reporting. That is, what would the failure of a particular project to deliver its benefits, or to deliver on schedule, mean for the organization? This is what the business owner of a project has to determine for his or her business group, and then to translate this risk upward to the portfolio level. This is why a red-rated risk for a project may not be a red-rated risk for the organization itself.

Going back to the example of Scott in the Antarctic, there were several side expeditions organized by Scott from his base at Cape Evans that were not directly led by him. These side expeditions had goals such as the laying of food depots, the trial use of motor sledges and ponies, and the undertaking of geographic or scientific research. For most of these side projects, the goal of going as far south as possible was not a priority, yet this was one (just one) of Scott's strategic objectives.

One of these side projects was the midwinter expedition to Cape Crozier, undertaken by Wilson, Bowers, and Cherry-Garrard. Its purpose was to collect penguins' eggs for scientific study. On that trip, which very nearly killed the three involved, the non-negotiable outcome was the collection and safe return of Emperor penguin eggs. Science was the primary goal of this trip. There was a very low tolerance of risk to that outcome permitted. Unfortunately, as it developed, this very low appetite for failure of the science traded off a little too much risk appetite for the men's own safety. Fortunately the eggs were obtained and the men, a little worse for wear, survived.

In modern business, the date when a new service goes live may not be as important as the quality of the new service when it does go live. If so, then the owner and manager of the project need to pull out all the stops to ensure that a quality new service is delivered. This is the area where tolerance of risk needs to be at its lowest. The successful delivery of new services, though, may not always be a low-risk appetite area for the organization at the strategic level, depending on the organization's strategic planning and what the particular services are.

INFORMATION SECURITY IN PROJECT-X

Information security may be a low-risk appetite area for Organization ABC at the strategic level, but because Project-X is managing only unclassified and non-personal data, or is itself experimenting in a protected and bounded way with new approaches to information security, information security in Project-X may actually be an area of high risk appetite. Experimentation with different information management approaches might actually be encouraged by Project-X. Table 6.1 compares Project-X's risk appetites with the organization's corporate risk appetites.

The Project-X example shows the importance of a project's owners and managers understanding what their low and high risk appetite areas are, relative to the greater organization. Most importantly, they need to understand that the organization's low and high risk appetite areas may not be, or even *will* not be, the same as that of their projects.

TWO KEY POINTS

Differentiating Project Risks from Organizational Risks

Appetite for risk in different areas of a project differs depending on the purpose of the project—one size does not fit all. Project risk appetites will not

Table 6.1 Project-X's risk appetite compared with the organization's risk appetite

Organizational and Project Risk Appetites Will Be Different				
Appetite Area:	Company Brand	Information Security	New Services	Profit Targets
Organizational *Risk Appetite—* high or low?	*Very Low*	*Very Low*	*High (service dependent)*	*Low*
Meaning:	*No failure permitted*	*No failure permitted*	*Some experiment-ation permitted*	*Profit targets must not be missed*
Project-X *Risk Appetite—high or low?*	*Medium*	*High*	*Low*	*High*
Meaning:	*Some failure is permitted (localized impact)*	*Project goal is to test new technologies. Data to be used is low risk*	*A new service must be delivered —it is the project's primary goal*	*NPV is not as important (this project) as the delivery of a new service*

be the same as corporate risk appetites. Without understanding this, opportunities to optimize outcomes, reduce costs, focus capabilities, and reduce the risk of failure will be missed.

If a project must deliver by a certain date (or else major organizational failure will occur), then risk appetite for schedule delivery must be low—on-budget delivery may not be as important, nor may some service quality deliverables.

Triggering Value Thinking That Wouldn't Otherwise Occur

During risk appetite discussions, think about the causes of and treatments for risk. Many times, these specific discussions wouldn't otherwise occur without this exercise. As such, better decisions (lower cost, higher value) are made. It's a law of risk management that is like a law of physics—any discussion of risk, reduces risk—and reduction of risk is money in the organization's back pocket, every time.

WHAT DOES MANAGED RISK APPETITE IN PROJECTS LOOK LIKE?

1. There will be a shared awareness of low risk appetite and high risk appetite areas.

Areas of low risk appetite (i.e., low tolerance of failure) and high risk appetite (i.e., higher tolerance of failure) are understood in the organization's projects and are a part of everyday conversations among project sponsors, managers, and teams. There is an understanding of risk appetite within specific projects and how organizational risk appetite relates to project risk appetite, and where and why risk appetite for some projects may be different from the organization's at the strategic level.

2. *Processes for identifying and managing risk appetite and for understanding the context of risk in projects will be in use.*

Establishment of risk context in projects is an integral part of project risk management processes, and recognizes that risk likelihood and consequence frameworks need to be tailored for each project.

3. *Minimum portfolio, program, and project management (P3M) standards will be in place for all projects, tailored for risk and value.*

A level of non-negotiable commoditization of project management and project risk management processes will exist to ensure that important thinking is not bypassed by managers who may be under pressure, lacking experience, or have high personal risk appetites in high-risk areas.

A MANAGED RISK APPETITE PROCESS

Addressing risk appetite in projects is not a difficult or expensive thing to do. Reflection and review of risk appetite is some of the highest return thinking one can apply in a project, and more so in complex and high-risk projects. A process for managing project risk appetite is shown in Figure 6.3.

WORKSHOP AND MAP RISK APPETITE IN SPECIFIC PROJECTS

For each project, hold a risk appetite workshop and identify areas of the project's performance for which risk appetite is low, medium, or high. Inputs to the risk appetite workshop should include:

- Organizational problem or opportunity statements that have triggered the project, or that are relevant to its scoping and delivery;
- Higher-level organizational risk appetite assessments, reports, or statements; and

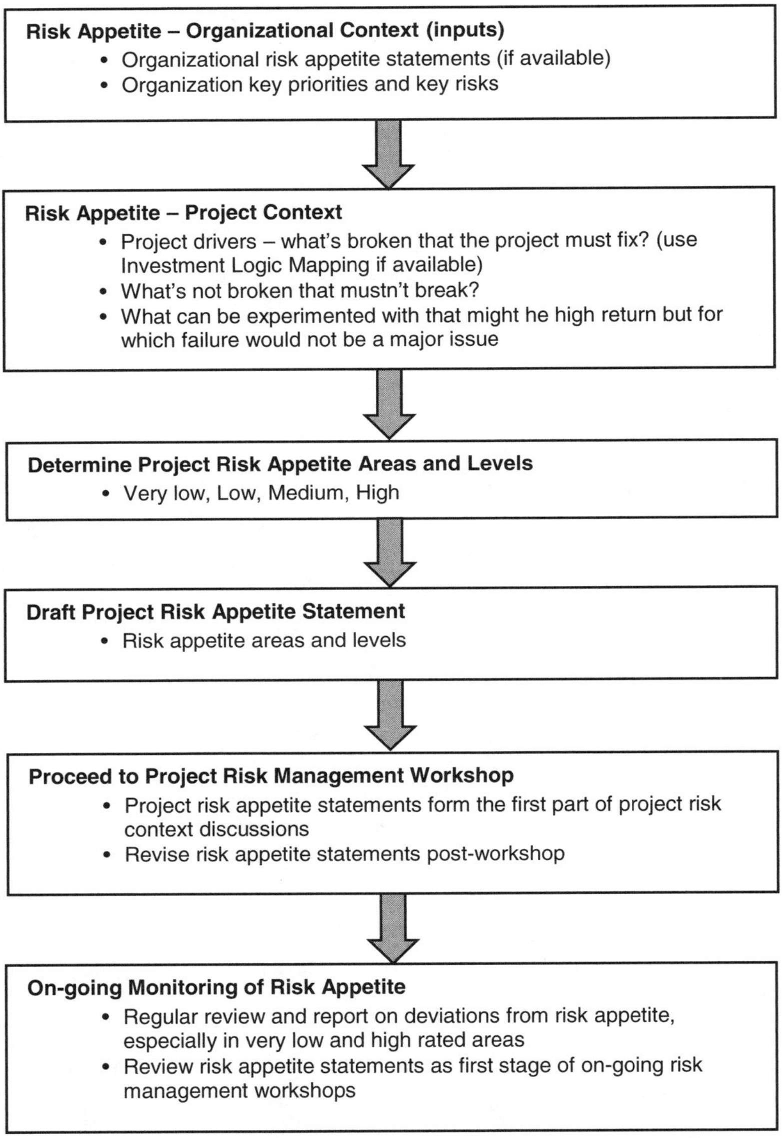

Risk Appetite – Organizational Context (inputs)
- Organizational risk appetite statements (if available)
- Organization key priorities and key risks

Risk Appetite – Project Context
- Project drivers – what's broken that the project must fix? (use Investment Logic Mapping if available)
- What's not broken that mustn't break?
- What can be experimented with that might he high return but for which failure would not be a major issue

Determine Project Risk Appetite Areas and Levels
- Very low, Low, Medium, High

Draft Project Risk Appetite Statement
- Risk appetite areas and levels

Proceed to Project Risk Management Workshop
- Project risk appetite statements form the first part of project risk context discussions
- Revise risk appetite statements post-workshop

On-going Monitoring of Risk Appetite
- Regular review and report on deviations from risk appetite, especially in very low and high rated areas
- Review risk appetite statements as first stage of on-going risk management workshops

Figure 6.3 A risk appetite process for projects

- Project Investment Logic Maps or other documents that weight the relevant importance of problems and benefits which the project is scoped to address.

An example assessment of risk appetite in a project (fictional) is shown in Table 6.2.

Remember that in Table 6.2, *appetite for risk* effectively equates (to an extent) to *tolerance of failure*; this is why it's important to identify where we don't want risks to be taken—the areas where our risk appetite needs to be low. Where there is low risk appetite (such as with the security of patient information management), there must be no failure. Where there is high risk appetite (such as with the aesthetics of the new consultation rooms), there is an opportunity for experimentation that may result in unscoped additional value (the upside of risk).

If risk appetite for an area is assessed as being high, statistically, this means more failures in this area are likely. Conversely, if risk appetite is assessed as being low, and the project's management is in line with this assessment, less failure in that area should be expected.

Table 6.2　Project-X's risk appetite compared with the organization's risk appetite

Risk Appetite Hospital Extension Project		
Risk Area	**Appetite for Risk**	**Notes**
Disruption to existing service delivery	Low	The existing customer base must be protected at all costs
Security of patient information management systems	Very Low	Brand damage in this area would be costly
Functionality and technology support for new consultation rooms	Low-Medium	Reliable, advanced technology is important to the new center's competitive advantage
Aesthetics of new consultation rooms	High	Opportunity for experimentation exists here
Total project costs	Low-Medium	The ROI of the new center is high, so investment cost is flexible
On-schedule delivery	Low-Medium	Existing rooms will be used in parallel with extension delivery
Increase patient numbers	Low	New patient targets must be met
Increase patient satisfaction	Low-medium	Satisfaction levels must be maintained, but opportunities to increase these should be tested

WHAT PORTFOLIO AND PROJECT MANAGEMENT OFFICE MANAGERS SHOULD ASK

- Is project risk appetite being discussed?
- Have project risk appetite statements been created?
- Are project risk appetite statements being managed?

And if you're just starting with these processes, the first one—*discussion*—is the most important.

WHAT SPONSORS AND MANAGERS OF PROJECTS SHOULD ASK

- What is it that we *must* deliver—that we can take *no* chances with—the *one* thing?
- Is there just *one* of these, or are there more?
- What must *not* go wrong—what things must *not* happen?
- What is the one area that we can experiment with to gain extra value?
- Is there more than one area that we might gain value from without creating risk?
- Do these value-added areas conflict with our low risk appetite areas?

In projects, risk appetite management works by reducing the capabilities-outcomes gap on a benefit-by-benefit basis. *It is a process that metaphorically stitches together the two sides of the appetite-ability failure gap—one risk and one benefit at a time.* Capabilities are strengthened where they count, and eased off on where they don't, avoiding the unconscious growth in complexity that can occur at the portfolio level in organizations which are focused solely on capability building.

At the portfolio level, smaller loss zones and smaller death zones for projects are created.

TIPS FOR MANAGING RISK APPETITE IN PROJECTS

1. Include project risk appetite in everyday language and reporting.

In some high-risk businesses, the term *risk appetite* may not be in common usage, but the word *context* and the broader language of risk awareness should be.

Include project risk appetite in project reporting and as a standing item on project steering committee agendas. Be sure to include the reasons for risk appetite being high or low in particular areas, and anything that may be a threat to the project (that is, where a project may be running close to the wind in a low appetite area). Ensure conversations on the topic of risks in projects and on areas of low project risk appetite and high project risk appetite are occurring regularly.

Consider the establishment of *risk safety officer* roles (or a similar accountability where a full-time-equivalent resource cannot be justified) in project and program management offices. Project *risk safety officers* should be responsible for monitoring and reporting against low risk appetite areas and threats to low appetite areas.

2. Ensure all three sides of the CORA triangle (capabilities, outcome, risk appetite) are addressed.

For capabilities: Is resourcing of the project, experience of personnel, and maturity of project management capabilities appropriate for the complexities of the required outcomes? Are capability gaps being addressed?

For outcomes: Are the problems or opportunities that the project is going to address understood? Are the complexities of subsequently proposed solutions understood, in terms of benefits that are to be delivered? Are these outcomes and benefits prioritized? This is so that importance is *not* applied *equally* to each of time, cost, and scope—including the specification of key benefits—because all benefits are not created equal.

For risk appetite: Have areas of low project risk appetite and high project risk appetite been identified using a work-shopping process? Is there a documented understanding of areas of risk that must not occur? Where must failure *not* occur? Is there a documented understanding of where experimentation can be encouraged? What concepts or approaches can be tested during stakeholder engagement, scoping, and piloting that may provide dividends, but equally where failure would not be fatal? Has project risk appetite been tested against higher-level organizational risk appetite? Has project risk appetite been used to inform project risk context establishment in risk workshops and in risk planning? Is risk appetite regularly reviewed?

3. Make sure everyone understands what high and low risk appetite means.

If risk appetite for an area is assessed as being high, remember that this means, statistically, that more failures in that area are likely. Conversely, if risk appetite is assessed as being low, and the project's management is in line with that assessment, less failure should be expected in that area.

4. Make risk appetite visible.

The drivers of risk appetite, and indeed risk appetite itself, are often unconscious processes. It is important to make risk appetite and its drivers visible.

5. What are your heaven-and-earthers?

In Scott Carpenter and Kris Stoever's 2002 New York Times bestseller *For Spacious Skies: The Uncommon Journey of a Mercury Astronaut*, they commented on how NASA technicians, managers, and engineers in the 1960s would *move heaven and earth* to bring astronauts safely home to their families. The reference was an endorsement of the level of commitment that NASA had to safety in the 1960s, but also a lamenting of the broken safety culture which the Columbia Accident Investigation Board (CAIB) found in NASA in 2003.

To move heaven and earth means to do everything within your power, to use all possible means, to ensure that a particular thing happens—or doesn't happen, as the case may be.

Scott and Shackleton were renowned for the concern they held for the safety and welfare of their men. Their low risk appetite in this area meant that they would move heaven and earth to ensure their men's safety.

What are your project's heaven-and-earthers—the areas where your risk appetite needs to be very low; where nothing must stand in the way of the risks to those areas being successfully managed—including the project being canceled if that is what is required.

6. Focus performance management incentives on what matters.

Having identified your heaven-and-earthers and where your risk appetite needs to be low and where it is able to be high, focus your performance incentives—whether they be cash bonuses, mentions in dispatches, or some other reward (including to ego…)—on the delivery of low risk appetite outcomes.

Gerald Wilde, a leading thinker on risk homeostasis, talks about the importance of incentive systems for reducing risk. They need to be focused on the right things. The mistake we sometimes see in the project management world, where some organizations include success bonuses or penalties in the performance agreements of project managers and owners, is that incentive systems have a narrow focus on the delivery of budget and schedule targets. If budget and schedule are made the primary goals, that's where the attention and energy of the project will go. Satisfaction of stakeholders, information security, or the reliability of the delivered systems will become secondary.

If we analogize this to climbing on Mount Everest, we can see how poor incentive frameworks can increase the chance of failure, not reduce it. If I am a member of a climbing expedition and my financial bonus (or my ego boost) is based on my achieving the summit, then not surprisingly, my focus is going to be on achieving the summit. The goal of others in also reaching the summit, and ultimately their safety, if I'm selfish enough, will take a lower priority. We actually see this behavior on Everest.

It's the same if I am the manager of a complex ICT-enabled business (EB) project. If my performance goals are all about delivery of something by a certain date, then I'm going to ensure that's what happens. Something at least, is going to get delivered.

A number of years ago, I was on the steering committee of a large and very challenging ICT-EB project. The complexities of the project's business goals were beyond the capabilities of the organization. The project sponsor's primary performance KPI (for his salary review) was that the project must be completed by June 30 of that year. With only two months to go until the end of June, all that had happened was the delivery of some expensive IT boxes and the creation of a substandard data warehouse. The members of the steering committee were astounded to hear the sponsor say, at the June meeting, that he had approved a minor scope change proposed by the project manager and that the project was now able to be completed by June 30, as scheduled.

The *minor* scope change was the removal of the requirement for customers to be able to access the new data warehouse. The customers complained, but they had been complaining about poor service in a number of areas for some time, and so their complaints about the new data warehouse went largely unheard.

The project sponsor received his performance bonus as planned—after all he had delivered the rescoped project by the required due date! Three years later, under a new CEO (in part, the result of ongoing service quality issues) and with the sponsor of the original warehouse project long gone, a new project was initiated to deliver the required customer connectivity that had been descoped the first time around.

7. *Ensure project management processes and practices are tailorable.*

Many organizational project management frameworks are process-rich and value-poor. The focus must be on practices and processes that increase awareness of risk appetite and that maximize risk reduction. None of the world's project management methodologies were designed to be dropped lock, stock, and barrel into organizations without first tailoring them to the organization's needs—and then separately, to the project's specific needs.

This particularly applies to such key practices as benefits management, risk management, portfolio management, quality management, and maturity management.

8. *Commoditize a minimum, non-negotiable set of process requirements.*

As with the national programs in Antarctica, and the higher-quality guiding companies on Everest, establish a core set of project management *safety* standards that are non-negotiable.

These might include a minimum set of requirements for the preparation and approval of business cases; the requirement for minimum monthly reporting on risks and progress; minimum levels of project management and project sponsorship training or experience; and the requirement for a minimum level of quality assurance review at key life cycle stages.

9. *Ensure people are held accountable for failures to follow minimum standards.*

It has only been through the increased commoditization of minimum experience requirements, practices and equipment, and climbing safety rules that death rates on Everest have declined in recent years. These measures would not have been successful without strict accountability management.

Individuals with high personal risk appetites will inherently be driven to cut corners, which can add risk to the organization's portfolio. High risk appetite individuals are also sometimes attracted to work in high-risk projects (see Chapter 7). These individuals can sometimes add value, but they can also add risk. Rules which prevent high risk-taking in low appetite areas for projects must be followed, if risks are not to be increased.

If people do not adhere to your minimum base-set of practices, or push for exemptions from them by using powerful but uninformed or inexperienced leaders in other parts of the organization, then your efforts to reduce failure long term are unlikely to succeed.

Sanctions to be considered might include that projects are simply not permitted to proceed to their next stage of delivery. Repeated infringements should result in performance management sanctions being applied.

10. *Understand how your P3M capabilities rate against the capabilities of others.*

How would you rate your organization's project management capabilities against the average organization's project management capabilities? Given that repeated surveys and international research over the past 20 years tells us that waste through failure of outcomes, budget, and schedule management in the average project exceeds 30%—is your organization better or worse than this?

If you have project sponsors, managers, or other stakeholders who have *been there* before, and they are becoming uncomfortable with the growing levels of risk they see around them, then their discomfort is likely to be a good indicator of risk levels. They are the equivalent of the experienced, high-altitude climbers who have climbed Everest before—they have experience and intuition—if they feel that your risks are increasing, then they probably are.

11. Manage the acquisition of a project risk appetite capability as a project in its own right.

Awareness and management of project risk appetite is a valuable capability for any organization. It reduces failure, increases success in the right areas, and reduces risk to brands. Creating a successful project risk appetite capability can often mean a challenging cultural shift for an organization. To successfully make that shift does not require significant financial, asset, or people investment, but does require senior level support and a structured approach.

There should also be measurable KPIs, by which the success of the creation of a risk appetite capability might be judged. For example, what percentage of projects has documented risk appetite statements?

12. Pay attention to comfort.

Risk appetite is fundamentally a comfort thing. It is the level of comfort that a person or organization has with the level of risk that they are exposed to. It's important to understand where feelings of comfort and discomfort with risk levels are coming from, particularly when there are different views on them.

If people are uncomfortable about having to comply with a minimum level of process in their project (for example, in the preparation of a business case or the completion of a project health-check review), that is, they would prefer the freedom to make their own decisions on the minimum process levels which should apply, but they have not managed or supported similar projects in a similar role previously, then their discomfort is probably a sign of their inexperience.

This is analogous to the low-skilled climbers on Everest who complain about safety rules and summit turn-around times. They are the ones who need the rules the most.

13. *Beware of optimism in complex projects.*

We know from much international research that the average organization has projects on its books which are beyond its project management capabilities.

If an organization is describing a project as *high risk* or *complex*, then by definition, there is going to be some degree of failure—a budget overrun perhaps, a late delivery, or maybe under-delivery of functionality or business benefits. In ICT-EB projects, all three are common.

There is little room for optimism in projects that are classified as high-risk in any organization. Optimism creates comfort, and comfort increases risk appetite. Optimism is such a significant issue in major projects that the British government (Her Majesty's Treasury) actually recommends *optimism bias* adjustments be made to the costs of all projects.

Her Majesty's Treasury's supplementary guidance on optimism bias in projects recommends a starting range provision for optimism bias in ICT projects of *10-200%*. That is, for a project with estimated capital costs of $100 million, the optimism bias adjustment process should start with a range of $110 million to $300 million. The guidance notes that the upper estimate is not an upper limit, and costs could be higher (or lower if adjustments for known contributory factors have already been made).

A more informal rule of thumb (origin unknown) for correcting for optimism bias in ICT-EB projects, states simply:

> *"Take the project's starting estimates from the business case, double the costs, halve the benefits, and if it's still a good idea, proceed..."*

I've seen many an experienced project manager, or battle-scarred past-ICT-EB project sponsor, nod their head affirmatively with a serious and knowing look in their eye when they hear this rule.

One of the most famous efforts to manage optimism bias in a high-risk project was Shackleton's reported advertisement for people to join him on his 1914–1917 Imperial Trans-Antarctic Expedition:

> "MEN WANTED: FOR HAZARDOUS JOURNEY. SMALL WAGES, BITTER COLD, LONG MONTHS OF COMPLETE DARKNESS, CONSTANT DANGER, SAFE RETURN DOUBTFUL. HONOUR AND RECOGNITION IN CASE OF SUCCESS. SIR ERNEST SHACKLETON"

The expedition failed, and all of the advertised discomforts occurred—plus some—but the men survived, and they did receive significant honor and recognition on their return.

14. Include a review of risk appetite awareness in all project quality reviews.

Independent quality checks on projects should be one of the non-negotiable process requirements mentioned earlier. For low-risk projects, such quality reviews may be light-touch—but for higher-risk projects, more detailed review should occur.

15. Employ people on the project who have risk appetites appropriate to the project's overall risk rating and its current phase.

Project risk appetite needs can vary depending on the stage of the project at the time. Sometimes the talents of a project manager can be misaligned with the phase of the project. An example of this is a project manager with a strong record of delivering high-risk technology projects being appointed to the scoping phase of a large ICT-EB project.

Success in the *delivery* phase of a project is often predicated on low risk appetite for the schedule, budget, or output dimensions of a project. Nothing must get in the way of the on-time, on-budget delivery of specified project outputs—assuming these have been determined to be important.

However, during the early scoping phases of a business transformation program, when stakeholder concerns are high and their successful engagement is critical to success, low risk appetite for time or cost parameters can be a mismatch to what is required. Low risk appetite for stakeholder buy-in is what is usually needed at this stage, and if the project proceeds at the expense of good stakeholder buy-in (a common failing actually), then the project's success will be at risk.

Shackleton may not have been the man to successfully complete the logistically complex and high-risk challenge of walking across the Antarctic continent in 1917 (we'll never know, because his ship was crushed by sea ice before he was able to land), but he was certainly the man to lead his 27-man team to safety in the most impossible of situations that resulted.

7

Denial

"From where comes your desire to risk? Is it the mountain before you, or the chasm within?"

Michael Elmes, Ph.D., Professor of Organization Studies,
WPI, Worcester, MA, USA

NORMAL NARCISSISM

Narcissism is a personality trait that we all have a little bit of. Freud described it as a natural part of the human makeup. In healthy amounts it is described as having a positive self-regard for oneself, healthy self-esteem, and a realistic confidence in one's abilities. In the academic literature healthy narcissism is sometimes called *normal narcissism*.

Unhealthy narcissism, such as is sometimes seen on the slopes of Everest or at the governance tables of troubled projects, is something different. It can add significant risk to already risky situations.

Service to oneself, at the expense of others who may need help, or at the expense of the greater team, can be a sign of unhealthy narcissism. Everest is a mountain where unhealthy levels of narcissism can sometimes be found. When service to one's personal goals dominates the urge to lend assistance to a dying man, it's time for reflection on what it is that drives us.

DAVID SHARP

Early on the morning of May 15, 2006, a climber lay dying on the upper slopes of Everest. David Sharp was found at 2:30 a.m., sheltering under an overhanging rock, 1,500 feet (500 meters) from the summit—well into the death zone.

Over 40 climbers were reported to have walked past David that morning. Several stopped, briefly, to see if they could help, but reported he was unresponsive. They returned to their climb. David was suffering from frostbite, hypothermia, and possible cerebral edema—a high altitude condition that confuses thinking, and if not treated, can lead to death.

At around 9:30 a.m., the first of those same climbers, on their way back down the mountain with their summits achieved, reached David again. Some reported they could see him shivering, still alive. Unfortunately, by then, many of the returning climbers were themselves exhausted. Some were even unwell. A few of the fitter ones tried to give David oxygen from their personal sets and to get him to stand up. Several climbers were in radio contact with their expedition leaders lower on the mountain, and the advice they were provided was that David was beyond help; the climbers should get themselves out of the death zone as soon as possible.

Two hours later a second descending group tried to help David. They attached one of their oxygen bottles to his regulator and placed his mask back onto his face. They tried to get him to stand but he couldn't, and so they, too, carried on down the mountain. Not long after this, a descending Sherpa and two climbers pulled David out into the sunlight, and gave him more oxygen. It was then that David spoke the name of the expedition he was with, and said that he just wanted to sleep. That was all they could get from him. Eventually they too headed down.

It's believed David most likely died sometime the following night. No one knows exactly when. His frozen body was found early the next morning by that day's summit climbers.

There was a lot of debate in the media and in the climbing world about David Sharp's death. Why hadn't the climbers tried as hard to save David on their way up the mountain as they had on their way down? On their way up, the climbers would have been fresher and stronger than they were on their way down and would have had spare oxygen. David would also have had more life in him.

Most of the world was stunned that a rescue of David was not attempted and they were stunned by the number of people who walked past him on their way to the summit. There was the suggestion that if someone had organized a number of the fitter climbers and their guides into a rescue team, and they had given up their summit attempts and those of their clients, a rescue of David might have been possible. The seeking of such a powerful goal—the summit of Everest—to the exclusion of caring for someone who is dying, or worse, to the exclusion of trying to rescue someone who might have lived, might be seen as a narcissistic behavior.

Sir Edmund Hillary, the first climber to summit Everest in 1953, was scathing in his criticisms of the David Sharp tragedy. Hillary was quoted by the media at the time:

> *"I think the whole attitude towards climbing Mt Everest has become rather horrifying. The people just want to get to the top. They don't give a damn for anybody else who may be in distress and it doesn't impress me at all that they leave someone lying under a rock to die."*

A leader of one of the larger climbing expeditions on the mountain at the time was quoted as saying that, had he been aware of David Sharp's situation earlier in the morning, when Sharp was first found, he would have investigated the chance of a rescue. Rescuers would have missed their opportunity to summit, but second attempts for everyone could have occurred later in the season which had only just started.

There was a counterview, that to save David was never possible. He had been out on the mountain in the death zone for too long. The logistics of rescuing a nonwalking climber from that altitude are significant. Few people have survived such experiences—but they have survived. Climbers assessed as being near death or unable to walk, after being found in the death zone after an exposed night out, have been saved. In fact, such a rescue occurred just 10 days after David Sharp's death.

From an altitude 600 feet (200 meters) higher than where Sharp died, and in more difficult terrain, a climber named Lincoln Hall was left for dead late one afternoon, and then was rescued the next day. Twelve months later, Usha Bista, a female climber from Nepal, was found close to unconsciousness at 27,000 feet (8,300 meters). She too was rescued. Hall and Bista's rescues were both major exercises that involved many people. The primary requirement for the rescue of someone who can't walk from near the summit of Everest, that is, for a rescue to at least begin, appears to be the will for it to occur from those in the vicinity, followed quickly by the will of others to help.

The problem with rescues on Everest is that for a climber to help with a rescue, they have to give up their own chances of summiting, if they haven't already summited. High on Everest there simply isn't the oxygen available to do both—i.e., to participate in a rescue and then to carry on with your climb. Faced with this, the collective weight of will required for a rescue to start on Everest can be hard to find.

To say that an attempt should not be made to rescue someone, when the evidence is strong that such attempts can be successful, and then to carry on walking to the summit yourself, is an unusual dynamic. Even in war, and especially among high-performance teams in war, great efforts are made to save comrades, to not leave anyone behind.

Everest's summit represents a powerful ego force for some of the climbers who go there—not all of them by any means, but some. The dynamics of climbers being reluctant to become involved in a rescue are complex. Personal survival is a factor, but so is the importance of not getting caught in queues (the cause of many failed summit bids), the importance of being able to tell people when you get home that you made it to the top, and the commercial importance of making sure your clients get what they have paid a lot of money for.

NORMAL NARCISSISM CAN BECOME ABNORMAL

Normal narcissism incentivizes us to want to be better people and to want to be successful in our work. Some of us have more narcissism than others. At the upper end of the continuum this can be unhealthy. Strongly narcissistic behaviors have been implicated in major disasters and are known to be damaging in business.

The upper end of the narcissism continuum is where the clinical condition *narcissism personality disorder* (NPD) sits. NPD is defined in the World Health Organization's International Classification of Diseases as a disorder characterized by *excessive self-love, egocentrism and grandiosity, excessive need for attention, and sensitivity to criticism*. The American Psychiatric Association's (APA's) diagnostic criteria for NPD includes: *fantasies of unlimited success, hypersensitivity to criticism, feelings of entitlement, exploitativeness, and a lack of empathy*.

In the 1960s, NPD was known as megalomania or severe egocentrism. Today it is believed to affect about one percent of the population, but is believed to have a much higher incidence among leaders and those who participate in high-risk activities (including projects). Narcissistically affected people are known to be attracted to high-risk activities.

The scale commonly used to measure narcissism is the Narcissistic Personality Inventory (NPI) developed by Raskin and Terry in 1988. The NPI, in its basic form, is a 40 question, multi-choice test (a number of websites publish freely available versions of it). The NPI is frequently used in studies of narcissism, but not usually for clinical diagnoses of NPD. The nearer one's score gets to the top of the 40 point NPI scale, the more NPD-like the listed behaviors become.

NARCISSISM IN THE WORKPLACE IS NOT UNCOMMON

Narcissism on mountainsides, in projects, and in business can look quite ordinary on the outside. Sometimes it may present as excessive passion for a goal, anger at things that get in the way, or an absence of empathy for team members who are suffering on the journey. When there is more of it, narcissism can become visible in isolated but concerning behaviors, and when there is lots of it, the isolated behaviors become visible patterns.

A number of years ago, an organization I was involved with underwent a major restructuring. A senior manager was brought in to manage the restructuring process and to handle the large number of redundancies (firings) that the process would require. The senior manager, Mr. Brillo, was the perfect man for the job in the eyes of the CEO. He was highly goal-oriented, with little empathy for the human toll that his job, or the way he would go about it, would create.

I will always remember Brillo's response to a comment offered from the floor, from one of the staff at a *town-hall* meeting called by Brillo for the announcement that a large number of them would soon be losing their jobs. Brillo had asked the group if there were any questions. A hand went up and a brave voice expressed concern at the turmoil that the restructuring process was creating in the minds of people with families. There was an expectation that Brillo might respond with some words of support. His response was much simpler. He stared silently at the questioner for a few seconds, and then scanned the room for the next question.

During the restructuring, staff emotional engagement with the organization, as measured in regular staff surveys, plummeted. Brillo got the job done, but the organization lost many of its best people and much value in the process. Those who stayed became a part of a new and unhappy culture.

Brillo became known for enjoying his angry outbursts and the ego attention that his restructurings involved—and for having little empathy for those who lost their jobs along the way. *Narcissistic rage* is the description given to outbursts of anger that some high-NPI-affected personalities can display. This rage can occur in response to perceived threats to the subject's ego.

Some years ago, I knew a manager of a large program who was known for relentlessly pressuring, sometimes angrily, people on her team who she perceived as not supporting her decisions. A senior member of her management team resigned one day and when I interviewed him to find the reasons for his departure, he replied with a little humor—"Grant, I don't need to come to work to be browbeaten like this, I can get it at home." He was a good man and a loss to the organization. His strengths and knowledge were seen by the program manager as a threat.

NARCISSISM AND RISK TAKING

A lot is written in the academic literature about narcissism and its connection with risk taking, whether it is in mountain climbing or in business. In 2014, Emily Grijalva and Peter Harms wrote a paper reviewing the literature on organizational narcissism and proposed a model to guide future research on narcissistic leader-follower relationships. Grijalva and Harms noted the consistent finding of researchers that narcissism is associated with a deep yearning for leadership roles. Their findings also included that narcissists are frequently overconfident and inclined to make risky investment decisions.

A 2004 paper entitled *Narcissism, Confidence, and Risk Attitude*, by Campbell, Goodie, and Foster, found that the willingness of narcissists to take risks, combined with their tendency to be overconfident, can (probably not surprisingly) result in *losses*. The authors noted the connection that researchers have found between threatened self-esteem and risk taking. The more narcissistic someone is (i.e., sensitive to threatened self-esteem) the more risks they will take to protect their egos.

In a 2009 paper entitled *Why Do Narcissists Take More Risks? Testing the Roles of Perceived Risks and Benefits of Risky Behaviors*, the authors (Foster, Shenesey, and Goff) found that narcissists engage in dysfunctional behaviors because of a *surplus of eagerness* and not because of any *deficit of inhibition*. That is, narcissists are usually aware of the downside of taking risks, but they perceive the upside of the value that might come from success (should it occur) to be higher.

The narcissist's upside, in the event of success, includes strengthened or protected ego, the benefit sitting behind much narcissistic risk taking. A comparison of normal versus high narcissism in decision making, and the role of the ego, is shown in Figure 7.1.

If the leader of a project has narcissistic tendencies, the subconscious bolstering of the leader's ego creates a value proposition for the leader that may be an unreasonable risk proposition for other project participants (particularly the project's investors). In an already high-risk project, narcissistically affected risk taking can also tip a project into failure.

SUNK EGO

This protection or bolstering of ego is an important factor in narcissistic risk taking. When people make decisions, a little bit of ego is often

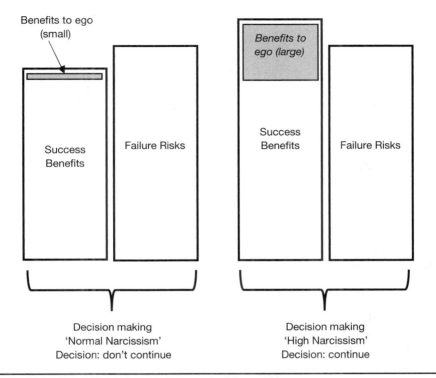

Figure 7.1 The effect of narcissism on decision making

invested—sunk—into the outcome. We all like our decisions to turn out well. If too much ego is invested though—if there is too much dependence on the outcome for the sake of the ego—behaviors can be distorted and risks increased.

Professional project managers are familiar with the *sunk cost* rule. The sunk cost rule in project management states that the amount of money which has already been invested in a project should not be a reason for continuing with the project if it is in trouble—that is, the sunk cost should not be allowed to affect a decision to terminate the project, if it is failing. Unfortunately, usually because of inexperience, sunk cost often influences continuance decisions in troubled projects.

Sunk ego works the same way. The sunk ego rule might read: *the amount of ego that one has invested in a project should not be allowed to influence one's need to terminate the project, if it is in trouble.* Unfortunately, it all too often does.

Climbing on Everest and complex information and communications technology-enabled business (ICT-EB) projects are both high-risk activities and they have a lot of things in common. Sunk ego is one of them, and another is their death rates. The death rate on Everest for people attempting the climb without supplemental oxygen is about the same as the failure rate (outright failure, not partial failure) of ICT-EB projects globally—just under one in every five.

Project owners and managers can learn much about the effects of narcissism in high-risk projects from the parallels that exist between risk taking on Everest and risk taking in project management.

SELF-HEALING CREATES DENIAL

As we noted earlier, narcissism is a personality trait that we all have a little bit of. When we have too much narcissism, it can cause us to take risks in a subconscious effort to protect or strengthen our egos. It can also cause us to put our self-healing ahead of the interests of our team, our businesses, and our projects. Importantly in risk assessments, narcissism can cause people to deny limitations, deny the complexity and risks of what they are attempting, and to deny risks that might be increasing.

Many books were written on the 1996 Everest tragedy, in which eight people died in a storm when they were caught in the open at the top of the mountain. These books include Jon Krakauer's 1997 best seller *Into Thin Air: A Personal Account of the Mt. Everest Disaster* and Graham Ratcliffe's more recent (2011) *A Day To Die For—1996: Everest's Worst Disaster*.

Most of the books and magazine articles focus on the tragedy of the eight lives that were lost. A number asked why so many needed to die. Narcissism is believed to have played a significant role.

Analysis of the 1996 Everest tragedy case provides useful knowledge for the owners and managers of high-risk projects. What does narcissism look like? What behaviors does it produce? What can be done to mitigate them?

THE 1996 EVEREST TRAGEDY

May 10, 1996, started well enough. The strong winds which were threatening to prevent an attempt on the summit had died down the previous evening. At around midnight, 33 climbers began their summit climb from Camp 4 on the mountain's South Col. At just over 26,000 feet, the South Col is only 3,000 feet below Everest's summit and in the death zone.

The midnight start for the climbers was necessary to ensure they'd be back from the summit before it became dark the following evening. Climbing upward in the dark while one is fresh is much less dangerous than climbing downward in the dark while one is tired. At lower altitudes, a climb of 3,000 feet might have been expected to take the climbers two or three hours. In the death zone on Everest, even using supplemental oxygen, it was going to take most of the climbers closer to 12, just to get to the summit.

Thirty of the climbers that night were from two commercially guided expeditions. Together they comprised six professional climbing guides, ten Sherpa guides, and 14 fee-paying clients. Many of the commercial clients had paid U.S. $65,000 or more to be guided to the top.

The experience of the commercial clients was mixed. A number had little or no experience with climbing at extreme altitudes (26,000 feet plus)—that is, mountains with death zones. There are about fourteen of these scattered around the world and they are sought-after by some climbers.

The guides understood the technical limitations of the clients and so kept the guide-client ratios high—about one guide or Sherpa for each paying client. There were also strict rules that had to be followed. Clients were not allowed to do their own thing or to get too far ahead, and the fixed ropes that were laid above the climbers had to be clipped into by the clients at all times to prevent falls.

To reduce the risk of clients running out of oxygen, and of them becoming fixated on the summit at the expense of their safety, there was a firm *turn-around time* rule. If a client, or any climber in the party, had not reached the summit by 2 p.m. on the day of the climb (guiding companies today are increasingly setting this at 1 p.m.), then they must turn around and descend, regardless of how close to the summit they might be. One of the reasons this rule is set so firmly is that the judgment of climbers in the death zone is often negatively affected by the extremely depleted blood-oxygen levels that climbers suffer at high altitudes, even when using supplemental oxygen.

As the 1996 climbers ascended, problems began to quickly occur. Some fixed ropes had not been put in place as expected and this caused delays. Bottlenecks built up as climbers queued to get across the unroped sections. Delays are a serious problem on a summit day on Everest because climbers only have enough supplemental oxygen to last them for a fixed amount of time. If supplemental oxygen runs out, energy levels and the ability to think plummet.

At about 11:30 a.m. on the tenth, after nearly 12 hours climbing, three clients made the decision to turn back. They were exhausted and could see the available hours were not going to be enough for them to summit. Their decision to turn back probably saved their lives.

At around 1 p.m., a few of the fitter climbers reached the summit. As they took pictures, they could see storm clouds approaching through the valleys in the distance. Not everyone understood the seriousness of what they were seeing. By 2 p.m., the designated turn-around time, only six of the 33 climbers had reached the summit. In breach of the turn-around rule, and unaware of the significance of the approaching clouds, climbers who hadn't reached the summit continued to climb.

The last of these reached the summit at 4 p.m. and a number of them were not in good shape. Several, including one of the senior guides and one of the experienced Sherpas, were physically ill. Oxygen levels for everyone were dangerously low—many would not have enough oxygen to get back to the tents on the South Col.

For the commercial clients who reached the summit late, had they not been exhausted and inexperienced, had the weather remained good, and had their guides and Sherpas stuck closely with them on the return journey, things might still have been okay. The trouble was that none of these things happened. As the climbers tried to quickly descend, widely spread out across the death zone, the storm hit in full fury at 4:30 p.m.

By 6:30 p.m., 19 climbers had still not reached the safety of their camp. A full blizzard, with winds gusting over 100 km per hour (60 miles per hour), was in progress, the sun had set, and it was night.

A group comprised of two guides, two Sherpas, and seven clients had managed to get down to the South Col, but could not find their tents in the storm. They sat down in the blizzard and waited. Two of the group died. One of the group, Beck Weathers, was famously left for dead *twice* by searchers over the next 12 hours, and then saved himself later the next day.

Higher up the mountain was a story of survival against the odds, of heroism, and then of loss. Rob Hall (no relation to Everest climber Lincoln Hall of 2006), one of the expedition leaders, had refused to leave a client who was struggling when the storm caught them at the summit. Hall was in intermittent radio contact with his base camp 10,000 feet below for the following 24 hours. During this time the weather continued to defeat attempts to rescue him.

Finally, at around 6:30 p.m. on the eleventh, after spending over 24 hours in the open in the storm at the top of the mountain, unable to be rescued and with an inevitably tragic end in sight, Hall's base camp was able to connect him by radio to his wife in New Zealand and they were able to talk. Hall is believed to have died later that evening.

Eight climbers died in the 1996 storm, but had it not been for the heroic efforts of several individuals, the death toll would have been a lot higher.

THE MECHANICS OF NARCISSISM

According to the psychoanalyst Heinz Kohut, the roots of narcissism are in our unmet developmental needs as children. The theory goes that an important function of a mother or father is to confirm their child's *innate sense of perfection*, and to be someone with whom the child can *merge*, or idealize. When this doesn't fully occur, as it apparently doesn't for most of us, to some extent at least, we then grow up with a subconscious sense of a damaged *self*—our inner selves feel just a little less loved by the world than we would like them to feel. The problem is that we subconsciously, mistakenly, take that perceived deficit to mean there must be something wrong with us.

Narcissism theory uses the term *mirror transference* to describe one of the ways in which we try to repair our perceived deficits. What people say about us, what we think they think about us, becomes the mirror by which we judge ourselves—that is, the mirror by which we judge how perfect, or imperfect we might be, and consequently how damaged our subconscious *senses of self* feel. Those perceptions become the mirror that we use to try to heal ourselves.

The theory (and the practice) says that the more narcissistic one is, the more important the mirror of others' opinions about us. If our subconscious perceives the image in this mirror to be less than perfect, then our subconscious will take the view that this needs to be fixed. The result is that the narcissist will work hard to strengthen and protect their image—their ego—as they see it in the mirror of others' opinions.

The other term used to explain narcissism theory is *idealization transference*. The theory of this (and the practice) is that if we grew up feeling that our parents were not someone with whom we could *merge* or idealize (maybe they weren't good role models), then we will look to compensate for this by seeking people, causes, or things that we *can* merge or idealize with. Examples of these include political causes, charismatic people, and sometimes, great mountains—basically anything that has a strong image or high public profile. Such things can and do include, of course, large and high-risk projects.

High-risk activities provide both mirror transference and an idealization transference healing opportunity for narcissistically inclined personalities. Again, we all do this a little, but when we do it a lot—adding risk (sometimes a lot of risk) to things that are already risky—then we can have a problem.

Large and risky projects can provide mirror transference and idealization transference healing opportunities to people with high normal narcissism personalities.

THE ROLE OF NARCISSISM IN THE 1996 EVEREST TRAGEDY

A paper by Michael Elmes and David Barry[1] entitled *Deliverance, Denial, and the Death Zone: A Study of Narcissism and Regression in the May 1996 Everest Climbing Disaster* (Journal of Applied Behavioral Science, 1999), provides interesting insights into the role of narcissism in the 1996 tragedy.

Elmes and Barry looked at the intersecting roles of narcissism and work-structure changes (climbing becoming a commercial commodity on Everest) in what occurred. In their conclusions they wrote:

> *"We attribute the drive of many adventure clients to reach the top of Everest to an effort at reparation of a damaged structure of self. From a Kohutian perspective, adventure climbing offered clients an opportunity to be at the centre of a doting world—both on the mountain and round the globe (a mirroring transference function)—and to merge with a potent self-object—in this case Everest itself, a symbol of ambition, success, and exclusivity (an idealization transference function)."*

The following section lists some of the narcissistic behavioral issues that Elmes and Barry found present prior to, or during, the 1996 storm, and compares them with the equivalent issues we sometimes see in high-risk ICT-EB projects.

NARCISSISTIC FACTORS IN COMMON: EVEREST 1996 AND MAJOR ICT-EB PROJECTS TODAY

Denial of Limitations and Vulnerabilities

Everest

Some of the 1996 Everest climbers were on their second or third attempt to climb the mountain. A number of the high-paying clients had a *strong sense of entitlement*, and it was reported that some had sued their guides when they failed to reach the summit.

There were examples of clients telling guides that they didn't need them, of clients who were physically incapacitated insisting they should still be able to climb, and of clients who did not support the high level of fitness and altitude preparations that Everest required.

High-risk ICT-EB Projects

A common problem we see in complex projects is the denial by some project managers, sponsors, or senior executives of limitations and vulnerabilities

[1]In the acknowledgments section, I note my conversations with Michael Elmes, and my thanks to Elmes and Barry for their support of this book's title.

in their projects. One of the challenges for the independent reviewers of these projects is how to tell a manager or owner that a project contains serious risks of failure. Sometimes such findings are perceived as reflecting on the experience and efforts of those receiving the report.

This can sometimes be the result of *sunk ego* at work, i.e., mirror transference—*I am what the mirror tells me I am, and I don't like what it is telling me.* High levels of defensiveness can occur in these situations and this can increase project risks.

Narcissistic Rage

Everest

Narcissistically affected individuals can sometimes react with high levels of anger when criticized. This type of anger is called narcissistic rage. Non-narcissistic personalities can become frustrated from time to time, but it is the origin and extent of the anger that differentiates the two.

Elmes and Barry found examples of client climbers who became angry when guides would not let them do what they felt they were *entitled* to do (for example, not being allowed to press on ahead up the mountain). A quote from one of the client's diaries noted in angry response, *"Now, it's sure as hell the end of being nice and kind, because I want to reach the top of that mountain."*

High-risk ICT-EB Projects

We sometimes see examples of anger, and sometimes extreme anger, from leaders or followers (team members) in modern-day projects under pressure. Projects have inherent restrictions placed on them—they often must finish within a tight budget, to schedule, and deliver an agreed scope. Under pressure, one or more of these will often need to slip. This can cause frustrations for an ambitious project manager or sponsor.

Failing projects sometimes require outside intervention. Sponsors and managers of these projects have often invested significant effort and sometimes ego in their projects by the time this happens. Frustration, anger, and rage sometimes result.

Participants Wanting to Be at the Center of Attention

Everest

Elmes and Barry noted that a number of the clients in the 1996 expedition appeared willing to be pampered and catered to by guides and Sherpas. This included the willingness of one client to be short-roped for sections of the climb (short-roping is when the guide in front of a client is attached to the client by a short rope, in effect partially pulling the client up steep sections of the mountain).

Elmes and Barry also noted how media hook-ups and instant media coverage helped to put the expedition at the center of a *large, admiring audience*.

High-risk ICT-EB Projects

Large and high-risk projects can have a similar effect on people. The bigger the project the more some people want to identify that they have a role in it. Interestingly, this can also extend to people wanting to identify that they have had a role in large project failures that have had high public profiles. The bigger the failure of a major project, the easier it appears to be to find (further down the track) someone who was there at the time.

A similar effect is sometimes seen in participants who exaggerate the size or profile of their project, or of their role in a project. Million- and billion-dollar projects hold particular attractions, as do projects that have either a *secret* profile or a strong public profile.

Difficulty Forming Close Team Relationships

Everest

Elmes and Barry observed that in the 1953 British Everest Expedition, during the group's three-week trek across Nepal to the mountain, the climbers formed close friendships based on respect for each other's skills and differences. In contrast, the participants in the 1996 tragedy had difficulty forming close relationships. They formed friendships, but did not become the type of team that was needed to support each other in the life and death situation which overcame them.

Concerning the night of the storm, an experienced member of the 1996 group wrote, "*If I had been on Everest with six or seven friends instead of climbing as a client on a guided trip, I never would have descended to my tent and gone off to sleep without accounting for each of my partners.*"

High-risk ICT-EB Projects

Although team building is a common activity in high-performance business operations, we do not see it given the same attention in high-risk projects.

Project teams are often formed as groups of individuals. Friendships form, but high-performance loyalties are much less common.

We find that when such teams are under pressure, due to a slipping schedule or budget (perhaps analogous to a storm on the top of Everest), they experience very high internal tensions. These can sometimes result in high staff turnover, or conflict between individuals. In general, there is a reduced ability to effectively manage new issues and risks.

WHEN SOMETHING HIGH RISK BECOMES A COMMODITY

It was not narcissism alone that created the risks and performance failings of that night in 1996. During the late '80s and early '90s, climbing on Everest shifted from being a highly skilled, team-based activity to becoming a commodity where low skills and minimal teamwork were common.

If enough money is paid, and the payer is prepared to do some preparatory work, anyone can *attempt* to climb Everest. A blind man has summited it, 13-year-old children have summited it, a double-amputee has summited it, and the oldest person to summit it was 80 years old. The efforts that these individuals made to succeed were large of course, but that is not the point. The point is that if you have the money, you can have a shot, guided by some highly skilled climbers. One doesn't need to be a skilled climber to climb Everest, nor to be a team player.

Elmes and Barry found the *commoditization* of climbing on Everest (i.e., its evolution to a commodity) to be a significant, interacting contributor to the 1996 tragedy. It allowed high levels of narcissism to be attracted to the mountain, along with lowered skills, increased competition, and reduced team commitment. They argued that as a result, the patience, perseverance, diligence, and high levels of collaboration which risky endeavors require were unable to be developed by the 1996 clients prior to their summit climb.

> "... as ambitious, self-inflated individuals, not only did clients ignore the most fundamental rule for climbing Everest—the 2 p.m. turn-around rule—they were insufficiently skilled to cope with the storm on their own and not cohesive enough as a group to assist one another."

Succeeding at high-risk endeavors requires teams to become *sophisticated work groups*—high-performing teams that are "reflective and purposeful, question leader-member relations, and recognize and publicly test fantasies and defensive reactions" (Elmes and Barry). This type of team can be found in high-performance military groups (special services and the like) and on Antarctic bases, but we do not see them very often on large or complex ICT-EB projects. Yet the risk of failure of these initiatives and the losses that can result from these failures are significant.

The following section lists some of the observations that Elmes and Barry made on structural factors that were present prior to or during the 1996 storm, and compares these with the equivalent structural issues that we sometimes see in high-risk ICT-EB projects.

ORGANIZATIONAL-STRUCTURAL FACTORS IN COMMON: EVEREST 1996 AND MAJOR ICT-EB PROJECTS TODAY

The Impact of a Commoditized System (Services Become a Commodity)

Everest

Elmes and Barry found a number of examples in 1996 of the performance of individuals, and teams, regressing (and moving into negative tension with each other) as a result of the climbing on Everest shifting from being a high-skilled team-based activity in the pre-'90s, to a highly commercialized, less-skillful commodity (focused on the fulfillment of individual goals) post-'90s.

This included the formation of a rule-based work culture (which became dysfunctional under stress) in one of the climbing parties, and of an autocratic-charismatic work culture (also dysfunctional under stress) in another climbing party. The effectiveness of teams was greatly reduced and risks greatly increased as a result.

Without the high-threshold filters of skill, experience, and a resume of prior success, narcissism in expedition participants was able to increase.

High-risk ICT-EB Projects

Project management (PM) is increasingly being viewed as a commodity. The answer to growing complexity and risk in projects is too often seen as the establishment of a project management office (PMO) to police complex process frameworks, or the sending of project managers and teams on mass-produced PM training courses. Excessive rule-based PM cultures, and at the other end of this continuum, autocratic leadership (sometimes charismatically led), both add risk to projects.

The intersection of PM as a commodity with highly narcissistic personal-ities who are attracted to high-risk projects increases the risk to these proj-ects. Project failures or the less visible *benefits under-delivery* is frequently the result.

Inexperienced Participants

Everest

Before the commercialization of extreme high-altitude (EHA) climbing in the 1980s and '90s, EHA mountaineering was the pursuit of highly skilled individuals. EHA leaders looked for talent and experience with ice climb-ing at high altitudes as a part of their climber selection criteria. John Hunt, leader of the successful 1953 expedition, looked for men with a particular temperament—those who were committed to the team and its mission, not just their own personal agendas.

By the mid-1990s, with the commercialization of EHA climbing dom-inating (and today a firm commodity), climbers had largely differentiated into buyers and sellers (clients and guides). The pre-'90's emphasis on in-dividual and team skills had moved to a post-'90's acceptance of low skills, and of reduced responsibility to the team and to each other. The ability to manage risks and crises greatly reduced as a consequence.

High-risk ICT-EB Projects

The absence of qualified, experienced, and skilled project managers and sponsors is one of the challenges of PM today. Short courses in PM basics, and certificates in foundation methodologies, are seen as a short-cut answer to reducing the risk of project failure.

Service to self is commonly seen as a priority over service to the team or to the project. Responsibility to the project team, as a cultural value, occurs only where it intersects with the needs of the individual. As a result, the ability of many projects to manage risks and crises is much reduced.

Competition

Everest

One of the impacts of the commoditization of Everest climbing has been the growth in commercial competition between different guiding compa-nies, and the need for operators to succeed in getting paying clients to the summit, if they are to stay in business. This can be especially so if companies are new in the market, or have experienced a recent failure. In 1996 this placed extra pressure on the leaders of the main expeditions, and is likely to have contributed to their decisions to keep climbing on May 10, in the face of the deteriorating weather.

High-risk ICT-EB Projects

There are similar pressures on the sponsors and managers of major projects. It's not uncommon for some participants in these projects to be experiencing their first high-risk ICT-EB project. This can increase pressure on individuals to keep going, regardless of the risks to the project, which may be growing around them. Competition between commercial suppliers of PM systems, and between technical and consultancy vendors, similarly increase risks.

PROJECT MANAGEMENT SHARES THE EVEREST PROBLEMS

In summary, as a high-risk activity, PM suffers from the same service-to-self, denial-of-risk, and commoditization problems that Everest suffers from.

- Narcissistic factors
  - ◊ Denial of limitations and vulnerabilities
  - ◊ Narcissistic rage
  - ◊ People wanting to be at the center of attention
  - ◊ Difficulty forming close team relationships
- Organizational-structural factors
  - ◊ PM as a commodity
  - ◊ High-risk leadership structures (bureaucracies, autocracies, homogenized)
  - ◊ Inexperienced participants
  - ◊ Competition among team members and among service providers

The intersection of factors from the above two groups has a multiplicative effect on risks in projects. The more normal narcissism we have, the greater the level of risk that we are inclined to take in our life's challenges—including in the projects we are involved with. We don't take risks, or engage in risky activities just because of narcissism, but it is a factor.

People who have high levels of normal narcissism have been found to be attracted to high-risk activities, including high-risk projects. Just because you are a high-altitude mountain climber or skydiver doesn't mean you have high levels of narcissism, but some do. Pulling off the impossible or something that is seen by stakeholders as high risk, can feel very self-healing.

So higher levels of narcissism can be *attracted-in* to high-risk projects, adding risk to already risky ventures.

ASSESSING THE RISK OF *DENIAL* IN YOUR PROJECT

Table 7.1 presents a list of denial factors that you may like to test for in your project. The factors listed are either narcissistic leader (or follower) behaviors, or structural factors, the presence of which, especially together, can increase risks in projects.

The presence of four or five denial factors could mean that you actually have nine or 10 of them, but the other factors are just not always visible—or

Table 7.1 Assessing denial risks in your project

Assessing Denial Risks		
Narcissistic leader-follower behaviors and structural factors	**Everest**	**Your Project?**
Defensive anger or rage	✓	
Difficulty forming relationships	✓	
Lack of emotional awareness or empathy	✓	
Decisions that appear unnecessarily high risk, or that perpetuate or increase an existing high-risk situation	✓	
Denial of high-risk levels	✓	
Denial of limitations, e.g., that capabilities are insufficient	✓	
Regressive team behaviors, e.g., anger/silence/conflict	✓	
Group-shift (when a particularly loud or influential individual changes the team's direction)	✓	
Group-think (when the group talks itself into staying its present course in spite of visible high risks)	✓	
Excessive process-policing	✓	
The core activity is treated as a commodity, e.g., for projects, is PRINCE2® or *PMBOK® Guide* seen as the answer to all your risks?	✓	
One or other of the following leadership styles is dominating: • Institutionalized (bureaucratic, hierarchical, rigidly structured) • Autocratic (either charismatic or dictatorial) • Homogenized (leaderless, fragmented, undifferentiated)	✓	

that a level of further denial is occurring. How are the behaviors/factors when the project is under pressure? This is a useful context to apply when testing for the presence of these factors.

The Risks and Issues You Should Expect if Denial Is an Issue

If you have more than a few denial factors in your project, you should expect the following issues and risks:

- The project's risk levels will be higher than they appear, or were identified in workshops
- A fall-off in project performance as complexity increases and risks eventuate
- An increase in team conflict as pressure increases
- A need for individuals to have to work harder to compensate for poor team effectiveness
- High staff turnover
- Lower performance resulting in:
  - ◊ Cost and schedule overruns
  - ◊ Lower benefits delivery
  - ◊ Increased likelihood of catastrophic failure

The Mitigations You Can Take

- Apply risk management techniques rigorously—e.g., use formal risk workshops (not someone's monthly *best-picks*); develop risk appetite statements; tailor risk criteria for the project concerned; designate risk owners; regularly review risk treatments; encourage risk conversations.
- Prepare proactively for more risks to happen, and for their impacts to be worse, (or to be hidden or down-played), and expect complex knock-on effects within and external to the project.
- At business case approval and business case revisions, ask the costs-doubling question: *If you doubled the current cost estimates* (for Everest this might include the number of digits you expect to lose to frostbite), *and halved the expected business benefits* (for Everest you might halve the expected likelihood of summiting), *is it still a good thing to do? If it is, then proceed.* This question helps take into account the optimism bias and underestimation of risks inherent in nearly all complex projects, when denial is an issue.
- Choose leaders and followers who exhibit servant or transformational leadership behaviors, and who have high emotional intelligence. These

skills increase a leader's ability to manage complexity, and the project team's openness on risk levels.

- Call out bullying behaviors early. When bullying is occurring, someone is trying to build or protect their ego at the expense of someone else—a classic narcissistic behavior. Team performance will drop.
- Introduce team building as a priority. Every percentage point of improved team effectiveness is 10 percentage points of reduced risk.

8

The Death Zone

"We would only stay there for as little time as was absolutely necessary, because whilst there our bodies would 'die a little every day'."

Ranulph Fiennes on his climb into the death zone, Everest 2005 (from his book entitled *Cold*)

The *death zone* is that region of portfolio risk appetite where the ambitions of projects exceed an organization's portfolio, program, and project management (P3M) capabilities by a significant amount. Repeated international studies (refer to Chapter 5) tell us that as many as a third of all projects operate in this zone. They are often larger or more complex than their sponsoring organizations are experienced in managing. The hazards of operating in the death zone are great—underperformance is a statistical *given* and the likelihood of failure is high.

Figure 8.1 shows three zones of project risk. In the death zone, risks are high and failure is common.

OVER-STRETCHED

Projects operating in the death zone exhibit many of the same features. The following account demonstrates a number of these, and shows how these factors can intersect to create very high levels of risk.

Some years ago, I was a government representative aboard an Antarctic *adventure tourism* cruise in the Ross Sea region of Antarctica. My role was to monitor and report on the activities of the tour operator, including compliance with environmental protocols and the safety of his activities. I also had the job of providing the tour leader and his passengers with access to a

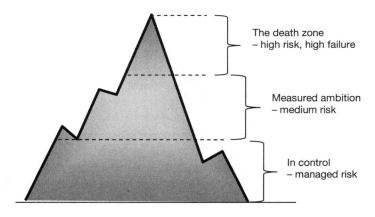

The death zone
– high risk, high failure

Measured ambition
– medium risk

In control
– managed risk

Figure 8.1   Project management zones of risk

number of locked historic huts dotted around the Antarctic coastline. One of these was Robert Scott's 1910 hut at Cape Evans—the hut Scott embarked from on his fateful trek to the South Pole in 1911.

When the cruise ship I was supporting neared Cape Evans, we were prevented from reaching the hut by about 10 km (6 miles) of frozen sea ice. This was an unsafe distance for the passengers to walk, since some of them were elderly, and a high degree of fitness is required for such a walk in Antarctica. The jackets and clothing of a number of the passengers were also not suitable for anything but the best weather that far south.

The tour leader's ship was not an icebreaker and had been prevented from reaching historic sites in the Antarctic by sea ice on previous trips. The effect of not reaching these sites can be disappointment for many passengers, a number of whom have interest in Antarctica's rich explorer history, and all of whom pay a great deal of money to travel there.

On this trip, determined not to be beaten by sea ice yet again, the tour leader had brought two eight-wheeled all-terrain vehicles (ATVs) with him. Each of these could carry four or five people. The leader's plan was that another 10 or 11 passengers would be towed behind the ATVs, sitting in five-meter-long, rigid-hull inflatable boats mounted on large sleds. Allowing for the tour leader, several tour assistants and myself, the two return trips required to get all 46 of the ship's passengers out across the 10 km of sea ice to Scott's hut.

This would be the first time the tour operator had towed large numbers of passengers a long way from the safety of his ship in this way, across sea ice of uncertain thickness and stability. A number of Antarctic explorers have died or had close calls in this same region when the sea ice they were walking on simply swept out to sea after wind or sea-state changes. Every year the sea ice in the area is expected to break away from the shore at some point and float out to sea. The most common month this occurs is February, the height of the Antarctic summer. The date of our trip was February 13th.

With some apprehension, I joined the tour leader as he set out across the ice with his first group of 30 passengers and support crew—most of them perched on the two boats being towed behind the ATVs. This first group of passengers became known as the *A-team*—hand-picked by the tour leader to be the fitter ones, in case there were problems. If the A-team made it to Scott's historic hut and back okay, the B-team would have their turn.

I had traveled in this area extensively during three summers and two winters working and leading trips across this very same ice, but those trips were in the winter and early summer, when temperatures were colder and the ice much stronger. I knew the main risk was not that the ice would be too thin to support the weight of vehicles or walkers (though this is always a risk), but rather, it was that if even a minor swell developed in the open sea nearby, it could cause the sea ice to crack and gaps to open. If the wind then changed—pushing the ice out to sea—we'd have tourists swimming (for a few minutes at least) or floating on pieces of ice in the open ocean.

My worries were not helped by the lack of assistance available to us if we struck trouble. For a substantial part of the journey, we would be traveling in a VHF-radio black-out area, where calls for assistance to the nearest national program bases of McMurdo Station and Scott Base, some 30 km (20 miles) away, would not be possible. Even if we could contact them, no real help would be available because the last remaining helicopters in the region had been flown out of Antarctica by jet transports a few days earlier. Our small cruise ship was also not an icebreaker—it had no ability to travel through closed pack ice.

As we traveled across the sea ice toward the hut at Cape Evans my fears grew. Soon after departing the ship, we reached a 10 to 20-meter-wide channel of open water. This should have been our cue to turn back—it was a sign the sea ice was thinning. A breakout of the ice was imminent. We crossed the channel using a precarious shuttling of vehicles and passengers in one of the boats. An ATV balanced on the top of a 5 meter runabout is not a highly stable arrangement—it reminded me of African river crossings made by Land Rovers balanced on wobbly rafts that I'd watched on TV documentaries as a child. We made it across the gap without losing anyone though, and the journey continued.

We eventually came to an area of ice covered in a mixture of slushy snow and sea water, signaling its thinness. A short distance later, we were prevented from going any further by about a kilometer (half a mile) of open sea, another sign of the lateness of the season and the impending breakup of the ice. Scott's hut was just visible on the far shoreline. Not to be defeated by this final obstacle the tour leader launched one of the boats into the sea and shuttled the passengers, in three or four groups, across to the land on the other side.

I unlocked the door to Scott's hut and proceeded to give groups of passengers a tour through this amazingly preserved *Heroic Age* hut. After a couple of hours everyone had seen inside the hut, and I joined the last shuttle boat to cross back to the ice floe.

As our boat approached the edge of the ice, there was a yell from the tour leader. "It's breaking up!" I turned around in the boat (having been facing the other way) to see large pieces of sea ice breaking away from the main floe. While I'd been in the hut, the wind had risen from its earlier near-calm to 15 to 20 km per hour (13 mph). The resulting chop on the open sea was what was breaking the ice up. For the moment, the sea condition was just choppy, but if a swell with a longer wavelength came up, we would be in serious trouble—it would fracture the floe into large pieces.

This had not been a sensible thing to do. Crossing 10 km (6 miles) of fragile sea ice at this time of the year, under-equipped; putting open leads of water between us and our ship; traveling with a group of tourists who had not been to Antarctica before; operating with no backup and little hope of rescue in the event of a floe breakup—we were practically asking for trouble.

There was a panic to get the boat out of the water. It was critical we get it loaded onto the sledge, and the tourists out of the area, as quickly as possible. During the rush to hook the boat-sledge up to the ATV, the ATV became stuck in slushy ice, wheels spinning. Stress levels were high. The leader yelled angrily at the ATV driver. With passengers and tour assistants helping, the ATV was freed and the boat pulled out of the water.

Although the ice was cracking, the breeze was working in our favor and holding the fractured pieces against the main floe. Everyone piled into the boat sitting on the sledge, and off we went, racing to get to firmer ice.

It was a hectic journey back. The increasing wind lifted powdered snow off the sea ice, creating a partial white-out. We could not see the ship, still some 8 km (5 miles) distant. Fortunately, the vehicle tracks from our outward journey were still partially visible in the snow. We raced along and the ship soon appeared out of the white haze in front of us.

A number of passengers had become cold in the increasing windchill. Two had lost their gloves or got them wet in the rush to get away from the breaking ice. I gave them spares which I'd been carrying since a trip I'd made with a different tourism group some years earlier. On that cruise, an 86-year-old passenger had brought a pair of sequined opera gloves with her in response to the tour company's suggested clothing list.

Shivering passengers clambered up the ship's ladder to head for the warmth of a hot shower in their cabins. The ship's doctor made a large bath available in the ship's first-aid room for anyone who felt they needed more intensive rewarming.

I was reboarding the ship myself, thinking how lucky we had been that the wind had not been stronger or changed direction, when a call came over the ship's public address system from the tour leader: "Would all passengers in the second group wanting to visit Scott's hut please assemble on deck for an immediate departure." I couldn't believe my ears. What about the open water, slushy ice, cracking floe, increasing wind, plunging wind chill, wobbly channel crossings, and the known propensity of ice in this area to just float away at this time of the year?

I found the tour leader and discussed the close call we'd had. He agreed there were issues, and asked if I would help him brief the passengers that the next trip to Scott's hut would need to be canceled. The B-team passengers asked if they might be allowed to go later if the weather improved. I believed the trip was too dangerous either way, but agreed to obtain a weather forecast by radio from Scott Base.

Fortunately (saving the tour leader an argument with the passengers, or so I thought…) the weather forecast warned of increasing winds. The tour leader then advised me that he wanted to take the B-team to the hut, regardless. Two of the B-team passengers had complained to him about not being able to visit the hut. They felt it was unfair that the A-team had gone, but not them. The tour leader appeared to be under some pressure. I advised him against doing any further trips, and said I would not be able to participate if he went ahead. The tour leader didn't like that at all.

He then asked for the key to the hut so that he could take the B-Team out, without needing me to come. I had no issue that the passengers were his to manage—it was his tour—but giving him the key to a hut that I was the custodian of was a different situation. I could just see the newspaper headlines: *Government rep gives tour leader key to hut on ill-fated sea ice journey for tourists*. It wasn't just a safety issue. There were legal implications for my employers. I declined to give him the key. This caused the tour operator to break into a rage—a good time to put the conversation on hold.

The tour leader could have taken the B-team across the ice to visit the hut without the key but he decided not to. As one of the B-team members later told me, they didn't want to take those risks unless they were able to look inside the hut. The perceived value of the goal had been driving them to overlook the consequences of a failure if it occurred—a consequence that might have included their lives.

The perceived value of the goal causes a lot of project owners to discount their risk levels. Risk appetite is different for all of us. When our leader, or our organizational culture, has a strong hunger for the goal, tolerance of risks can be very high—until they turn into issues. This is why it is important to document risk appetite before a project is approved. What must happen, what must not happen, and what can we experiment with that doesn't matter too much if it fails, but which may pay large dividends if successful.

The B-team trip did not go ahead. Most of the passengers understood why this was so. The A-team passengers shared their experience with the B-team. The tour leader's anger, though, was never quite resolved. It was a long trip home.

This Antarctic sea ice trip exhibited some classic signs of a venture into the (metaphoric) project death zone:

- The goal was ambitious—a 10 km journey using an experimental method of transportation across fragile sea ice with a large number of inexperienced passengers at the worst possible time of the year.
- The success rate for this type of initiative was poor—people had failed tragically in this area at this time of the year in the past.
- There were high levels of residual risk—the consequences of a serious incident occurring, should it occur, were high—people's lives.
- Major issues were occurring that had not been expected—the main one being the breaking up of the sea ice opposite Scott's hut.
- The cocktail effect was being experienced—multiple risks were intersecting. The ice began to break up; a vehicle became stuck; the wind that broke up the ice then picked up blowing snow which reduced visibility; and passengers became very cold even with the speedy return to the ship.
- There were several near misses—unexpectedly thin ice, slushy ice, ice breaking up, and a critical ladder nearly lost in the water on one of the lead crossings.

HIGH PROPENSITY FOR RISK

As discussed in Chapter 4, a person or organization's risk appetite is influenced by the risk personality (propensity for risk taking) of the project's leaders or the culture of the sponsoring organization—unless it is set by a managed process first. A person or organization's risk personality can be shaped by a number of factors (Chapter 4), including:

- Their background and experience (or lack of experience);
- The pressures they are under (from customers, managers, or peers);
- The perceived value of the goal (for them personally, or for the organization);
- Their level of *normal narcissism* (and noting high-risk activities can attract people with high normal-narcissism personalities).

There were a number of signs that risk appetite on the sea ice trip was being driven from a base of high risk propensity.

- The tour leader's limited experience with sea ice travel (sans cruise ship)
- The pressure the tour leader was under from his customers to take the second team out
- The perceived value of the goal for the tour leader (commercial) and his passengers (various)
- Defensiveness and anger at the suggestion that there were capability limitations (*denial*)

I estimated that there was less than a 50% chance that the B-Team would have made it to Scott's hut and back okay that day—largely because of the forecast for strengthening winds and the breaking ice that we had already experienced. If I had thought they had a 90% chance of doing the trip safely, I still wouldn't have given the tour leader the key to the hut.

A 90% chance of success is a 10% chance of failure. A 10% chance of a failure on that sea ice, with next to no chance of outside rescue, and with the price of failure being the lives of ordinary tourists, some elderly, was not acceptable.

THE PROJECT DEATH ZONE AT WORK IN PROJECTS

Many project owners know their projects are high risk, and are aware of the published failure rates for high-risk projects, but they don't believe failure will happen to them—*failure is something that happens to other projects*—as the saying goes. A positive mindset is to be commended, but the need to be in the death zone, and the capabilities needed to operate there, should always be tested.

How does one know one's project is in the death zone without undertaking some kind of complicated capabilities-versus-ambitions analysis?

Common Symptoms of Projects Operating in the Death Zone

1. The project is big and/or ambitious.

If the project is an initiative that uses significant new technology, something that hasn't been done before, or something that no one has done before, it is at high risk.

Large projects have a much higher failure rate than small projects. Studies vary on how *large* is defined in a project, but for information and communications technology-enabled business (ICT-EB) projects it's broadly in the range of $10 million to $100 million. Large, of course, is a relative term. If your organization doesn't commonly do projects over a million dollars, then a $2 million project may be large for you. Any ICT-EB project over $100 million is large for any organization, and significant inefficiencies and high risks should be expected.

Don't attempt something that an experienced organization wouldn't attempt, particularly if your team doesn't have stronger skills, experience, and capabilities than other organizations.

2. The project has a large number of residual risks.

Residual risks are the risk levels that remain after your risk management plan and risk treatments have been taken into consideration. A large number of red and/or amber residual risks may signal a project that is working in the death zone.

3. Issues are occurring that were not identified earlier as risks.

Risks are problems that haven't happened yet. When they happen, they are known in project management as issues. Issues that arise *out of the blue*, without first appearing as a risk on a risk register, can happen on any project. But when they arise regularly in this way, or if they are individually large, your project's ambitions may be extending beyond your organization's capabilities.

4. The project is experiencing the cocktail effect.

Issues, risks, and new issues combine in projects exponentially, creating new and unpredictable failure modes. This effect is similar to how different alcohols and medicines combine in cocktails to create unpredictable and dangerous effects. Are you seeing issues and risks combining unpredictably to cause larger problems?

Watch out for large numbers of high and/or medium risks in a project. Sometimes we see organizations that are happy when their projects only have one or two high-rated risks. But then we see that they have 10 to 20, or more, medium-rated risks—any one of which, if it eventuated, could do some serious damage to the project. If there are 10 or 20 of these, then two or three of them might statistically be expected to occur. The combined effect of two or three medium risks occurring in a large project can be serious. Their combined cocktail effect can result in modes of failure and impacts which leaders don't see coming.

Projects that experience the cocktail effect often deliver late or over-budget, and/or have significant numbers of unhappy stakeholders at their closure.

5. There have been near misses.

In the aviation industry, an increase in near misses is a sign of increased risk in the system. It is an early warning that a major incident may occur, if preventive action is not taken. Project management studies tell us that a project that is running over budget or over schedule, just one-fifth of its way into delivery, is very unlikely (statistically) to succeed on time or on budget—even when managers attempt to address the slippage at the one-fifth point.

Pay attention to near misses. They are a sign that a major failure is not far away.

6. Staff turnover on the project is high.

High staff turnover is an early indicator that all is not well on a project. At the very least, high staff turnover adds costs and delays to projects. Extra costs or delays can push high-risk projects over the edge. High staff turnover is also symptomatic of troubled leadership.

7. There is commercial optimism in spite of high risks.

Recognize that any advice for you to proceed, provided by those who are exposed to the financial upside of your success but not to the downside of your failure, is going to be optimistically biased.

8. There is a low sense of urgency in spite of high risks.

A sense of urgency is an important element of emotional climate in high-risk projects. If clear and large risks are known (or sensed), an absence of urgency in the atmosphere of discussions and planning is not a good sign. Actual risk levels may be higher than risk reports indicate. Risk mitigations may not be fully effective because they are unlikely to receive the necessary prioritization.

9. Resources are inadequate or are being poached for other projects.

If a high-risk project is having key resources (test environments, people-hours, management attention, or funding) diverted to other projects or operations in the business, then high levels of risk should be expected. Diverting resources from high-risk projects adds exponentially to a project's risk levels.

10. Maturity of experience and capabilities is low.

When the capabilities and experience of those working on a project is low, against the level of risk and complexity that the outcomes require, then the risk appetite gap is, by definition, *high*—and so statistically, increased failure should be expected.

COMFORT KILLS

Experiencing comfort in the death zone is not a good thing. *Pride cometh before a fall* is a 2,000 year old saying, which modern risk homeostasis theory strongly supports. Gerald Wilde, the father of modern risk homeostasis theory, wrote that when a person is feeling comfortable with the level of risk they are experiencing, they will act to increase that risk. This is not always a conscious process.

Special service soldiers put it more bluntly—*comfort kills*. If a soldier in the battlefield relaxes at the wrong time, or at any time, if he lets himself get too comfortable, his risk levels can increase without him noticing. For example, he might decide things have been kind of quiet over the last few days and he no longer needs to worry about walking in the open. Or he might decide that no mines have been found under roads in a new area of operations and so soldiers no longer need to check for them. Experienced soldiers will tell you that comfort in these situations can get you killed.

The same holds true for mountain climbers who are approaching or descending a summit. Most deaths occur when climbers are descending. They feel they have done the hard part, they have achieved their goal, and that they can now relax a little. Their guard then drops, just a little, and mistakes happen.

In the project management of high-risk initiatives, no one should be too comfortable. If you are, is it because you have done this exact same thing before and you have a strong team, reliable leadership, and the organizational maturity to succeed? Or, is it because you haven't experienced this process before and are unaware of what lies ahead? Or, has someone who doesn't carry the same risks of failure as you given you optimistic advice that the risks can be managed?

If you've done something with this level of (high) risk recently, and gotten away with it, this can also create risky comfort. An *80%* chance of success may well result in success—perhaps several times in a row—but where the success of your business, or a once-in-a-lifetime project, or when human lives are at stake, a *20%* chance of failure (which is the downside of your 80% chance of success) should be unacceptable.

Increased comfort was a likely issue for the tour operator on the sea ice trip. On the first visit out to the hut, he had escaped an extremely risky situation. This was likely to have increased his comfort with taking a second group into the same area, with the additional risks of increasing wind and less-capable passengers (the B-team).

MITIGATING THE RISKS

So how do we stay out of the death zone, or at least reduce our time in it, in this modern world of commercial pressures and complexity?

How to Reduce the Risks

1. Don't go there.

The rule for project leaders or teams who find themselves heading into the death zone is simply *don't*. If at all possible, don't do it, or do it a simpler way.

2. Run a risk appetite assessment and management process.

An effective way to avoid finding yourself in the death zone is to document the project's risk appetite as a part of the project's approval process—what must happen, what must not happen, and what we can experiment with that doesn't matter too much if it fails, but which may pay large dividends if it succeeds. If the risk appetite is documented and monitored ongoing, risks and issues that are unnecessary or that may be fatal can be treated.

3. Monitor the project for signs of the death zone, and for signs of risk propensity.

The signs that a project is operating in the death zone, or has high risk propensity, can be revealed through testing. Table 8.1 provides a summary of these for you to use for self-assessment.

4. Seek informed and independent advice.

Find someone with experience regarding the type of project you are considering—including both its scale and approach—and seek their advice on the risks involved and of ways to manage them. Make sure the person you seek advice from has no commercial or other interests in the project, or in the sponsoring organization, which might cause their advice to be conflicted.

5. Ensure there are robust business casing and quality assurance processes.

This should include a two-stage business case where the focus of the first stage is on the comparison of options and alternatives to proceeding. Only after an evaluation and approval of this stage should a detailed proposal be prepared requesting approval of the preferred approach. Quality assurance that includes a review of the project at each of the project's primary decision points (stage gates) is a must.

6. At the portfolio level, budget for a level of failure.

For projects in the death zone, a level of failure is a statistical given. At the *whole of organization* (or whole of division) portfolio level of investment, a

Table 8.1   Factors that may indicate your project is operating in the death zone

Monitoring for signs that your project may be in the death zone	
Factor	**Yes/No**
The project is big and/or ambitious	
The project has a large number of residual risks	
Issues are occurring that were not identified earlier as risks	
The project is experiencing intersecting risks ("the cocktail effect")	
There have been near misses (in the subject project, or earlier projects)	
Staff turnover on the project (or in the business) is high	
Commercial optimism is high	
There is low or no "sense of urgency" when clear risks exist	
Resources are inadequate or are being diverted to other projects	
Maturity of experience and capabilities is low	

high average rate of failure should be budgeted for when projects that are operating in or near the death zone are present.

Table 8.1 provides a list of factors that may signal your project is operating in the death zone of project risk. Three or more *yes* responses in Table 8.1 is a cause for concern. Five or more *yes* responses may mean you are running a very high risk of failure.

Table 8.2 provides a list of factors that may signal high risk propensity in your project.

Table 8.2   Factors that may indicate high risk propensity in your project

Monitoring for signs of high risk propensity (the project's "risk personality")	
Factor (refer to Chapter 4, Risk Appetite, for further info)	**Yes/No**
There is a lack of experience with this scale/type of project	
The project or its leadership is under high levels of stakeholder pressure	
The goal is perceived to be high value to individuals, or to the organization	
There are signs of high levels of normal narcissism in individuals or in the organization's broader business culture	

9

The Level-3 Organization

"Only one in five organizations report having a high level of benefits realization maturity."

Capturing the Value of Project Management,
PMI's *Pulse of the Profession®* report 2015, pmi.org/pulse

SCOTT

Scott was a successful manager of complexity. He had the value-add and soft skills that success with complexity requires—personal vision, an ability to lead, tolerance of ambiguity, and a talent for managing stakeholders at all levels.

Scott's soft skills were complemented by strong technical management skills. He was experienced with process and planning frameworks and controls, talent management, and the management of new technologies. In project management today, we call these structured management capabilities, their consistent use in organizations, and the ability to tailor them in different contexts *project management maturity*.

Project management maturity is critical for any organization that manages projects. The more complex the project, the more critical maturity is. High maturity is correlated in international studies with high levels of project success, while low maturity is correlated with high levels of project failure. There are a number of methodologies available for assessing whether the maturity of an organization's project management abilities is high or low.

GREATER MATURITY MEANS GREATER SUCCESS

In 2012, PricewaterhouseCoopers (PwC) surveyed over 1,500 people from 38 countries covering 34 industries to produce their third global survey on the state of project management. The resulting report *Insights and Trends: Current Portfolio, Programme, and Project Management Practices* included the key findings that:

- Higher maturity yields higher performance and
- Organization maturity is directly correlated with organizational success.

PwC found that as organizations increased their maturity by increasing their internal controls and processes, those organizations became better able to respond to changing project demands and to decrease the amount of time they spend on adapting to change. Increased success was the result. PwC also found that when an organization has a methodology in place to improve project performance, and the organization is one that focuses on continuous improvement, it will have a competitive advantage and be better suited to meet the modern world's constantly changing business environment.

The Project Management Institute (PMI) has been undertaking similar global surveys of project management since 2006, publishing the findings in their regular *Pulse of the Profession®* reports. The *Pulse* surveys are a significant work. The 2014 edition of *Pulse* surveyed over 2,500 project management leaders and practitioners from North America, Asia Pacific, Europe, the Middle East, Africa, Latin America and the Caribbean.

The *Pulse* reports define high-performing organizations as those that have *80%* or more of their projects delivered on time, on budget, and meeting all specified goals. In 2014, the *Pulse* research found only *12%* of organizations could be classified as high performers. In 2013, the figure was only *8%*.

Low-performing organizations are defined in the *Pulse* reports as organizations that have *60%* or fewer projects delivered on time, on budget, and meeting specified goals. The 2014 *Pulse* research found a rather large *29%* of all organizations were classified as low performers. That figure was *22%* in 2013.

Correlated with the poor project success rates, PMI found that only *8%* of the low-performing organizations reported they had mature project management processes. Across all the organizations surveyed, only *20%* self-assessed as having a high maturity of project, program, or portfolio management. Similarly, only *25%* reported they used standardized project management practices.

PMI's *Pulse* data correlates well with P3M3®-based maturity frameworks which report that *80%* of all organizations are at Level-2 or below on P3M3's *1–5* point scale (1 being low, 5 being high).

International surveys and research papers regularly report that project management maturity is correlated with success in project management, and with organizational success overall. Clearly from the large numbers of low performers, low maturity is highly correlated with project and organizational failure.

SCOTT, A FOUNDATION OF ORGANIZATIONAL MATURITY

Scott had strong leadership skills and an inherent ability to manage the scoping and stakeholder ambiguities that characterize complex projects. He also had a mature understanding of planning structures, processes, and controls which the successful delivery of complex programs requires. He obtained these working for one of the most mature organizations of his time, the British Royal Navy.

Scott was the product of an innovative, structured approach to officer training that the Royal Navy was known for in the mid-1800s. Arthur Herman, in his 2004 book *To Rule the Waves: How the British Navy Shaped the Modern World*, described officer training in the Royal Navy of Scott's time as a formalized professional training system which produced technicians "whose expertise and specialized training the navy would need in an increasingly complex world." Herman noted that although British naval officers were steeped in tradition, they were on "the cutting edge of modern science and technology."

David Howarth, author of *British Sea Power: How Britain Became Sovereign of the Seas*, wrote that the British Navy, "were always eager for discovery, not only in fighting and exploration but in surveying, navigation, astronomy, the sciences of the sea, and the design, construction, and organization of ships and their machinery and equipment." Capability competence (maturity, as it is known today) was something that the Royal Navy strove for.

In 1881, at the age of 13, Scott entered the Royal Navy as a naval cadet. After surviving a four-year apprenticeship, he was promoted to the rank of sub-lieutenant and entered the Royal Navy College at Greenwich, graduating from the college near the top of his class.

Scott wanted to specialize as a torpedo officer, an emerging technical branch of the Navy. Self-propelled torpedoes that were powered by compressed air had just been invented. In 1877 the Royal Navy's HMS *Alexandra* was the first capital ship to carry tube-launched torpedoes. The relationship between Germany and Britain was also beginning to cool and in the 1890s the Royal Navy built over 200 torpedo boats in an effort to stay ahead. Torpedoes were a technological innovation that the Royal Navy was leading.

When Scott was trained as an officer, it was at a time when rapid advancements in weapons and technology were intersecting with rapidly evolving ships. These had to operate in complementary synchronization with growing numbers of other ships, of increasing variety and specialization, over ever-expanding areas of ocean, to achieve uncertain outcomes in a frequently uncertain political world. Royal naval officers were no strangers to ambiguity and complexity.

When Scott completed his officer training, he joined a torpedo training ship where he studied torpedo launching, attack and defense tactics, and new technologies such as *advanced electricity*. Promotion within the Navy in those days was dependent on either family connections or technical expertise. Scott didn't have the family connections, so he was determined to be the best technical expert that he could be. His first specialist posting was as a torpedo lieutenant on the HMS *Vulcan*. Carrying six torpedo boats, *Vulcan* was the most heavily armed and technically advanced cruiser of its time. Scott quickly became regarded as an expert on torpedoes and mines (which then were the forerunner of torpedoes) and in 1885, he was asked to write the section on mining for the Royal Navy's Torpedo Manual. Scott followed this with a number of sea postings and in 1897, was posted to the Channel Squadron's flagship HMS *Majestic*.

In 1896, Clements Markham, President of the Royal Geographical Society, after a chance meeting with Scott aboard one of Scott's ships, asked the ship's Captain Egerton what he thought of Scott as a potential polar leader. Markham had been trying to get support from the government for a British expedition to the Antarctic for some time and was keeping an eye out for possible expedition leaders. He liked what he saw in Scott. Egerton replied, "He is just the fellow for it—strong, steady, genial, and scientific, a good head on his shoulders, and a very good naval officer."

Several years later (June, 1899), quite unplanned, Scott bumped into Markham on the streets of London. Markham told Scott that the British government had finally agreed to provide official support for a British Antarctic expedition, and that they were on the lookout for someone to command it. The next day Scott wrote to Markham advising his interest in the role. Markham was keen to have Scott but the recruitment process was not a quick one. It would be another year before Scott's appointment as leader of the 1902 British National Antarctic expedition was confirmed. That month, the Navy also promoted Scott to the rank of Commander.

The expedition was scheduled to depart only 12 months after Scott's appointment date. In a world with no computers or internet, no fax machines or printers, Scott had to plan a major geographic and scientific exploration program, staff and resource it, and be ready to depart in less than a year. The expedition's ship was still being built—and five weeks before the expedition was due to depart the expedition's steering committee was still arguing over the expedition's exact aims.

Many major projects suffer these same problems today. Scott rose to the challenge. He went on to lead two of the world's most successful Antarctic geographic and scientific research programs.

Scott was a classic *heroic manager* of complexity (refer to Chapter 10), but his success was not due to heroism alone. Success on the scale that Scott achieved requires mature capabilities management, processes, and controls. These were skill areas which Scott had been thoroughly trained and experienced in through his time in the Royal Navy. He brought a very mature set of capabilities to his complex project challenges and built strong teams and work systems to support them.

PROJECT MANAGEMENT MATURITY TODAY

Today, there are maturity models available for assessing many different dimensions of an organization's capabilities, from software engineering to cyber defense, to change management. There are a number available for assessing organizational project management maturity, and many of these include options for the assessment of program management and portfolio management.

Two of the more commonly used project management maturity assessment models are PMI's OPM3® (Organizational Project Management Maturity Model) and Axelos's (née the British Government's) P3M3® (Portfolio, Programme, and Project Management Maturity Model). P3M3® assesses maturity using the generic five-level scoring system first developed by Carnegie Mellon University in the 1980s for the U.S. government to use in the assessment of the quality of software supplier processes.

Five-level assessment scales, where 1 is low and 5 is high, are common in maturity models. Most of these use or are based on the following generic scoring structure.

- **Level 0 – Nil:** There is nil, or minimal awareness of the capabilities and processes necessary to be successful.

- **Level 1 – Aware:** There is awareness of the processes and controls necessary to support success, but they are only partially in use. Capabilities overall tend to be ad hoc.
- **Level 2 – Repeatable:** Recognized processes and controls are in use in most parts of the organization, and are repeatable within respective business groups, but they may vary from area to area. Centrally defined monitoring, processes, and controls are not commonly used.
- **Level 3 – Defined:** The organization's centrally defined processes and controls are embedded and in common usage in all areas. Processes exist for tailoring them to the size, risk, and value of subject initiatives.
- **Level 4 – Managed:** Processes and controls are actively managed. Data is collected (frequently quantitative) on process and control usage and their effectiveness, and the data is used to manage and improve performance.
- **Level 5 – Optimized:** Processes and controls are continually optimized in response to changing business needs and trends.

Whether you are using the P3M3® model, the OPM3® model, or some other model, the above capability levels reflect the journey of capability improvement, from low-awareness through to continuous optimization, that organizations should be traveling.

GOOD PROJECT RESULTS CAN OCCUR AT LEVEL-1, BUT NOT CONSISTENTLY

Good results at Level-1 will often be due to the heroic efforts of individual project managers—managers who can champion success in spite of the organizational constraints that surround them. These constraints can include unpredictable resources, changing scope requirements, and variable senior-level support.

Success for projects being delivered in Level-1 organizations is not usually defined in measurable ways. Business cases will sometimes not exist, or if they do, will not include complete cost or benefit information. Exploration of alternative solutions is often missing or weak.

Project costs are often not fully known when projects are approved—project operational costs are frequently not collected, and often only capital costs are recorded. Similarly, the project's budget may not include operational costs, or the whole of life cycle costs. Many projects would not be approved if the full costs to the organization—of the new business capabilities being created from project initiation through to the end of the new asset's/capabilities' usable life—were fully known.

Similarly, the degree of success of a project in a Level-1 organization is not usually able to be assessed because the business outcomes that the project is tasked to deliver are often not specified in measurable ways. Frequently the business case will say *faster, better,* or *more,* but without key performance indicators (KPIs) being specified, success is undefined and cannot be tested. To approve a project on the basis of such qualitative metrics is like someone buying a television that has *bigger screen* or *more channels* written on the box. One must define how much bigger the screen is or how many more channels will be available.

Project success in a Level-1 organization is often *felt,* not *measured.* Precise costs and benefit metrics are frequently unknown. Sometimes the unwritten metrics for project success in Level-1 organizations in government are *time, cost,* and *newspapers* (replacing the more usual *time, cost,* and *quality*). As long as the project hasn't seriously blown its budget, hasn't overrun its schedule by too much, and has managed to stay out of the newspapers, no one looks too closely, and the organization moves on to the next project. The true costs of Level-1 projects are unknown, but are usually higher than the figures reported.

Importantly, success in Level-1, when it happens, must be seen as an individual capability. Success at Level-1 is not an organizational capability. If the heroic manager leaves, or if the context changes (e.g., change of sponsor, or change of business structure), large failures can occur.

LEVEL-2 IS BETTER, BUT IS SOMETIMES MISUNDERSTOOD

Level-2 is better than Level-1 because although project management processes and controls are different in different business areas of the organization, they are repeatable (reliably) when used within those areas. Importantly, to achieve Level-2, all parts of the organization must be using some kind of repeatable process and controls framework.

Because of this, true Level-2 organizations are sometimes difficult to find. What Level-2 is actually saying is that a level of maturity exists across the organization being reviewed, but is implemented differently in different areas. This achievement requires some kind of process and control authority being present in *all* areas that are being assessed (without which, ad hoc Level-1 should be the correct maturity result).

Sometimes Level-2 ratings are given out by less-experienced assessors when they see pockets of good processes being used in different parts of the organization, or when they see a centrally mandated framework which has not yet succeeded with full uptake in all areas. The assessor may feel that the organization's enterprise project management office (PMO) is on its way to achieving success, and that a rating of Level-3 is not far off, and so Level-2 is a fair interim score. But if significant parts of the organization are still managing projects without a repeatable, standardized process, then Level-2 is the wrong score.

Often Level-2 organizations are large or diversified organizations, perhaps geographically spread, or comprising culturally different business groups. The different business groups in these organizations may well have their own PMOs and different project management frameworks.

Small or mid-sized organizations that were originally Level-1, and are aiming for Level-3, do not always achieve a full Level-2 score (organizationally) as an interim score while on their Level-3 journey. Level-2 may be found in common process areas, or within a key business group of the organization, but when an organization that was at Level-1 is aiming for Level-3, Level-3 is usually the next all-of-organization score that is achieved.

In Level-2 organizations it can be difficult to compare the performance of projects across the organization because different business groups sometimes use different cost, schedule, and benefit assessment standards in their business cases and reporting. Effective resource management, budget prioritization, and portfolio management can be difficult in Level-2 organizations.

LEVEL-3 IS WHERE CONSISTENT, MEASURABLE VALUE OCCURS

Level-3 is achieved when project management processes and controls are being managed using a centrally defined framework across the organization for all projects. It is the level of maturity at which consistent, measurable value occurs.

In Level-3 organizations, budgets are reliably based, costs are reliably tracked, and benefits are specified using SMART (simple, measurable, achievable, relevant, and time-bound) metrics. Decibel-based resource-management (whoever yells loudest gets the resources)—a common issue in many organizations—is replaced by structured prioritization.

Importantly at Level-3, processes and controls are able to be scaled to the needs of framework users. If a project is not at high risk of failure, or its possible failure is not high risk to the organization, then it should not be subject to the same business case standards or rigor of quality assurance review which a higher-risk or higher-value project should be.

Level-3 is the level at which the benefits of improving project management maturity can reliably be valued. Project costs, schedules, and benefits are specified in measurable ways before business cases are approved, and benefit realization reviews occur during project delivery and after projects have been completed.

Level-3 is also a cultural change. It requires a centralized, supported and supportive, engaged organization for it to be successful.

Level-3 also requires a similar level of maturity within operational, business-as-usual groups. If these groups are not collecting and tracking business performance KPIs, the business improvements delivered by projects will not be able to be assessed—an important element of Level-3 maturity.

WHAT IS THE DOLLAR VALUE OF INCREASING MATURITY?

Unless high-quality business cases and project performance baselines are created before a project is approved, the value of benefit realization reviews is greatly reduced. The real costs of projects, and project management success rates across organizations, cannot be reliably calculated.

Many people ask, "What is the value to my organization of moving from maturity Level-1 to maturity Level-2? Or moving from maturity Level-2 to maturity Level-3?" It is not possible to answer that question with an accurate dollar figure because projects created at Level-1 do not specify accurate cost, schedule, or benefit metrics—and at Level-2, that data is not consistent across the organization. What we can say is that in the average organization, nearly one in five projects fail outright (sometimes noisily, sometimes quietly), about a third fail to some notable degree, and less than a third are deemed complete successes.

In Level-2 organizations this wastage is less, but true Level-2 organizations are not common (half of all organizations are at Level 1.5 or below). True Level-3 organizations are also not common, but their wastage is again, much less.

Having sponsored and performed a large number of maturity assessments, I find the following are useful figures for articulating the scale of the opportunity that increasing maturity provides organizations:

- Level-1 to Level-2: a 30% reduction in organizational project costs (comprising reduced or avoided project costs, increased benefits delivery, increased customer satisfaction, and higher-return strategic decision making).

- Level-2 to Level-3: a *30%* reduction in organizational project costs (this is on Level-2 costs).
- Level-1 to Level 3: a *50%* reduction in organizational project costs.

In moving to Level-4 or Level-5, value continues to accrue for organizations. True Level-4 and Level-5 organizations are uncommon, mainly because achieving and holding true Level-3 is challenge enough for most.

It is sometimes misunderstood that Level-4 or Level-5 as a maturity level is reserved for high-technology organizations such as those that might be found in the aerospace industry. An organization that sets itself the goal of active management and performance improvement of processes and controls, and of proactive, managed responses to business trends can be expected to accrue significant business benefits over organizations that don't. There is no reason that Level-4 or 5 maturities should be the preserve of only high technology industries.

Because of its high returns, becoming a *Level-3 organization* should be the goal of all businesses involved in project management, and especially for those involved in large, complex, or high-risk projects. Level-4 or 5 can then be considered—once Level-3 is achieved and sustained.

MOVING TO LEVEL-3

The following points are important to note in the planning of your journey toward becoming a Level-3 organization.

Define the Scope of the Organization to Be Maturity-Improved

The definition of organization is not limited to the whole of a trading or operating entity. It may refer to a business group within an organization, a discreet business function, an internal service-delivery group, or any combination of these. In most maturity assessments that we undertake, the *organization* under review is defined as the business area, or areas that is/are under the sphere of oversight of a particular PMO, higher-level enterprise project management office (EPMO), or portfolio management group.

The scope of the business organization to be improved or assessed needs to be defined, and it need not be the full business entity. Keep in mind that the wider the scope, the greater the variety of business subcultures that you will need to bring along for the ride, and that low-performing areas that are included in scope of a maturity assessment will bring down maturity scores.

Obtain a Professional, Independent Assessment of Your Current Maturity Levels

You don't have to use a five-level maturity tool. PMI's OPM3®, for example, uses a percentage-based scoring framework. The critical things are:

1. That you create a baseline of maturity against which you can have your organization reassessed sometime in the future, and
2. That you obtain professional advice on how to go about maturity improvement.

Improving portfolio, program, and project management (P3M) maturity is a business change project, and as with any business change project, advice from someone who has done it before (preferably many times before), in an organization similar to your own, will greatly enhance your chances of success.

Ensure That Project Capability Improvement Is Managed as a Formal Project and Has a Strong Business Sponsor and a Professional Project Manager

These roles may not be full-time (depending on the size of the organization to be improved) but they should be filled by professional and experienced people.

Sometimes we see the role of capability improvement delegated to the PMO as a business-as-usual work-stream, but if there is not structured management—i.e., a business case, success KPIs to meet, a budget (importantly its own budget), a schedule, formal change management (maturity improvement is a culture change project), and quality reviews—maturity improvement projects are at risk of failure.

Focus on Buy-In and Uptake, Not on More Processes

To those who are new to project management maturity, it is sometimes misunderstood as meaning *create more processes*. Becoming the *process police* is the quickest way to get your PMO shut down or restructured. Process effectiveness is the product of processes *and* their uptake. This is shown in the equation below, and in the worked examples that follow.

> *Process effectiveness = the percentage of processes documented (those that need to be documented should be documented simply and be able to be scaled/tailored by users) × the percentage of process uptake by users.*

If a PMO has documented *80%* of relevant processes, but their uptake by users is only *20%*, then the PMO is only *16%* effective!

If a PMO has documented *50%* of relevant processes, but their uptake by users is *90%*, then the PMO is *45%* effective—and is strongly placed to grow.

A PMO that starts off with 45% effectiveness and 90% customer support is in a much stronger position than one that is only 16% effective and has only 20% customer support. In fact the correct approach to take with a low-performing PMO is often to close it down or restructure it (the action taken for nearly 60% of all PMOs in their first two years of operation).

Don't Expect to Sustainably Increase Maturity at a Rate Faster than 18 Months Per Level

Increasing organizational project management maturity means changing the culture. To change the culture in any organization, or in a business group within an organization, takes time. To increase maturity by a single level takes a minimum of 18 months. To increase from Level-1 to Level-3 (with interim improvement milestones planned) will take three years at best. High-return milestones and quick wins can be achieved along the way, but a stable, full Level-3 rating is rarely achieved more quickly.

Part of the problem is that when starting from Level-1, an organization is starting from a level of inherently low project management ability. As project management capability improvement is itself a project, its initiation and delivery is likely to be bumpy in an organization with low inherent maturity. This is another reason why having external support for scoping and planning capability improvement is important.

Prioritize the Professional Development Framework

It is important to the success of the journey to Level-3 that the experience, training, and capabilities of staff are considered a priority element in the capability maturity improvement journey. Without this, the people using the new framework (from business analysts to project sponsors and portfolio governance committee members) are unlikely to fully value or support the reasons why the framework is the way that it is, or be able to intelligently apply (including tailoring and scaling) its guidance.

As PMI noted in its 2013 *Pulse of the Profession* in-depth study on talent management, talent management is a driver of organizational success. Alignment of talent management to strategy increases project success rates, and reduces organizational dollars at risk in projects by up to 50%.

THE MOST IMPORTANT LEVEL-3 LEVER

The key differentiator between successful Level-3 organizations, and the Level-1 and 2 organizations that would like to be Level-3, is the presence in the organization of a senior-level champion of P3M capabilities—someone who understands, at their core, the importance of strong P3M capabilities in high-risk environments (most of the modern business world), and who is prepared to go to bat for improved capabilities at the senior leadership table.

A P3M champion should preferably be a member of the senior leadership team, and critically, enjoy the full support of the chief executive on the importance of P3M capability building. P3M champions are rarely full-time roles at the CX level, that is, Chief Projects Officer, or Chief Change Officer. More often, they will be a CFO, CIO, Chief of Strategy, or similar officer, who has responsibility for P3M capabilities in their area and possibly across the organization.

Ideally the P3M champion should actually *be* the CEO. They will not usually hold this as a formal accountability and are more commonly found chairing a senior-level portfolio investment committee or similar group. There are few tasks more important for a CEO than overseeing which parts of the organization's strategy should be funded, which parts shouldn't, which strategic initiatives are on track, and which aren't.

When CEOs champion these things, that's when we see Level-3 success really happening.

CRITICAL SUCCESS FACTORS FOR BUILDING P3M CAPABILITY

Project management studies, particularly *Researching the Value of Project Management* written by Thomas and Mullay, which was published by PMI in 2008, have identified a number of factors that are critical to the successful establishment of PMOs (project or program management offices) and successful P3M capability building in organizations. These factors include:

1. Having a PMO function in the organization that is perceived as being able to provide expert advice
2. Having a PMO function that is not perceived as being too controlling
3. Having a PMO that has a supportive organizational culture
4. Having a PMO that is known for continually improving value

When scoping a Level-3 capability improvement program, these success factors should be tested for—and the absence of any of them should be addressed as a priority in an early stage of the project.

THE ROLE AND LOCATION OF PMOS

PMOs are high-return functions when they are well executed in organizations. They have a key role to play in projects that are tasked with delivering P3M capability maturity.

There is no *generic* right or wrong set of functions for a PMO to manage. Scoping of PMOs can and should vary greatly. PMI's 2013 *Pulse of the Profession: PMO Frameworks* report provides a useful set of PMO framework information for practitioners to consider when reviewing or establishing PMOs.

A PMO's functions should focus on what it is that is broken in the organization that leaders want the PMO to fix. Often an organization's portfolio and project problems are not clearly defined when a PMO is established, and this can create risks for the PMO's success. A senior-level workshop, held early, can be high-return for resolving PMO scoping ambiguities.

There is also no right or wrong part of the organization in which a PMO should reside. The best location is usually within the business group whose leader most understands the importance of P3M capabilities. Many PMOs are born within information and communication technology (ICT) groups because that is where many change and complexity challenges exist.

Later in the PMO's life cycle, if it's a good PMO, non-ICT business groups will see its value and want access to its services. An EPMO is then sometimes proposed. If an EPMO is approved, it may be relocated from the ICT group to the Chief Finance or Chief Strategy leader's group. This can be a mistake, however, if the new EPMO is not supported with the same passion in the new group that it was receiving in the ICT group.

The results of moving a PMO too soon can be compared to transplanting a fragile potted plant from a greenhouse to the outside world. If it is moved too soon or if care is not taken in its repositioning, its performance and the corresponding support for it can quickly wilt.

It is worth noting that the acronym PMO is sometimes associated with organizational pain due to the high number of PMOs which are poorly set up, then fail or undergo major restructuring. In the light of this, you may want to consider giving your PMO a different name. If so, focus on the PMO's core function. What does it do that is helpful? Examples of alternative name combinations include *Project Advisory Services*, *Change Support Office*, or *Portfolio Reporting and Support Services*.

Level-3 organizations accrue significant savings, risk reduction, and strategic advantages over Level-1 and Level-2 organizations. The challenge is getting to Level-3. Whether you use the Axelos P3M3® model, PMI's OPM3®

model, or one of the many others, the important thing is making the move, seeking professional advice, and giving it senior-level sponsorship. Table 9.1 summarizes the success factors needed for moving to Level-3.

If any one of the Level-3 factors is missing, plans for the creation of a Level-3 organization, along with the significant returns that it provides, can be at risk.

Table 9.1   Success factors for moving to Level-3

Moving to Level-3	
Success Factor	**Yes/No**
Is it understood that maturity improvement requires culture change?	
Are the business boundaries of maturity improvement defined?	
Has experienced maturity improvement advice been sought?	
Is maturity improvement being managed as a formal project?	
Is there a senior business sponsor, and an experienced project manager?	
Is the capability focus on buy-in and on uptake, and not on processes?	
Is maturity improvement planned at 18 months/level or slower?	
Is the professional development framework prioritized?	
Is there an effective P3M champion at the senior leadership table?	
Is there a PMO in place that possesses the four key success factors?	

10

The Heroic Manager

"The undertaking was new and unprecedented. The object was to explore the unknown Antarctic Continent by land. Captain Scott entered upon the enterprise with enthusiasm tempered by prudence and sound sense."

Clements R. Markham, Sept. 1913

The hero project manager is *a highly skilled practitioner who operates almost single-handedly to create project success*—a definition provided by Dr. Lynda Bourne in her paper *The Future of the Hero Project Manager*, which was presented at the Project Management Institute's (PMI's) 2010 Global Congress in Italy.

The term hero or heroic project manager is used in the world of project management to describe a manager who can get the most difficult of projects across the finish line, satisfying or exceeding stakeholder expectations in spite of the poor governance and low change maturity of the organization that surrounds them. Bourne describes hero project managers as being able to deliver *despite organizational obstructions,* and quotes the definition of *hero* from the Oxford dictionary as *a person distinguished by exceptional courage and strength, a leader—a person who guides and inspires others, a mythical being, and (also) a fighter and a champion.*

That description sums up the hero project manager well. Courage is important. Hero project managers frequently accept high levels of personal risk to achieve success with projects in difficult business (or physical) environments. Hero project managers have good judgment on when to take these risks. They intuitively know what is required in situations—what the right thing is to do—and then they do it.

Complex projects cannot be delivered by portfolio, program, and project management (P3M) maturity alone. The ambiguities and multiple stakeholder interests that characterize complexity are too great. Recent project management research and the experience of explorers, past and present, are aligned on this. Successful delivery of complex projects requires heroes.

THE WORLD'S GREATEST LIVING EXPLORER

Sir Ranulph Fiennes is widely referenced as *the world's greatest living explorer*. He was the first man to reach both the North and the South Poles by surface travel and, on a separate journey, the first man to cross the Antarctic continent unsupported. He has led over 30 major expeditions, including the first polar circumnavigation of the earth in 1982. In 2009, at the age of 65, Fiennes became the oldest Briton to reach the summit of Everest. His explorations and adventures have raised over 14 million pounds ($23 million) for a variety of charities.

In overcoming the major management and operational challenges that he had on his many high-risk explorations—the political, bureaucratic, logistical, financial, stakeholder, risk management, environmental, safety, resourcing, and financial challenges (most of them simultaneously)—Fiennes is the quintessential *heroic project manager*.

The heroic manager has to be able to take control and trust his/her judgment when it matters most. Decisions cannot be made by bureaucratic adherence to process, or by debate. Managing high-risk, complex initiatives is more art than science. Heroic managers need to be able to make decisions in the face of significant ambiguity and risk, to be free to make those decisions, and to promote and implement them in ways which inspire their teams to follow.

In his 2013 book, *Cold: Extreme Adventures at the Lowest Temperatures on Earth*, Fiennes recounts the story of how, during the 1979–82 Transglobe Expedition (man's first circumnavigation of the earth through the north and south poles), he had to make one of his highest-risk decisions. As the leader, he had to decide at which point, after walking across most of the north polar ice cap, he and his trekking partner Charlie Burton should cease walking, set up camp, and wait for the ocean currents to carry their tent and their ever-shrinking slab of ice the rest of the way to their ship.

If they made camp too soon, the risk was high that their chosen slab of ice may not drift far enough south to reach the ship. If they left the decision to camp too late, i.e., if they kept walking south in order to reduce the distance that they would have to float, then the risk was high that they might not find a piece of ice large enough to survive the three months that they expected to need to float. If their piece of ice was too small and it cracked into smaller pieces, there was a good chance they would drown.

Fiennes had already completed 90% of the Transglobe Expedition, overcoming huge logistical and physical challenges and dangers crossing the frozen Antarctic continent, two sides of the planet, and now the floating north polar ice cap. It would be a tragedy for them to fail now with the finish line in sight—or worse, die in the process.

Fiennes and Burton had differing views on what they should do. Burton believed that they should keep walking and get as far south as possible. He was worried that camping too soon would result in them being cut off from the ship. Fiennes, normally the one with the greater risk appetite in these things, was worried by the rapid deterioration of the floating ice which he saw around them. If they did not look for a suitable floe to camp on soon they may not find one at all. Fiennes wrote in his book *Cold*:

> *"This was not time for indecision. The ultraviolet rays of the summer sun were daily weakening the cohesion of the floes… Only by quickly locating a big chunky ice platform for our floating base could we hope to survive such a risk-ridden, unpredictable ride."*

Fiennes and Burton understood that the decision was Fiennes' to make, and if it was the wrong decision, all fingers would point at him. Many an Arctic explorer had died getting this *walk or float* decision wrong.

Fiennes made his decision. They would look for a suitable ice floe on which to camp. Eventually one was found and he and Burton settled in for the long drift south. The decision was the right one. They floated southward for three months on the drifting floe, walking the last few hundred meters across broken ice to the waiting ship, after it had battled north through the ice to meet them.

When the journey to success is complex and high-risk, good judgment and an ability to lead, are critical.

In his book, *Beyond the Limits: The Lessons Learned from a Lifetime's Adventures*, Fiennes described the difficulties that he and Burton experienced and the process that he applied toward making his camp-versus-walk decision (as well as many others). Fiennes called the chapter of the book where he described some of these difficulties *Dictator or Democrat*.

In selecting that chapter title, Fiennes, I'm sure unconsciously, demonstrated two other key characteristics of the heroic manager: self-awareness and humility.

From Bourne's paper and those of others, and the repeated picture of heroic leaders in exploration and adventure, we can see five recurring attributes for heroic managers:

- Courage
- Good instincts (judgment)
- The ability to inspire others
- Self-awareness
- Humility

COMPLEXITY REQUIRES HEROISM

To be successful in project management, to have low rates of project failure and good rates of benefits delivery, requires an organization to have good project management maturity—structures, processes, and controls. To be successful at managing *complex* projects however requires more.

PMI's 2013 *Pulse* report *Navigating Complexity* stated that to improve the success of complex projects, organizations need to have not only mature P3M capabilities, but also:

- Engaged sponsors who actively support the project
- Leaders who are able to establish the vision, mission, and expected outcomes in ways that people can understand, and that teams can align with
- Effective stakeholder communication

The above resources mapped directly to the characteristics which PMI's report found defined complexity in projects. The more significant of these were:

- Multiple stakeholders
- Ambiguity of project features, resources, and phases
- Significant political/authority influences
- Significant external influences
- The use of new technology

These characteristics are featured in many studies discussing complexity in project management. To successfully deliver complex projects one must have a leader who can manage these resources, often simultaneously. The description *heroic* is well suited to the leader who can do this. Fiennes was able to do this; so was Scott of the Antarctic.

SCOTT, THE HEROIC PROJECT MANAGER

Captain Robert Scott's 1901–04 Discovery Expedition and 1910–13 Terra Nova Expedition were both complex undertakings. The following section reviews complexity characteristics in Scott's expeditions (characteristics no different from modern projects today) and looks at how Scott managed these.

Multiple Stakeholders

Both of Scott's expeditions required the management of challenging and diverse stakeholder groups. These included government and private sector funders, the British public, and the public and governments of countries which supported the expeditions, including Australia, South Africa, and New Zealand.

There were a number of steering committees that oversaw the expeditions. One committee was still arguing over the Discovery Expedition's aims just five weeks before its departure, and another had decided on the type of boat that one of the expeditions was going to use before Scott had even been appointed. There were also the influential Royal Society and the Royal Geographical Societies, whose support was required before the planning for either expedition could commence.

Scott inspired confidence in the expedition from his supporters and financiers. Critically, he also inspired confidence from his internal stakeholders—the people who sailed with him and lived and worked with him in Antarctica. These included people with civilian backgrounds and people with military backgrounds. There were sailors who were used to doing as they were told, and scientists who were used to challenging things. There were sailors with Royal Navy backgrounds and sailors with Merchant Navy backgrounds, and scientists from a variety of scientific disciplines with diverse and sometimes competing interests.

Scott knew there was no point at which he could relax his *engagement game*. He had a sincerity about him which shone through when he met people and talked with them about his plans. He constantly sought people's views and, as a result, people felt listened to and engaged.

Ambiguous Scope

Scott's 1910–13 Terra Nova Expedition suffered from a number of ambiguities. The expedition was not a single expedition to claim the South Pole for Great Britain. It was a large program of geographical exploration and scientific research that included an attempt on the Pole as a part of that research program.

Unfortunately, many of the British public then, and many observers and some historians since, have not understood the primacy that the expedition's research program held for Scott. The British, and Scott on behalf of the British, had always wanted to be the first to the Pole, but the entry of Amundsen to Antarctica at the last moment was not the race that many at the time (and many since) painted it to be. Amundsen kept his plans to go to the Pole secret from Scott, and in fact, secret from his own financial backers, until the last possible moment.

It was only when Scott's men stumbled across Amundsen's camp by accident in Antarctica, finding it just a few hundred kilometers along the coastline from their own and 100 km (60 miles) closer to the Pole, and possessing no scientific or geographical objectives, that they realized Amundsen planned this to be a race—and one which he planned to win, by surprise if at all possible.

One of Scott's strengths was his focus on the success of the program's scientific and geographical exploration goals. When he found out Amundsen's true intentions, he was disappointed, but he refused to be distracted. Scott's clarity of purpose was one of the reasons he became the hero that he did, in spite of the negative myths created about him by some authors of the 1970s and '80s (for a robustly researched exposé of these, see Fiennes' 2003 biography *Captain Scott*). Although Scott lost his life, his scientific and geographical achievements were some of the greatest of his time.

Resourcing Problems

The management of the Terra Nova Expedition's resources, and how they were to be distributed between the various subexpeditions, contributed a lot to the complexity of the program.

The expedition started with three motorized sledges that had been developed specifically for dragging supplies across ice and snow. Unfortunately, while unloading the sledges from the ship, one of them was placed on sea ice that was unable to support its weight. It dramatically broke through and sank to the bottom of the Ross Sea. Scott was lucky it didn't take several of his men with it. The expedition was down a third of its motorized sledges before they had even begun. The remaining motorized sledges suffered from design problems that reduced their value. The testing program for the motorized sledges had been cut short in Europe before the expedition's departure.

Scott's pony resourcing didn't fare much better. The ponies were an important part of the expedition's transport plans. The expedition had departed for Antarctica with 19 ponies, but by the time the South Pole journey itself started, nine of the ponies had been lost to accidents or illness.

Image 10.1 One of Scott's experimental motorized sledges in Antarctica in 1910, Mount Erebus in background (Photo provided under license from the Scott Polar Research Institute, University of Cambridge).

Political/Authority Influences

Members of the expedition's steering committee, the Admiralty, the Royal Society and the Royal Geographic Society, politicians, foreign governments and business sponsors, all sought to exert influence on Scott about his objectives, about how he would operate, and regarding who he would take with him.

Scott managed these political and authority forces well. He couldn't keep everyone on his side all of the time, but he achieved the sponsorship and financial support that he needed, even at times when both support and money were in short supply.

External Factors

Scott's highest external risk factor—his greatest external uncertainty—was the continent itself. Antarctica is beautiful, but its geography and its climate are highly unpredictable. This is still the case for people working and traveling there today. These ambiguities were worse for Scott because he was exploring areas that no one had visited before.

There was one environmental event that had a major impact on Scott that he was not able to manage. This was the one that took his life and the lives of three of his polar expedition party—the period of ultra-cold weather that struck the party on their return from the Pole. Painstakingly researched by Dr. Susan Solomon in her 2001 book, *The Coldest March*, this period of cold weather was exceptional—the ultimate Antarctic *rogue wave*.

Scott's sledging teams kept high-quality records of the temperatures they encountered wherever they went. The temperatures were collected using calibrated thermometers that were rechecked for accuracy on their return to Britain. The data was collected, and later analyzed and published, with the oversight in Antarctica of the meteorologist Dr. George Simpson (later to become Director of the UK Meteorological Office). These temperature recordings were an important part of Scott's broader science program.

Solomon compared Scott's temperature records with more recent Antarctic records collected from the same areas that Scott traveled through in 1912. Solomon found that only one year in 35 had been as cold as the one that killed Scott. For the three weeks from February 27 to March 19, 1912, almost every daily minimum temperature that Scott experienced was 5 to 10°C (10 to 20°F) colder than what should have been typical. On his return from the Pole, Scott should have been able to expect days of around −30°C (−20°F). He instead got days of around −40°C (−40°F). This three-week period of ultra-cold weather occurred when Scott was at his weakest. The compounding effect of the cold on the complexity of Scott's return was dramatic. Solomon tells it best in this quote from her book, in the chapter entitled *A Chillingly Unusual Month*...

> *"In a more typical year, there would have been some days of cold discomfort, but there would also have been warmer days to nurse frostbitten feet and, most important, many days in which to make far better and easier progress toward home across an infinitely more tractable surface. One weather-related problem thus added disastrously to another, because the unusually cold temperatures went hand in hand with both the lack of southerly wind to fill the sail and the terribly difficult surfaces that brought their progress to a crawl when they could least afford it."*

The difficult surface that Solomon refers to above is the crystalline-roughness that snow takes on at temperatures colder than −30°C (−20°F).

When snow is warmer than −30°C, skis (and sledge runners) are able to slip smoothly across a thin film of liquid water that forms on top of ice at warmer temperatures. Below −30°C this film does not form easily and the surface becomes like sand at the beach.

Days when Scott should have been able to cover 15 miles of man-hauling, he was only achieving six, because of the extreme cold, in essence, turning the snow to sand. When Scott and his men finally succumbed to the cold and hunger at the end of their journey, dying in their tent, they were just 12 miles from a major supply depot containing food and fuel—and from there, just a few miles more to the safety of one of the expedition huts. The exceptionally cold weather delayed them beyond anything that their contingencies could provide for.

The Use of New Technologies

The ambiguity of technology choices, business models, and scope that confronts the modern project manager is a recurring source of complexity, risk, and failure. Professional project managers of major information and communications technology-enabled business (ICT-EB) projects know about the problems of new technology systems not living up to expectations, or to the promises of their vendors.

Modern businesses want to extract as much cost and benefit advantage as they can from the new systems and technologies that they have available to them. But it's risky to be at the leading edge of technology. The *leading edge* is frequently known as the *bleeding edge* because of the price people pay to be there. The returns can be high, but the possibility of failure is exponentially higher.

On his Terra Nova Expedition, Scott had problems with a relatively simple but *new* technology which was almost his undoing. This was concerning the way that fuel cans were manufactured and how their lids sealed. Antarctica created complications with the new sealing techniques that no one had foreseen. The problem was with the soldered seams on the cans and the leather washers that were used to seal the new screw caps.

The older cork bungs that had been used to seal the fuel cans on Scott's earlier (1901–04) Discovery Expedition had been prone to spillage whenever the cans were bumped or tipped over. The new *high-tech* metal screw caps and their leather washers were supposed to have been an improvement. In Antarctica, with its extremes of temperature from the low −50°C range (−60°F) in winter to as high as 0°C (32°F) in the summer, thermal cycles of expansion and contraction of the metals used to make the cans and the screw caps loosened some of the screw caps, allowing the fuel in some cans to evaporate. This was compounded by the leather seals on the screw caps drying out and cracking, especially when the fuel cans were left exposed to the sun. Unfortunately, this happened often because the fuel cans were painted red and Scott's men would sometimes place them on the top of supply depots to make the depots more visible.

The seams of the fuel cans were also prone to leakage. They were soldered by hand back then, and the quality of the seals was sometimes poor. A small pinhole in the soldering could pass unnoticed at room temperature, but in the freezing cold of Antarctica, cracks and gaps widen, and some of the pinholes became leaks. These leaks could be fatal to an explorer who was dependent upon a full can of fuel for cooking and melting snow on a long polar journey.

As Scott traveled from depot to depot on his return from the Pole, he found that a number of the fuel cans stored at the depots were half empty. No damage to the cans could be seen. This put pressure on Scott, and reduced the amount of time his polar party could spend heating food and melting snow, but the issue itself was not fatal. Scott's planning had allowed enough fuel contingency for him to manage his way around it. This issue was an example of the way that even simple technologies, when they are new, can create risks and increase complexity.

Scott also had a number of transport decisions to make. His various geographical and scientific explorations depended on efficient and reliable transport. Efficiency was critical in order to maximize the range of the journeys, and reliability was critical, if the journeys were to succeed. Nearly all of Scott's planned journeys were at the maximum range of his capabilities.

Scott had to consider the trade-offs of range and reliability, and the uncertainties and risks of terrain that no man had yet visited. Scott's options included dogs, ponies, man-hauling, skiing, and a new type of petrol-engine car with continuous-loop tracks called a *motorized sledge*.

Scott decided from the beginning not to be dependent on dogs to tow the sledges. He was keeping his technology *off-ramps* open with this decision. Although dogs were known to handle snow and Arctic conditions relatively well, they were new to Antarctica and were known to struggle in the difficult terrain that typified that continent—especially crevasses. Eight months before the commencement of the Polar journey, during a supply-laying trip in February 1911, Scott lost nearly an entire dog team of 13 dogs down a crevasse.

Many believe that this incident was the deciding factor in Scott's decision not to use dogs to haul their sledges all the way to the Pole. Dogs were fast

Image 10.2   Two of Scott's dog teams preparing for departure (Photo provided under license from the Scott Polar Research Institute, University of Cambridge).

on flat ground, in good snow conditions, but they would not be the primary transport for Scott's journey with the terrain uncertainties that he faced.

The fact that Amundsen succeeded with his *dogs or nothing* approach to reaching the Pole involved extraordinary levels of luck. Had Amundsen failed to find a dog-friendly glacier that he could use to climb from the Ross Ice Shelf at sea level, up to the expansive polar plateau at 10,000 feet, he would not have reached the Pole and might even have perished.

As it was, Amundsen was in such a hurry to beat Scott to the Pole that he set out too early in the spring and nearly lost his dogs to the extreme cold that occurs in Antarctica at that time of year. He had departed for the Pole on September 8, much earlier than even his second-in-charge had advised—and hit temperatures of −56°C (−70°F). He was forced to turn back, but only after five of the dogs died in the process and many of the others suffered severe cold damage to their feet. Amundsen didn't restart his polar journey until October 19.

It became fashionable in the 1980s to criticize Scott's decision to use man-hauling as his main method of pulling sledges to the Pole, but these criticisms were based on a lack of awareness of the operational context that Scott was working in (and a widely published, but poorly informed, biography written on Scott at the time).

Scott's other transport option was the new and experimental *motorized sledge*. Also called a *polarized car*, it used a petrol engine and innovative (at that time) continuous-loop tracks. The motorized sledges proved useful but the expedition had cut the sledge testing program short in Europe due to time pressure, and the sledges proved unreliable in the difficult terrain of Antarctica.

Scott's ability to consider, in careful detail, his technology options and risks against the ambiguities of the environment and its terrain, and not to allow himself to be distracted or pressured by spurious external events, were important factors in the success of his broader program.

SCOTT'S ACHIEVEMENT IN THE FACE OF COMPLEXITY

Apsley Cherry-Garrard, author of *The Worst Journey in the World*—the book in which he told so well both his and Scott's Antarctic stories—commented on the scale of Scott's success in planning and delivering the Terra Nova Expedition:

> *"On the whole I believe this expedition was the best equipped there has ever been, when the double purpose, exploratory and scientific, for which it was organized, is taken into consideration... Your difficulties increase many-fold directly [when] you combine the one with the other, as was done in this case."*

Edward Larson, a Pulitzer Prize winning author, wrote about the scientific achievements of Scott in his 2011 book, *An Empire of Ice: Scott, Shackleton, and the Heroic Age of Antarctic Science*. Larson described both of Scott's expeditions as complex enterprises where:

> *"Science wove through every part of them, both influencing and being influenced by their other aspects."*

These difficulties and interplays characterized the complexity of Scott's undertakings, differentiating them from many of his contemporaries. In spite of this complexity Scott's expeditions were hugely successful. Larson describes them as *modern and forward looking enterprises* that:

> *"helped to shape the twentieth-century view of Antarctica, and its place in the global system of nature."*

The importance of heroism to the success of the modern ICT-EB project, or any undertaking involving high levels of complexity, is the same as it was for Scott. Multiple stakeholders, scope and resource ambiguities, political influences, external forces, and new technologies challenged Scott in the same way they do modern complex project managers. It was Scott's leadership, personality, experience, insightfulness, and tenacity that got him through. These are the attributes that managers of today's complex projects also need.

HEROISM AND THE MODERN ICT-EB PROJECT

I have consulted on a large number of complex and large ICT-EB (and non-ICT) projects. The ones that did well all had experienced, wise project managers at their helms. They were classic hero project managers—doing for their projects what Scott did for his expeditions. They delivered success in spite of the organizational constraints, stakeholder challenges, and scoping ambiguities that confronted them.

Two years ago an organization called me in to advise on quality assurance (QA) planning for a major ICT-EB project. The organization was large, and so was the project; it cost just over $100 million. The project was also complex. Its goals were to move the organization to an internet-based sales strategy, reduce the organization's cost of sales, improve the experience of its customers, and grow its customer base. When I was called in, a business case had been completed but the organization's board was nervous about its risks.

I met with Jane, the project's Director of Change, to get a better understanding of where the project was at and what their goals were, before giving them advice on project QA. After receiving an overview from Jane, I asked if I might be able to meet with the project manager to get his or her thoughts as well.

Jane responded by asking, "Who do you mean by the project manager? We haven't been out to tender for the new systems. I'm the project manager until that happens." The project had been running for nearly a year since Jane's team had been given approval to write the business case. It was behind schedule and the business case wasn't telling a consistent story. There were no QA reviews planned of the project's past or current activities. The scoping of the project was complex. Different group managers had different views of which of its multiple goals was the most important.

This project desperately needed a hero project manager to gain some traction. The business case was focused on a single technology answer and down played the extent of business change required. There had also been no engagement with potential supply chain partners on possible solutions and the CIO's enterprise architects were concerned that the project's costs had been underestimated.

This was a project that might get lucky and get through, a bit like Amundsen did with his dogs to the Pole, but in my opinion, significant success for them would be unlikely on their current course.

My primary recommendation was for them to recruit an experienced big-projects project manager—a hero project manager. That person needed to be someone who could manage upward to Jane, to the CIO, and the organization's board; sideways to supply chain partners and potential solution providers; and downward to the project's scoping and delivery team.

A hero project manager can be great for creating vision, simplifying goals, and driving difficult projects forward. Many owners of major projects don't understand that projects start at the time when someone decides that a business case might be needed to obtain some funds for an idea. Projects don't start when a decision is made to tender to the market, or worse, after a contract has been signed to deliver something—by then 90% of the risk is built in. A project's destiny of success, or failure, is set well before it's tender documents are released.

HOW IMPORTANT IS HEROISM TO YOUR PROJECT?

The more complex your project (within the context of your organization) the more important heroism is to your success. We say *within the context of your organization* because what might be complex in one organization might be business-as-usual in another.

Table 10.1 combines some of the complexity attributes listed in PMI's report, and the reports and research of others, to create a framework for estimating relative complexity in a project.

For your project—assessed relative to your organization's previous experiences, successes, and current comfort levels with what is proposed—how would you score your concerns for the attributes listed in Table 10.1?

The maximum score for an attribute, signaling an overwhelming concern, is 10. Scores over 8 should be used when you feel there is an aspect of *concern*. A score over 6 signals that you feel there is an aspect of *challenge* involved. For example, low organizational P3M maturity (say 0 or 1 on a 5-point scale) would be a concern and so should receive a high score.

Because complexity factors are interactive and contribute exponentially to total complexity as new factors are added (or as single factors increase in score), high scores are to be avoided. Your maximum possible relative complexity score is 100. If you've scored anywhere near 100 you need to think seriously about whether your project should proceed.

The following score ranges reflect the exponentially compounding nature of complexity:

Table 10.1 Estimating the relative complexity of a project

Estimating the Relative Complexity of a Project		
	Scott's 1911 score	Your score today?
Multiple stakeholders, internal and external	8	
Ambiguity of project features, resources, phases	9	
Significant political/authority influences	7	
Other external influences/factors outside your control	9	
The use of new technologies, methods, and approaches	8	
The scale of indicative costs	6	
Schedule pressures	6	
The newness or innovation of the outcomes sought	9	
The uncertainty of the project's risk appetite	6	
The maturity of the delivery-organization's P3M capabilities	6	
TOTAL SCORE:	**74**	**xx**

The OK range

0–33: A lower likelihood of experiencing significant loss. An experienced project manager is important.

The Challenge range

33–66: Some losses should be expected. A heroic manager is needed.

The Concern range

66–100: High risk of loss, or outright failure. A heroic manager is critical, and from the earliest possible stage.

The fact that Scott was able to achieve as much as he did in the face of the complexity that he faced (scoring 74 using the above assessment) shows his abilities as a leader and his worthiness of the label, using today's project management term, *heroic manager.*

KEY LEARNINGS ON THE HEROIC MANAGER

1. A heroic project manager is a must have, above mature organizational project management capabilities, for successful delivery of complex projects and programs.

2. Heroic project managers and heroic project sponsors are passionately engaged, establish a vision, inspire teams to follow them and to align with the vision, and are adept at managing ambiguity and multiple stakeholders.
3. Key characteristics of the heroic project manager are courage, judgment, the ability to inspire others, self-awareness, and humility.
4. To succeed with complexity today, heroic management must still be underpinned by a foundation of organizational project management maturity.
5. Heroic managers have to be supported by capable and supportive project steering committees whose role includes representing the project's risk appetite interests.
6. Without clear project risk appetite statements and the guidance they provide, the value of the heroic manager can be greatly reduced and complexity risks increased.
7. The greater the complexity of the project, the greater the need for heroic management.

11

Advanced Basics

"To face a thing because it was a feat, and only a feat, was not very attractive to Scott: it had to contain an additional object—knowledge."

Apsley Cherry-Garrard, *The Worst Journey in the World*

Captain Robert Scott of the Antarctic employed all the latest knowledge, experience, and technologies that were available to him on his 1910–1913 Terra Nova Expedition to Antarctica. These included the use of the newly invented motorized sledge; experimental combinations of men, ponies, and dogs for hauling supplies; new diets to beat scurvy; high-energy diets to beat altitude and stress; hi-tech cookers and fuel containers; and new strategies for keeping team members motivated.

The 1924 British Mount Everest Expedition did the same—employing the most up-to-date climbing knowledge and technology that they could find, including high-altitude supplemental oxygen sets, new climbing clothing, and new diets.

The 1953 British Mount Everest Expedition was even more advanced. Led by Colonel John Hunt, they employed a major-assault approach to the climb. They used large numbers of highly skilled climbers, literally tons of equipment, modernized oxygen sets, newly developed rebreather sets, and advanced weather forecasting.

Naturally, modern Everest climbing expeditions do the same. Every percentage point of advantage that can possibly be gained is looked for: real-time weather forecasts, light-weight climbing equipment and oxygen sets, high-energy foods and drinks, and advanced medicines and treatments. These treatments include the use of dexamethasone (dex) as a very effective treatment for some altitude illnesses. Unfortunately dex is also used by some climbers to enhance their performance at altitude—the payback being higher risk.

Managers of complex projects need to keep up to date with the latest knowledge, experience, and techniques for managing projects—not just in their own countries, but globally. Project management is a rapidly evolving practice in both soft skill areas (such as governance/leadership, and the psychology of change) and hard skill areas (such as methodologies, techniques, frameworks, and standards). We regularly see valuable new project and portfolio management approaches developed by governments and businesses around the world that leading practitioners in other countries still have not picked up many years later.

These *advanced basics* can greatly reduce a complex project's risks. Two areas that have advanced significantly in the last few years, and that are particularly high-return, are business casing and quality assurance.

THE IMPORTANCE OF THE BUSINESS CASE

Two common business case problems are:

1. The business case is written only after the solution to the perceived business problem has already been developed, leaving no opportunity for an intermediate business case to explore alternative ways to solve the problem. Is there cheaper, lower-risk, or higher-return ways to fix this? Do we really need this expensive new information and communication technology (ICT) system? Maybe we can change the way we do business, or partner with someone else's systems? The answers to these questions are often missing or not robustly developed when the first business case submitted for approved is allowed to propose the detailed solution.
2. The business case isn't prepared at all.

One of the drivers of these problems is the rapid evolution of the complexity of projects in the last 10 to 15 years. Ten years ago business cases were *nice-to-haves* on many projects, not required in any quality sense on others, and were only of good quality in limited instances. When business cases were done back then, they were largely just structured descriptions of an asset that someone had already decided to buy. Many business cases in those days provided limited confidence that the solutions they proposed were the highest-return, lowest-risk solution to the problem.

Today, the size, complexity, and risks of projects are many times greater than what they were 10 to 15 years ago. A business case process that unpicks the drivers and solution options for a project is imperative. One of the reasons this sometimes doesn't happen is that many of the CEOs and senior executives sponsoring these initiatives today were brought up in different times. They were ordinary staff or middle managers 10 to 15 years ago, when the complexity of projects was a lot lower and mature business cases were less important.

Some of these leaders today, though well-meaning and trying to do the best for their organizations, will push back against investing too much effort in a business case. The reply they sometimes give the portfolio or project management office (PMO) manager who is asking for a business case to be written as part of a minimum process is:

> *"Why are you making us do a business case? You are holding us up.*
> *Just let us get on and do/build/buy what we know is the right thing*
> *to do."*

This reply, often given for the complex business change projects of today, is analogous to an aircraft departing on an international flight without a flight plan developed and filed. Many years ago flight plans were simple things, but not today. Airlines cannot hope to stay in business long if their planes don't fly the most economic flight paths, have optimized fuel weights, pass all safety checks, and have every seat full.

Business cases require time and cost to develop, but they pay returns many times over.

TWO-STAGE BUSINESS CASES

The gleam that first appears in someone's eye when they propose an idea for a project is not triggered by the excitement of an open-ended question about a business problem they have found. It signals an idea they have for something that needs to be bought. The thought of testing to see if others in the organization care about the problem enough to have their share of the organization's funds diverted to make this purchase is usually some distance down the proposer's idea list.

This problem is sometimes called *solutionitis*—where the focus of the proposer is on the solution instead of on the problem or the opportunity. To prevent solutionitis, business cases should always be done in two stages.

The Stage-1 business case should present: "Here's what I think needs fixing (or what I think is the opportunity) and here is my *long list* of ideas (perhaps seven or eight) that I have for fixing the problem." The purpose of a Stage-1 business case should not be to request funds (unless those funds are to undertake further business case work) but should be to ask (and propose an answer for) the question:

> *"Do others think we should fix this problem as well, and what other ways to fix it should we be considering?"*

Closely followed by:

> *"Is everyone okay with us spending more time and money on developing the costs and benefits of the preferred option, or couple of options, from the long list that the Stage-1 business case provides?"*

Only after the Stage-1 business case has been socialized, had an independent review, and been approved by the investor, should work on the Stage-2 business case—detailing the proposed solution—begin.

We've had people say to us, "But the CEO (or the board) is insisting that we go buy this thing. Why are we bothering to do a Stage-1 business case?" The answer is because the CEO or the board will not have looked in detail at alternative ways to solve the business need that may be cheaper or lower risk. That's not their job, it's your job. Often the CEO's or the Board's proposed solution has been raised to them by an outside individual or vendor. Sometimes the origin of solutionitis is an unstructured discussion by the board or well-meaning deputies of the CEO that then results in a lobbying process for change, with the purchase of a new system as its focus.

In some cases, if the solution of what needs to be purchased really is a no-brainer, then the Stage-1 business case that argues the need for investment and tests alternatives will only be two or three pages. The point is that it should still always happen. The business need and the assessing of alternative ways to go about things should still be independently tested and approved before work on a Stage-2 business case is allowed to proceed.

A good business case process will search out all the factors that might have impact on the costs, benefits, and risks of the project to the business. Are there economies of scope that might be gained by combining the problem to be solved with existing project works or external business partners? Are their cheaper ways, lower-risk ways, or higher-return ways of meeting the same need? This is why it is important that a robust testing of the business problem or opportunity, and options for solving it, should occur as a stage-1 business case.

Frequently we hear that business case writers are under pressure and do not have time to do a Stage-1 business case, or do not have time to consult fully on what it proposes. The result is increased risk and loss at the portfolio level of the organization. For a large or high-risk project it is analogous to a climber arriving at the bottom of Everest late in the climbing season, and lobbying an expedition to be allowed to climb the mountain after only a few days of preparation and limited assessment of different routes to the top. Are there other ways to climb that might involve partnering with others, creating an entirely new route, or using a new route which someone has just put in on the other side of the mountain—perhaps with fixed ropes and free oxygen stations already in place all the way to the top?

Sure, you could charge ahead without the Stage-2 business case, but don't expect the recommended solution to be the safest or highest-return way to solve the problem.

Sometimes the issue is cultural for specific organizations, since business cases are regularly solution focused. If this is the case, then at the portfolio level, the *all projects level*, the organization should expect a higher rate of project failure, more expensive projects, and delivery of fewer benefits.

The Stage-2 business case, after the Stage-1 business case has been approved, should contain the developed detail for the proposed investment. That is, a detailed description of the proposed scope (or of the project's first stages, with detail of how later stages are going to be progressively elaborated), detailed costs, detailed benefits (with quantitative measures), and risks to success.

INVESTMENT LOGIC MAPPING—THE STAGE-0 BUSINESS CASE

Investment Logic Mapping is a high-return process for assessing the need for a project, along with what that project is going to do for the business. It was developed by the Department of Treasury and Finance (DTF) in the Australian state of Victoria to reduce the time and costs taken to develop business cases, and to strengthen the returns of new investments. A detailed description of the method is available on the DTF's web-site (www.dtf.vic .govt.au).

An Investment Logic Map (ILM) tells the story of a proposed investment on a single A4 (letter) sheet of paper. It is sometimes referred to as the *Stage-0* business case. While a Stage-1 business case talks about options for solving a problem or taking advantage of an opportunity; and a Stage-2 business case talks about the detailed scope, costs, benefits, and risks of the recommended investment; an ILM asks, "what is broken (or what is the pressing opportunity), where is the evidence for it, and do we care?" It tests the need for anyone to even begin work on a business case.

The value of an ILM is to be found in its simplicity, the conversations that it forces, its independent facilitation, and the bluntness of its process. The ILM is developed within a single, two-hour workshop—or it is not done at all. The rules for running ILM workshops are very firm and include that they should be completed within the two hours allotted.

A big part of the value of the mapping process is the common understandings (or the agreed disagreements) that the workshop's conversations produce. The one-page ILM, which summarizes those conversations, is written up by the facilitator and distributed within 48 hours of the workshop concluding.

The ILM contains:

- The problems the business is looking to solve with the proposed investment (a maximum of three problems is permitted in an ILM), using structured cause-and-effect wording.
- The benefits that will accrue to the business when the problems have been fixed (again, a maximum of three is permitted in a single ILM), with business improvement metrics indicated.
- The strategic responses that the organization should take to solve the problem and secure the benefits (five or six of these are permitted). An important principle of the ILM process is that discussion of strategic responses should include ways to reduce the *demand* for the investment to even occur. Responses should not just focus on purchasing something to solve a problem, the drivers of which have not been fully explored.
- The potential solutions, including the systems and assets which flow from the strategic responses. An important principle of the ILM method is that no *solution-people* are allowed to attend that first two-hour workshop (e.g., ICT architects for a potential ICT-enabled business [EB] project, or civil engineers for a building development project).

The mapping process includes a requirement that the three problems which the map contains are each weighted with a percentage, with the three percentages (if the maximum of three problem spaces is used) totaling 100%. These weightings show users of the map which problem the organization considers most important, and which is considered least important. For example, the need to replace aging technology may be considered most pressing, and if so, it would be weighted with a high percentage, while the need to improve customer service, even though it is considered high-return, may be given a lower percentage than the aging technology problem. The meeting participants agree on the weightings as part of the work-shopping process.

The three benefits in the map are subject to a similar weighting process. For example, improved customer service may be weighted highest (say 60%), while a healthy net present value (NPV), a side effect of improved technology efficiencies, may be weighted 30%. These weightings may also be the other way around—it depends entirely on the agreed upon view of the meeting's participants.

The prioritization information that the weighting percentages provide is very useful for informing scope-change, dependency, and trade-off decisions throughout the project's life cycle. Image 11.1 presents a fictional ILM showing how they are structured.

An important condition of the ILM process is that the *investor* must be present during the two-hour workshop. The investor is the person in the organization who will own the project's budget and be accountable for delivery of the project's business benefits. The investor should be the person who has the most to gain, or lose, from the success or failure of the project, if it is approved. Most organizations would call this person the *sponsor,* or the *senior responsible owner* (SRO) and sometimes (using the PRINCE2® parlance) the *project executive*. If the sponsor is not available for the two-hour ILM workshop, or instead delegates to one of their team or maybe a project director, then the ILM workshop does not proceed. The presence of the sponsor is critical to agreements being reached and decisions being made concerning wording and priorities in the workshop.

The lay out of an ILM differs slightly between projects and programs, and a version is also available for an organization's high-level investment portfolio. The portfolio-level ILM asks, "what are the strategic problems or opportunities that the organization exists to solve?"

A second or third workshop is sometimes held as a part of the ILM process, to further develop benefits thinking or solutions thinking (at which time solution-oriented participants are allowed to attend). The bulk of the ILM, however, is completed in the first workshop and a single workshop is sometimes all that is required.

For the cost of getting senior executives around a table for two hours, the ILM process is very high return. Discussions of important business needs, problems, and priorities happen in ILM workshops—discussions that, were it not for the ILM process, often wouldn't otherwise happen. Sometimes, early on in the workshop process, we see just how little senior executive agreement there is regarding the specific business problem that the project is actually trying to solve.

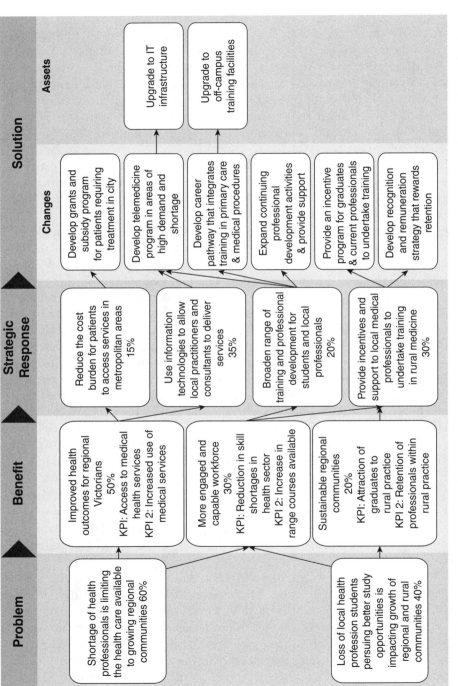

Image 11.1 A fictional Department of Health ILM "Improving access to health services in rural Victoria" (source: The Department of Treasury and Finance, Victoria, Australia)

If, during the ILM workshop, agreement cannot be reached on the business need, benefits, or strategic responses, then the ILM workshop has still been a success. A business case that would likely have cost the organization thousands, or for larger projects millions of dollars to develop, only to be redone or canceled at a later date, isn't allowed to start. Sometimes the meeting participants go away and further thinking occurs, but sometimes there is the realization that this just isn't the right time, or that the idea was a daft one from the beginning.

THE 16 QUESTION CHECKLIST

Reviewing business cases for project proposals can be an expensive and time-consuming process. Expensive assessment reports can be commissioned and still not provide investors with confidence that the investment is high return or safe.

Regardless of the form of the business case, or the type of project it proposes, there are four areas where confidence must always be sought. They are that:

- There is a real problem and it needs to be addressed at this time;
- The benefits that would be provided by successfully addressing the problem are of high value to the organization;
- The way the problem will be addressed is both strategic and innovative; and
- The solution is likely to be delivered within the specified time and cost expectations.

The ILM we discussed earlier is structured around these four areas. The DTF (the authors of the ILM process) have further developed these four areas into a 16 question checklist that can be used to assess the quality of any business case. The checklist contains four confidence points for each of the four areas above. Similar to the ILM process, the 16 question checklist is brilliant in its simplicity. The checklist is shown in Table 11.1.

A reviewer enters *Yes, No,* or *Partial,* in response to each of the 16 questions. This tool provides a systematic approach to analyzing business cases. It assists in informing the assessment of business cases, including whether further work is required. Using the 16 question checklist can save a lot of cost and variability in the review of investment proposals, and substantially increase delivery confidence.

Table 11.1 The 16 Question checklist (source: The Department of Treasury and Finance, Victoria, Australia)

PROBLEM	BENEFITS	STRATEGIC RESPONSE	SOLUTION
1. Is it clear what the problem is that needs to be addressed, both the *cause* and *effect*? **Yes***Partial*/**No**?	**5.** Have the benefits that will result from fixing the problem been adequately defined? **Yes***Partial*/**No**?	**9.** Has a reasonable spread of *strategic interventions* been identified and packaged into sensible strategic options? **Yes***Partial*/**No**?	**13.** Consistent with the preferred strategic option, has a reasonable *spread of project options* been analysed? **Yes***Partial*/**No**?
2. Is there *sufficient evidence* to confirm both the cause and effect of the problem? **Yes***Partial*/**No**?	**6.** Are the benefits of high value to the organization? **Yes***Partial*/**No**?	**10.** Is there evidence to demonstrate that the strategic options are feasible? **Yes***Partial*/**No**?	**14.** Is the recommended project solution the *best value for money way* to respond to the problem and *deliver the expected benefits*? **Yes***Partial*/**No**?
3. Does the problem need to be addressed *now*? **Yes***Partial*/**No**?	**7.** Are the KPIs SMART and will they provide strong evidence that the benefits have been delivered? **Yes***Partial*/**No**?	**11.** Were the strategic options *evaluated fairly* to reflect their ability to respond to the problem and deliver the benefits? **Yes***Partial*/**No**?	**15.** Is the solution *specified clearly and fully*? (all business changes and assets) **Yes***Partial*/**No**?
4. Does the defined problem capture its full extent/scope? **Yes***Partial*/**No**?	**8.** Have key dependencies critical to benefit delivery been considered? **Yes***Partial*/**No**?	**12.** Is the *preferred strategic option* the most effective way to address the problem and deliver the benefits? **Yes***Partial*/**No**?	**16.** Can the solution really be delivered (cost, risk, time frames etc.)? **Yes***Partial*/**No**?

STANDARDIZING THE PROJECT LIFE CYCLE AND USE OF STAGE GATES

Two things we frequently see missing from projects are:

1. The use of a common decision-making life cycle, and
2. The use of good (or sometimes any) stage-gated quality assurance.

The term *gated life cycle* is sometimes used to describe the decision making and quality review life cycle of projects. Decision-making life cycles are not the same as project or program *phases*, which tend to be higher-level descriptions of *activities*, rather than descriptions of a particular *decision* that needs to be made and assured. A project should not be allowed to proceed through a decision gate, into the next life-cycle stage, until defined quality and confidence-of-success criteria have been met.

The following is a typical stage-gated decision-making life cycle in common usage in many project management frameworks.

- *Idea-Gate*: Early consideration of the concept.
- *Gate-0*: Consideration of the strategic need and of the supporting investment logic (ILM).
- *Gate-1*: Consideration of the Stage-1 business case; options for solving the business need, and the *indicative* scope, costs, benefits, and risks of the project—should it be approved.
- *Gate-2*: Consideration of the Stage-2 business case; the detailed case for investment, its scope, costs, benefits, and risks.
- *Gate-3*: Consideration of the decision to commit to a delivery or acquisition plan—possibly including consideration of a decision to sign a contract with a specific prime contractor.
- *Gate-4*: Consideration of the decision for a new system, or major changes to an existing system, to *go live*—e.g., the operation of a new ICT system, the release of a new customer service, or the opening of a new building.
- *Gate-5*: Consideration of the decision to declare the project a success. The primary activity of this review is benefits realization. This gate is not to be confused with the project's closure report which usually occurs just after the project has gone *live* (while the project manager is still involved). The benefits realization review (in support of the Gate-5 decision) will usually happen six to 12 months *after* project closure (sometimes later). Sufficient time needs to have elapsed after go-live for benefits realization data to be available to reviewers.

A project should not be allowed to proceed through a decision gate before an appropriate level of review has occurred (tailored to the project's size and risks), and confidence in ongoing success has been obtained.

An organization's project management practices must be able to be tailored to the size, value, complexity, and risk levels of the projects using them. Sometimes *tailorability* is missing, creating extra work for low-risk projects that shouldn't require it. At the other end of the tailoring continuum, care should be taken that the tailoring process doesn't provide for exemption from minimum best practice management standards or their review. Sometimes we see lower-risk projects being exempted from quality assurance (QA) reviews of major life-cycle decision points. QA reviews should never be completely omitted from a project's key decision points. If a project is small and low-risk, then review of life-cycle decision points can be appropriately scaled, but must still occur.

If an early stage-gate review is exempted, say because of time pressures that the project is under, the risk is (and we often encounter it) that the project suffers expensive scope changes as it advances, or it struggles to maintain stakeholder support, increasing its risk of failure. If the final Gate-5 review of the project's success is exempted, then the organization will not know what the project's actual return on investment was (and with the average high-risk project under-delivering benefits by 30-50% this is important information to assess) and opportunities to reward good performance, or to hold people to account, will be missed.

Gate-5 reviews can provide benefits in a number of ways, not just in identifying losses. One organization we worked with advised us that their complex, multimillion-dollar ICT-EB project had gone live without any hitches. They were not sure they agreed with our recommendation that they should still commission a Gate-5 benefits realization assessment. We discussed with them that a Gate-5 review would be a good opportunity to present a success story back to the wider organization and to enable success-learnings to be shared.

The organization's portfolio manager agreed and a Gate-5 review went ahead. Some useful *causes of success* were identified in the review and were able to be shared with the sponsors and managers of other projects. We also found that one or two of the services delivered by the new project weren't running as smoothly as senior management had thought. Resolution of the problems with the new services was able to be prioritized as a result of the Gate-5 report.

THE IMPORTANCE OF EARLY STAGE-GATE REVIEWS

There is increasing recognition of the need for robust review processes to apply to large and complex projects at the earliest opportunity in their life cycles. The British Lord Browne of Madingley summarized the problem succinctly in his 2013 paper entitled: "Getting a Grip: How to Improve Major Project Execution and Control in Government". Lord Browne listed two drivers of his report's recommendations for improving the execution and control of major projects. These were:

1. *"The lowest standards that are set at the start of a project are the highest standards that can be expected for the rest of the project. Investment of time and resource in a rigorous process at the outset is essential for success."*
2. *"Nobody ever stops or intervenes in a poor project soon enough. The temptation is always to ignore or under-report warning signs, and give more time for things to improve to avoid revealing bad news, rather than to intervene decisively at the earliest opportunity."*

The Major Projects Association, in their 2014 paper "Project Initiation: Making the Right Start" wrote it as:

"Poor project initiation can lock in failure for all subsequent phases."

They went on to quote from the National Audit Office's 2011 paper "Initiating Successful Projects":

"The quality of project initiation is highly predictive of project success."

Once a project has commenced (not its delivery stage, but its concept proposal stage), it is very difficult to alter its course later. High-level processes, combined with high levels of sunk ego (refer to Chapter 7), can create a momentum in large and high-risk projects that is hard to turn.

QUALITY ASSURANCE IN PROJECTS

The key to good QA planning in projects is to ensure projects have quality (*the ability to succeed*) designed into them from the beginning, and that there are processes for reviewing—and assuring—the project's journey to success along the way.

A QA plan is a must for all projects. QA is a formal component of Projects in Controlled Environments (PRINCE2®), Managing Successful Programmes (MSP®), and the Project Management Body of Knowledge (PMBOK®), yet it is either missing or poorly done in many projects. QA reviews, at a minimum, should occur at each of the organization's gated life-cycle decision points. All organizations should have a standardized gated project life cycle.

Quality defined in simple terms is *fitness for purpose*. It is, as the definition suggests, a control area that provides an investor confidence that a project is going to succeed in delivering the business outcomes that the organization needs, not just those that were written down in an early version of the business case. QA also provides confidence that a project is fit to enter its next stage of delivery. QA reviews, at the project's key decision points, are critical in this regard. Is the project still on track to succeed? Is it on track to deliver its stated business outcomes on time and within budget, and on track to proceed to the next stage? These are the questions that QA reviews should be scoped to answer in the three or four gated reviews that occur before the solution is implemented.

MAJOR QA REVIEWS AND INDEPENDENT QUALITY ASSURANCE

Independence in formal QA reviews, which should be undertaken at all gated life-cycle decision points, is critical on high-risk projects. For this reason, it is recommended that they be performed by someone contracted from outside the organization and certainly from outside the business group sponsoring the project.

Independent quality assurance (IQA) reviews should be undertaken by experienced professionals who specialize in this type of work. IQA on major projects is not retrospective auditing of compliance with processes (although audits may be a component of broader QA planning), but includes a significant component of risk judgment and the provision of forward-looking advice. Complexity, the reduction of it, and the assurance of success in its delivery cannot be reduced to *compliance with a process*. We can check that a high-altitude climber has all the right equipment, and that he or she has attended a climbing course, but the climber's experience, how they work with or lead others, and the route they plan to take to the top, are questions that require high levels of experience and judgment to assess.

To organizations who are looking to engage IQA specialists on high-risk projects, we say that they should hire *brains* not *brand*—they should engage with the market to retain the services of specialized IQA individuals. IQA on high-risk projects is about the depth of the reviewer's experience and the quality of their judgments. Suitably wise and experienced individuals are not easy to find, but they pay for themselves many times over.

THE INDEPENDENCE OF THE IQA REVIEWER

To be independent, a QA reviewer must not provide so much advice during a review, or become involved in assisting the project to such an extent, that they can't return for a future QA review and feel comfortable criticizing what they find, should this be needed.

If an IQA reviewer is too involved in advising on the shape of project deliverables, or on recommending technical or other solutions, there is a risk that they can become conflicted when returning to do later IQA reviews. Some of what they have to review at a later date will actually be their own work, or the result of directions that they themselves have recommended. This creates a conflict of interest for the reviewer.

The decision of what is *too much* advice or involvement for an IQA reviewer requires good judgment, and should be discussed between the IQA reviewer and the IQA owner before an IQA engagement is confirmed. It may be, for example, that facilitating a risk workshop (where no content input from the facilitator is provided) is allowed, but that facilitating a large number of such workshops might create a conflict risk. Similarly, attending a steering committee meeting to understand the culture and dynamics of a project's governance might not be a conflict risk, but attending as a regular member might be.

One way of managing such risks, while still obtaining the value of experienced, senior-level involvement in these areas, is to have providers from different advisory companies (or internal business groups for smaller projects) undertaking these different roles. This should be considered when it is agreed that a conflict risk may exist.

PROJECT SUCCESS SHOULD ALWAYS BE AN IQA FOCUS

IQA should not be scoped to review just one stage of a project, or one stage's outputs, in isolation from its broader business goals. For example, IQA should not be scoped to review only the business case, or only the go-live plan. IQA, to be good quality QA, should be scoped to assess all the elements of a project that are relevant to the quality of the project at that time, its potential to succeed longer-term, and its readiness to move into the next stage of its life cycle. There may be a focus on a key output or deliverable, but assurance of broader success should be in scope.

Approaches for structuring project QA reviews include:

- *PMBOK® Guide's* 10 knowledge areas
- P3M3®'s seven capability perspectives
- MSP®'s nine governance themes
- Issues raised by earlier reviews
- Specific areas requested by the QA owner

Sometimes elements from all of the above are used in a single review, and sometimes a different structure may be used altogether. The important thing is that a QA review must walk its own talk, that is, be fit for its own purpose—the provision of assurance of success. No two projects will serve the same purpose, contexts, and risks, and neither will the QA reviews of those projects.

SELECTING THE RIGHT *OWNER* OF AN IQA REVIEW

When scoping an IQA engagement it is important to consider who will own the QA report and the control of the review. The owner must determine the scope of the QA engagement (usually liaising with a QA specialist for advice on this) and, post-report, ensure that the report's recommendations are actioned.

The best person to own a primary stage-gate QA engagement (where a go or no-go investment decision is being made) is the owner of the relevant business group's portfolio of projects who is *at least one level higher* in seniority than the project's sponsor. This may be the project sponsor's boss, or a more senior manager's representative, e.g., the organization's portfolio owner. This higher level of ownership is needed because the impact of a project failing is not restricted to just the project's sponsor. Risks to the higher-level business group's strategic outcomes, budget, or brand can sometimes be significant. Ownership of stage-gate QA reviews lower than this can increase conflict-of-interest risks.

Technical and process QA reviews, which are not informing go or no-go investment decisions, may be commissioned and owned directly by sponsors or project managers. These reviews may even review aspects of the sponsor's performance, as long as the review's findings are not being used by a more senior stakeholder for investment decision making, or to inform the sponsor's performance management.

In cases where the project sponsor may be a deputy chief executive or vice president, the owner of the QA report should be the CEO. The CEO's QA ownership role may then (but not always) be delegated to the organization's audit and risk (or a similar) group. Even when the CEO's IQA ownership role is delegated, the CEO themselves should always receive drafts of the IQA report, not just the final version, and should have regular discussions with the delegated IQA owner.

When the CEO of an organization is the active sponsor of the project (for a major organizational transformation perhaps) the organization's higher-level governance board should be the IQA owner. The organization's board should be considered for the ownership of the IQA of any project that presents a risk to an organization's viability or brand.

CONFLICTS OF INTEREST IN IQA

Project managers, more senior project or program directors, and sponsors of projects should not be the owners (or controllers) of IQA reviews of their own projects—*where the results of those reviews are to be used to seek endorsement of the project, or funding from a higher-level source*. These roles can become conflicted if an IQA review finds problems with the performance of a project or its risks. Everyone wants what is best for a project—but when that best, for whatever reason, hasn't been able to occur or it requires extra work that may put someone's annual performance bonus at risk, project decision makers can become conflicted when owning or controlling IQA.

Commercial advisory conflicts also need to be considered. When commercial IQA providers are appointed by an IQA owner, the provider will be under an inherent commercial pressure to preserve the relationship with the IQA owner (lest they are not reappointed for the IQA of the project's next phase, or of projects elsewhere in the organization). This pressure can unconsciously (and sometimes consciously) cause an IQA provider to soften the wording of IQA recommendations, or to dilute them among less serious matters.

Some years ago, we were commissioned to do a post-mortem on a failed project and of the role that inadequate IQA might have played in the project's failure. During the post-mortem, we became puzzled as to why the project's IQA reviewers appeared not to have commented on a contracting risk that seemed to have been growing in the project for some months before its ultimate failure. When we visited the author of the IQA report to ask about this, he thumbed backward and forward through his copy of the very large IQA report. He then proudly pointed to a page in the middle of the report saying, "Here it is on page 72." The issue identified on page 72 should have been a stand-alone bullet point in the executive summary. We now call this the *page 72 effect*.

WHEN THE IQA REPORTING LEVEL IS TOO LOW

In a different organization, we were asked by a project's sponsor to undertake an IQA of a major business transformation project. One of the conditions the sponsor wanted to place on us was that we weren't to make any recommendations that slowed them down. This wasn't a term we felt we could agree to, so we declined the work. About a year later, we were called in by the organization's head of risk and assurance to assist with a dispute that had arisen between the project's sponsor and the IQA company that had *won* the IQA work that we had earlier declined.

We commenced the engagement by attending a meeting with the sponsor, his management team, and the IQA provider. We sat down across the table from the IQA provider's CEO and his company's senior IQA reviewer. The project's sponsor (a senior group manager) and his senior managers filled the other two sides of the very large table. It was at this meeting that we saw the extent of pressure we would have been under to produce a positive IQA report for the project.

The sponsor was visibly annoyed with the IQA company's senior reviewer, a highly regarded consultant in the projects-IQA space. The reviewer had written in his IQA report that the project's proposed transformation was too focused on one particular information technology (IT) solution, when there appeared to be less complex and cheaper solutions elsewhere in the market.

This recommendation conflicted the sponsor in three ways:

1. It suggested rework that would delay the delivery of an important strategic capability for the sponsor's organization. The delay would not go down well with the CEO, board, or shareholders.
2. It suggested a performance failing by the sponsor, putting at risk the sponsor's annual performance bonus, and his promotional prospects.
3. It threatened the sponsor's ego, and this sponsor was renowned for receiving such threats poorly.

The meeting did not go well. The sponsor insisted there was no time to look at alternative IT solutions, that the reviewer should have been aware of this, and that if the proposed new system wasn't in place by the end of the year, the organization was going to fail. The reviewer replied that nothing the IQA team had seen suggested that the organization was at risk of failure—the current systems were working fine. He also restated their IQA view that there were potentially very large savings to be made if a wider assessment of the market was undertaken.

The sponsor then became visibly upset. He stood up, leaned over the IQA provider's CEO (ignoring the reviewer himself) and said, "See, this is what happens when you send us junior staff!" A rather awkward silence ensued as the IQA CEO struggled to figure out how to respond. The reviewer himself, to his credit, stayed silent. I think he could have been forgiven if he had stood up himself and left the room. Someone broke the silence by changing the subject, and after some discussion, it was agreed that a piece of work would be undertaken by the sponsor's staff to review any less complex or cheaper alternatives that might be available.

About six months later we heard the project had been broken up into smaller, more manageable chunks that wouldn't require the purchase of an enterprise-level ICT system. The organization didn't fail, as the sponsor had claimed it might (there was no evidence for this claim), and instead, probably saved many millions of dollars adopting a more evolutionary approach. Unfortunately, the IQA provider was not used again by that organization, but we commended their courage in the face of the pressures they were under.

On another project's IQA process that we reviewed, we found that the first draft of the IQA report had correctly identified a number of issues and risks that were threatening the project's success, but that most of these issues and risks were missing, or were significantly minimized, in the final report. When we asked the IQA reviewer about this he was visibly stressed. His words to me were, "Grant, for the last three weeks (the period during which the IQA report changed from its draft to its final version) I have been used as a piñata by the project sponsor pressuring me to change my report."

In multimillion-dollar transformation projects the pressures on project sponsors and project managers to meet deadlines can be huge. The losses in these projects globally are equally large, and it's the job of the IQA reviewer to find the sources of these losses in a project and provide advice on them before they occur. The roles of the sponsor and manager who are under pressure and the IQA reviewer are, therefore, not always well-aligned.

The (average global) one in five chance of a complete project failure that a project manager or sponsor may be comfortable managing will be unacceptable for most portfolio owners (for whom such probabilities mean the failure of eight out of every 40 projects). For large and complex projects, every percentage point of conflicted interest that sneaks into a project during an IQA review is 10 percentage points of additional risk downstream. These conflicts are significantly reduced when the IQA reports to a level above the project's business sponsor.

GATE MENTORING

Gate mentoring, not to be confused with IQA of a project's stage gates, is a process by which a team of from two to four independent consultants, not from the same consulting organization, come together for generally two to five days (no more), and undertake a series of highly confidential (and nonattributable) interviews of the key stakeholders and managers involved in a project at a particular decision point. These interviews are followed by a series of in-confidence discussions between the project's sponsor and the gate-mentoring team, where the gate mentors provide their thoughts and opinions on the risks of the project and how the sponsor might navigate these.

The value of a gate-mentoring process is in the discussions that occur between a small group of very experienced project mentors and the project's sponsor.

Unlike IQA, gate mentoring is a process where the consulting discussion is specified to occur directly with the project sponsor, and with no one else in the room, in order to preserve the process's confidentiality principle. It is a mentoring process for the benefit of the sponsor, not for the benefit (directly) of the CEO or managers above the sponsor. Gate mentoring can be very successful in large and complex projects because of its informality, confidentiality, and the mentoring nature of the discussions with the sponsor. To reduce the risk of commercial conflicts of interest which IQA can suffer from, a gate-mentoring process should specifically prohibit commercial engagement of gate mentors onto the project (or near it), either before or after the gate-mentoring process has occurred. Gate mentors can return to participate in gate mentoring of later decision points in the same project, but not in that project's delivery or its IQA.

Gate mentoring is not intended to be a formal QA process (and shouldn't be), but is intended to mimic more the type of conversation that a senior executive might have with a friend (a highly experienced one) over a beer or a glass of wine in a bar somewhere.

Gate mentoring can take many forms. The British government's Office of Government Commerce (OGC) (the then-owners of the IP for PRINCE2®, MSP®, and P3M3®) formalized a highly successful version of gate-mentoring in the release of their OGC Gateway® process in the early 2000s.

BENEFITS MANAGEMENT

If you can't measure it, you can't claim it in your business case. That's the simple but effective rule that increasing numbers of portfolio owners are applying to their business case approval processes. If it's a financial benefit, it will be a relatively straightforward process to specify the expected returns in the business case and to assess their successful delivery at the Gate-5 benefits realization assessment.

If it's a nonfinancial benefit, nonfinancial metrics should be specified. These might be *more customers*, *more users* of an online system, or faster response times. Sometimes people misunderstand the meaning of *intangible*. If your project includes intangible benefits, this doesn't mean they can't be measured, it just means they are difficult to measure. They should still be measured. If the business benefits are complex, then measurable proxies should be used. If *happier customers* is the benefit, then customer satisfaction needs to be measured—and base-lined before the project commences.

Over 60% of government projects are NPV-negative, that is, they are approved not because they generate cash but because they provide a nonfinancial benefit to their sponsoring organizations or the societies that they serve. These projects should still have full sets of benefit key performance indicators (KPIs) against which their success or failure can be assessed.

Benefits management has a close and critical relationship with QA. The success of a project will be judged by the effectiveness of its benefits delivery. If benefits are not defined and there is no benefits management plan, then it is very difficult to define or assess quality. Quality is *fitness for purpose*—if the purpose is not defined, quality cannot be defined either.

No project should be without a benefits management plan. What are the benefits? What are their KPIs? How will we measure them? When will see them? These are the questions the benefits management plan should answer.

If benefit metrics are not known when the business case is submitted, but confidence exists in the need for the investment to occur, at least in some form, then only enough funding to develop benefit metrics should be released. Resubmission of the business case for a further Gate-2 approval after benefit metrics have been determined should be a condition of partial funding releases.

WHO SHOULD BE THE SPONSOR OF THE PROJECT?

The sponsor of a project should be *the most junior person who has ownership of the budget that is funding the project, ownership of the business benefits that the project is going to deliver, and ownership of the risks that failure of the project might create*.

We use the term *most junior person* not to mean that the project sponsor should be a junior person, but that they should not sit too many levels above the business group that will own the new capabilities and benefits that the project is delivering. The sponsor should have a direct ownership interest in the project, owning and operating the budget that is funding the project, the project's benefits, and its risks.

Sometimes a CEO is appointed as the sponsor of a project, but the sponsorship role needs to be one of active leadership, not a figurehead. CEOs in medium- and large-scale enterprises are usually not well-placed in this regard. It is also useful to hold the CEO in reserve for considering project issues of exceptional interest to the business. Often this is effected through the CEO's role as chair of the organization's senior leadership team, or as chair of a major project (program) ownership group—the committee of joint-business owners which sits *over* the project's steering committee for large or complex change initiatives (the sponsor of the project would normally report to that committee at regular intervals).

EFFECTIVE GOVERNANCE OF PROJECT STEERING COMMITTEES

One of the most common risks (issues actually) that we see in project management is the governance of steering committees and the accountability-control relationship between the steering committee and the project sponsor.

The project *owner*, or the owner's representative, usually carries the title of *sponsor* (the label *senior responsible owner* [SRO] is also sometimes used). Whatever the label, the role is accountable to the investors in the project for the project being successful. The project sponsor chairs the project's steering committee with this goal in mind.

Steering committees for projects should not be voting democracies. The role of steering committee members is to provide *advice* to the sponsor and to assist the sponsor to achieve success. Good governance requires a single point of accountability, and a voting steering committee does not provide this (neither does a steering committee making decisions by consensus). The place for voting or consensus-based decision making in a project, if it is to happen at all, is at the joint-ownership level. Sometimes this will be the organization's senior leadership team, or even its board. Increasingly, for larger projects serving multiple business groups or different organizations, an independent ownership board is established, specifically for the project.

This ownership board sits above the project steering committee and is recognized in best practices such as MSP®. The ownership board is comprised only of people who have a key financial or benefit ownership interest in the project. Important strategic, scoping, and risk decisions are made by this group, and they may vote on these things.

The sponsor's role is to be a *champion* of the project—to manage the high-level political relationships that characterize large and complex projects, and to support and assist the project manager. The relationship management focus of the sponsor is *upward and outward*.

And that brings us to the critical role of the project manager—the role responsible for the day-to-day management of the project, and delivery of its time, budget, and scope outputs. A common area of weakness in project manager appointment decisions is *fit*. The choice of the project manager must align—fit—with the culture of the organization sponsoring the project and with the goals and areas of complexity that characterize the project (refer to Chapter 12). The relationship management focus of the project manager is *downward and outward*, but with a fair amount of upward also included!

RECRUITMENT OF THE PROJECT MANAGER

Some common project management recruitment mistakes we see are:

1. Appointing as project manager someone from within the affected business area (for example, a line manager) who has no project management experience, or no experience with managing complexity of a type that is similar to the subject project;
2. Appointing an experienced project manager, but not experienced with the same type of project risks (or in the same industry or sector) as the subject project;
3. Appointing someone who has a history of successful *delivery* in a similar environment, but the phase of the project they are being appointed to is *pre*delivery—that is, it involves stakeholder engagement or scoping which may not be strengths of the delivery specialist; or
4. Appointing someone who has a history of successful *initiation or scoping of a project* in a similar environment, but the phase of the project they are being appointed to is a *delivery* phase—that is, it involves structured management of complex time, cost, and output deliverables, which may not be strengths of the stakeholder and scoping specialist.

All project managers are not equal, and neither are the different phases of a project.

THERE IS NO SUCH THING AS AN *IT* PROJECT

IT (ICT) projects should always specify the business benefits they are providing for the organization. IT infrastructure or IT KPIs are not a reason on their own for investment. What does an IT KPI mean for the business? If it's a KPI that contributes to a business outcome, then that should be specified. If IT investment is contributing to a high-level program, then that program should be specified, and a clear benefits relationship map provided.

Even a simple server or desktop upgrade is an exercise in reducing operational business risk. What percentage will business outages be reduced?

What percentage will service maintenance budgets be reduced? What percentage will user satisfaction increase? IT should be seen as a *means* to a business-goal, not the business-goal in itself. When projects are approved on the basis of IT outputs alone, business benefits are not maximized, or do not occur at all.

QUANTITATIVE RISK ANALYSIS

One of the most underutilized techniques for reducing cost and schedule risks in projects, including ICT-EB projects, is *quantitative risk analysis* (QRA).

QRA is often confused with *quantitative risk management* (QRM). QRM is a process by which numerical values and sometimes costs are attached to different levels of risk in a project. QRA, however, is a structured and relatively specialized technique for determining a project's likely cost (or time) outcome. QRA specifies the project's likely cost as a *range* of possible cost outcomes, with the probabilities of each outcome specified.

Typically in the business case, the 50 percentile cost estimate (called the *P50* cost) is used as the project's cost, and the project's P10 and P90 figures are also given. The business case would usually provide the graph of the different QRA-developed cost probabilities. Text-wise, it might read, for example, the estimated P50 cost of the project is $12 million, with a 10% chance (P10) that the cost will be $9.3 million, a 90% chance (P90) that the cost will be under $15.2 million, and a 10% chance that the project will come in at above $15.2 million.

The single-point cost figure that most projects or their business cases traditionally come up with is called the *deterministic* cost. But no one knows exactly what the final cost of a project will be until all the bills on the project have been paid. Specifying the cost of a project as a *range* of possible cost outcomes makes much more sense. Deterministic cost estimates in projects are notoriously optimistic. Stage-1 business cost estimates for ICT-EB projects, created before an organization has commenced any market engagement, are known, on average, to vary by as much as plus 100%, or minus 30%. Although, we have yet to find the major ICT-EB project that has come in at the 30% under budget figure.

Figure 11.1 shows a typical QRA of project costs. *A'* is the unintentionally low deterministic estimate that non-QRA cost processes commonly present in the Stage-2 business case. *B'* is the P50 (50 percentile) estimate that a QRA process produces. This is the estimate of the project's cost, which is as likely to be over budget as it is under budget. It is the single-point figure

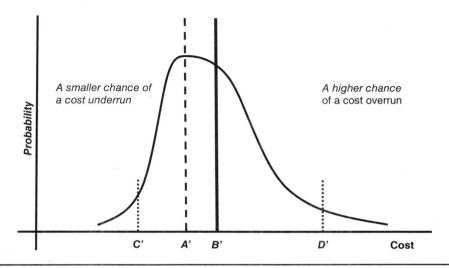

Figure 11.1   Typical early-stage QRA of costs for a high-risk project

that, if a single-point figure is to be used, should be the one. **C'** is the P10 estimate and **D'** is the P90 estimate produced by the same process.

QRA is sometimes run only on detailed business cases, but the risk of this is that a deterministic cost estimate may have already been quoted in an earlier Stage-1, indicative business case. If a single point cost estimate has already been published, a QRA process performed at a later stage will find itself under pressure to produce a P50 that is not more than the earlier single-point estimate. This pressure can introduce errors into the QRA process—sometimes large ones. Cost errors in projects can quickly contribute to project failures.

For this reason we recommend that an *indicative* QRA process is run during the development of the Stage-1 business case, usually focusing on the most preferred indicative option at that time.

How the QRA process is run is very important. At a high level, a QRA-of-costs process starts with the project's cost model, and puts this through a workshop where risks to the costs of each element in the cost model are discussed. A minimum, a maximum, and a mid-point cost for each cost element is then agreed on by the workshop participants, along with a function curve that describes the cost element's likely distribution of cost-probabilities. The various cost element function curves are then aggregated using a Monte Carlo algorithm. The output of this is the cost-probability curve for the project's total costs.

No specialist QRA knowledge is required by the workshop's participants, but specialist knowledge and solid QRA-of-projects experience is required by the workshop facilitator—the QRA consultant.

QRA is not sensitivity analysis. Sensitivity analysis should not occur until after a QRA process has been completed. One of the outputs of a QRA process is a list of the top-most cost-influential cost elements. The availability of this information greatly improves the usefulness of sensitivity analysis.

A common error in QRA processes is the failure to base the process on the project's cost model, and to instead start with a list of the project's risks, and to then cost the variability of each risk instead of the variability of each cost element. Costing risks, instead of costing cost elements, does not produce a valid QRA output and can result in substantial cost-range errors.

Commissioning a QRA on a project's cost model does not have to be an expensive process and the returns of the process are high. The greatest benefit of doing a QRA is that the process actually *reduces* a project's costs (its actual costs), by forcing discussions of cost risks which, but for the QRA process, wouldn't otherwise occur. These discussions increase awareness of cost risks and precipitate thinking on how cost risks might be treated. Less cost risk means less cost, right away—more money in the organization's back pocket, which but for the QRA, wouldn't be there.

Almost as significant as the reducing of a project's costs, a QRA greatly increases the accuracy of a project's cost estimate, and provides a statistically derived contingency figure by subtracting the P50 estimate from the P90 estimate—being a much more useful and scientifically based approach than the traditional *plus or minus 10%* technique.

Here is a quick word on project contingency estimates. If a true *P50* project-estimating process such as QRA is being used, and it is being applied correctly, project contingency budgets should not be issued to the project or it's sponsoring business group, but should be held *at the center*, e.g., by the CFO, the portfolio finances committee, or similar group. This is because when a P50 estimating process is used, the actual cost of the project will statistically be as likely to be under the P50 figure, as over it. If the contingency figure is then allocated to the project before any cost risks have eventuated, it will invariably get spent. The result of this would be—across the organization's project-investments portfolio—a massive overspend.

If the contingency budgets are being held at the center, this does not mean they should not be able to be drawn on by a project if a risk that was captured during the QRA workshop occurs. If a QRA risk eventuates, it simply means a conversation with the center needs to occur before any contingency sums are drawn down. This ensures that scope changes are not funded by contingency budgets—unless specific scope uncertainties were included in the QRA process (this is more likely during a Stage-1 indicative business case, than during the final Stage-2 detailed business case).

SHOW ME THE PROJECT THAT IS 20% FINISHED AND I'LL TELL YOU ITS FINAL COST

There is a common rule of thumb in project management regarding the cost or schedule performance of a project. It goes something like: *After 20% of a project is complete, you can extrapolate its budget or schedule overruns to the finish of the project*—i.e., if a project is running 10% behind schedule, or 30% over budget, those percentages are surprisingly close to how the project will be found at the finish line. The reason for this is that it is extremely difficult for the managers of slipping projects to pull a project back into control, unless major changes in management approach or project scope occur.

KEY LEARNING ON ADVANCED BASICS

1. Project managers should be using the latest soft and hard skill practices to increase the success of their projects.
2. Business cases must specify metrics for the business improvements that the project is going to deliver.
3. The business case should be done in two, separately approved stages; Stage-1 for strategic drivers and options and Stage-2 for seeking approval of the detailed scope, costs, risks, and benefits.
4. Investment Logic Mapping, or a similar process that achieves agreement on the problem the project is intended to solve, should be used before either a Stage-1 or Stage-2 business case is written.
5. The 16 question checklist, or a similar investment proposal review process, should be used to review business cases early in their development.
6. A standardized, stage-gated life cycle, based on key decisions to be made at each life-cycle stage, should apply to all projects.
7. Process requirements at different stage gates should be tailorable to a project's risk and value needs—tailorability should not provide for exemption from key processes.
8. Early stage-gate reviews are critical for all large, complex, or high-risk projects.
9. All projects must have active QA plans.

10. IQA at key stage-gated decision points must occur for all large, complex, or high-risk projects.
11. To ensure independence is preserved, QA reviewers should not provide a level of advice in QA reviews that make it difficult for them to criticize aspects of the project at the next IQA review.
12. To reduce conflict of interest risks, IQA of major life-cycle decision points needs to be owned by and reported to a management level above that of the project sponsor.
13. Gate mentoring, when complementing IQA, is very high-return in complex and high-risk projects.
14. Benefits management is critical to the success of projects—without benefit KPIs the project's level of success and true return on investment cannot be assessed.
15. The decision of who should sponsor a project, and the level they are at, is important to effective project leadership.
16. For effective governance, project steering committees should not be run as voting democracies, but instead should be advisory to the project sponsor.
17. For large or complex change, projects or programs may have a higher-level (voting) ownership board comprising senior finance, benefit, and risk stakeholders.
18. Recruitment of project managers should include consideration of their strengths regarding the management of different life-cycle stages and in different contexts.
19. QRA of costs is a high-return process that decreases project costs and increases the accuracy of project cost and contingency budgets
20. QRA should be applied indicatively on the Stage-1 business case and fully on the Stage-2 business case.
21. A project that is running late or over budget when it is 20% complete requires major work if it's performance is to be turned around.

12

The Circle of Project
Management Ethos

"It's easier to understand what we believe when we draw what we think."

Stephen Cummings, Ph.D., Professor of Strategic Management, Victoria
University of Wellington, N.Z. (Author of *Strategy Builder: How to
Create and Communicate More Effective Strategies*)

COMMITMENT

It's difficult for us to commit to something if our heart's not in it. This is
true of anything in our lives—our relationships, our jobs, and our projects.
The problem with projects is that without full commitment from everyone in the team—maximum emotional engagement—risks that are already
high become higher. Loyalty and trust are reduced, communication isn't as
strong, thinking isn't as enlightened, and people don't work as hard.

Success is maximized when personal and organizational values align with
the values of the project, its purpose, its actions, and the strategy it is using.
When these elements are aligned, a virtuous circle of reinforcement is created. Ethos—the collective spirit or *personality* of the project—is strengthened. Risks then reduce, and when you're operating in a high-risk space,
every percentage point of risk reduction is money in the organization's back
pocket.

Professor Stephen Cummings applies this model to corporations in his
best-selling book *Recreating Strategy*. Cummings calls it the circle of corporate ethos. The importance of coherent ethos to business success was first

written about by Campbell, Devine, and Young in their 1990 paper "A Sense of Mission." Campbell, Devine, and Young proposed a model for strengthening the successful delivery of mission in companies. The model is comprised of four elements—purpose, strategy, behavior standards, and values—and became known as the Ashbridge Mission Model.

Campbell, Devine, and Young wrote that when the four elements are aligned with each other, a company's mission becomes easier to manage and success becomes more likely. Commitment of employees is deepest when there is a match between the values of the employees and the values of the company.

In projects, the purpose and values of a project may not be the same as the purpose and values of the sponsoring organization. For example, an organization's competitive advantage may be the quality of the service it delivers to its customers, or the world-beating functionality of its new products; while a project within that organization may be tasked with reducing costs in an area of the business, and the budget for delivering that project may be limited. Another project may have the goal of delivering a set of new internal information and communication technology (ICT) capabilities by a critical date (a desktop upgrade, for example). There will be minimal appetite in the organization for that date being missed. The success of these projects will require a strategy, supported by actions and values, that are likely to be different from those required to support the higher-level corporation.

The circle of project management ethos can be written as:

Project Purpose → *Values* → *Actions* → *Strategy* → *Project Purpose*

The higher risk the project, the more important it is that the elements of the circle are aligned. Sometimes organizations will set the primary recruitment criteria of their search for a new project manager to be that all candidates must have a pedigree of delivering past projects *on-time, on-budget, and with all benefits delivered*. When criteria like this are set in isolation from the values and context of the project itself, problems can occur.

For example, problems can occur when the leader's ethos doesn't fit with the goals of the project or the values and approaches of those governing it. A good telecommunications project manager won't necessarily do well on a health-policy project, and a project manager who has been successful in scoping major business change won't necessarily do well delivering the same project to time and budget (if time and budget are critical deliverables). The selection of the leader, their values and ways of doing things, is central to a project's circle of ethos.

WAS IT ABOUT THE SUMMIT OR THE ENJOYMENT OF CLIMBING?

On May 29, 1953, the first man to reach the top of the highest mountain on earth was Ed Hillary. Hillary was knighted by the Queen for his achievement, six weeks after he summited, becoming the famous *Sir Edmund Hillary*. Not many people know that the only other person to be knighted on that expedition was the program manager—the expedition's leader—John Hunt.

The 1953 British Mount Everest Expedition was the ninth British attempt to summit Everest, and it was huge. It was comprised of 14 British climbers, 24 Sherpa climbers, over 300 Nepalese porters, and 7.5 tons of equipment.

There were actually three climber-pairs planned for the expedition's summit attempts. Hillary and his partner Tenzing Norgay were the second pair to try for the summit. The first pair, Bourdillon and Evans, ran low on oxygen after having problems with an experimental closed-circuit oxygen system. They were forced to turn back only 300 feet from the summit. Three days later the second pair, Hillary and Tenzing, made their attempt. They were using more proven but heavier, open-circuit oxygen sets. They were also arguably the strongest climbers on the mountain—individually and as a team. When they had their shot, they went for it. It was a great success for the expedition when they succeeded, and for the British Empire as a whole.

Sitting behind that success was the man who actually made it happen—John Hunt. Hillary and Tenzing were really only the tip of a gigantic pyramid of logistical planning and risk management.

The selection of the expedition's leader was the job of the Joint Himalayan Committee (earlier called the Mount Everest Committee). The Himalayan Committee was a joint committee of the Royal Geographical Society and the Alpine Club. Their appointment of the 1953 expedition leader was an exemplar of everything that shouldn't happen in a recruitment process. Everything, that is, except for the choice of the man they finally appointed to do the job.

The committee recognized that the choice of the leader was critical. The expedition's risks were large: logistical, environmental, technological, team leadership, safety, political relationship, cross-cultural management, public interest, and media. Any one of these, poorly managed, would be reason enough for a project to fail even today, but the 1953 expedition had them all.

The Committee's search for a leader was eventually narrowed to two men: Eric Shipton, the British public's (at the time) hardy and independent climbing hero; and Colonel John Hunt, a man unknown to the public and to most of the climbing world.

Shipton had climbed on four of Britain's previous Everest expeditions and was known affectionately by the British public as *Mr. Everest.* Two years earlier, in 1951, at the age of 43, he had led a successful reconnaissance expedition to the south side of Everest with a view of launching an attempt on its summit in 1952. Unfortunately for Shipton, the Swiss booked the sole 1952 Everest climbing slot that was available. The Nepalese government was only permitting one attempt by a foreign climbing team on Everest each year and the British had left their 1952 booking until it was too late.

As an alternative in 1952 (while they waited to see if the Swiss succeeded), it was decided that Shipton would lead a training expedition to the unclimbed Cho Oyu. Cho Oyu is not far from Everest, and at 26,906 feet, is only 2,000 feet shorter. If the Cho Oyu climb was successful it would be the highest summit achieved in the world at the time (assuming the Swiss didn't succeed on Everest first).

The British Cho Oyu Expedition was a disaster. No one died, but the expedition failed to ascend even the mountain's lower slopes. Shipton's leadership was criticized for the failure. Some members of the Cho Oyu team were frustrated by what they saw as a lack of planning and drive from Shipton, and some of his actions after the expedition were perceived as being too focused on his personal enjoyment of climbing and lacking commitment to the greater national cause that was Everest.

Before 1952 everyone had assumed Shipton was the man to lead the Everest attempt in 1953, but now there were doubts. Members of the Himalayan Committee began to challenge that Shipton was the right man to lead the scale of expedition required to succeed on Everest.

Shipton's style was also at odds with the style of the Himalayan Committee. The committee operated using formal management approaches and existed for the support of major expeditions, but the management of structure and complexity were not Shipton's thing. He liked to climb with small teams, and his leadership style was sometimes criticized as being too democratic. Democracy has its place in the leadership of high-performing teams, but sometimes leaders have to make decisions, tough decisions, on their own.

In 1951, a relatively unknown army colonel named John Hunt came to the attention of Basil Goodfellow, the Honorary Secretary of the Alpine Club. Goodfellow had met Hunt in Switzerland in 1951, and had climbed with him there for several days. Goodfellow felt that Hunt was just the type of driven leader that the British needed for Everest.

Hunt was very different from Shipton. He was a distinguished and decorated soldier, but was not well-known in the climbing world. He had nonetheless, climbed extensively in the Himalayas and in the Alps, and had experience leading large, complex initiatives. The introduction of Hunt as an alternative to Shipton split the Himalayan Committee down the middle. Each time the committee met, though, the pro-Hunt faction grew.

Mick Conefrey, author of the detailed 2012 book *Everest 1953: The Story of the First Ascent*, summed up the Himalayan Committee's evolving view:

> *"The Himalayan Committee wanted someone utterly focused on winning the race, someone who shared their sense of ownership of Everest, and who was demonstrably well-organized. This wasn't Eric Shipton but it was a good description of Colonel John Hunt."*

Hillary liked Shipton and had enjoyed climbing with him in 1951 and 1952. He believed that, in climbing, Shipton had few equals, but in his early autobiography (*Nothing Venture, Nothing Win*) he described Shipton's approach to big expeditions as *lethargic*. He also wrote:

> *"Shipton was not happy as leader of a big expedition. He didn't enjoy large-scale organization."* And, *"With Shipton as leader our (1953) expedition would not have been as well prepared* (as it was with Hunt) *before departure."*

When Shipton returned from the failed Cho Oyu Expedition, which he didn't do immediately, staying on in Nepal to do more climbing (a factor which irritated the committee further), he was summoned by the committee for a meeting. It is believed that word of their doubts about his selection as leader for the 1953 expedition had reached him before that meeting, because at the meeting he was very open with the committee about the possibility of someone else taking over as leader.

George Band, the youngest member of the 1953 team, wrote in his book *Everest: 50 Years on Top of the World*, that Shipton had said to the committee:

> *"My well-known dislike of large expeditions and my abhorrence of a competitive element in mountaineering might well seem out of place in the present situation."*

Shipton was reported to have then told the committee that it might well be time to hand the expedition over to a *younger man with a fresh outlook*. Band believes Shipton sealed his fate at that meeting.

Surprisingly, the committee didn't exclude Shipton from the leadership race right away. It probably reflects the committee's confused approach at the time, and their own disrupted ethos, that they left Shipton thinking by the end of the meeting that he was still the leader. While Shipton departed thinking this, the committee wrote to Hunt and offered him the job.

More committee meetings and conflicting letters followed. Shipton was offered a *co-leader* role working alongside Hunt, and then Hunt was offered the role of sole leader. But then members of the committee who were absent from the Hunt-confirmation meeting protested Hunt's appointment and another committee meeting was called. The leader decision was finally confirmed at that meeting, once and for all, by a vote of six to two in favor of Hunt.

Initially, Hunt's appointment was not well received by the climbing team. Shipton had already written to most of them saying he was looking forward to having them on his team. When Hillary heard that Shipton was being replaced by the essentially unknown Colonel Hunt, he thought Hunt might be a *Colonel Blimp*—a satirical 1930's cartoon strip that stereotyped senior army officers as being pompous and not very bright.

It took the combined efforts of the Himalayan Committee, strong relationship building from Hunt, and post-decision support from Shipton, who by then, had advised he would not be participating in the expedition, to keep the climbing team together.

As the arrangements began to build, people began to see Hunt in action. They saw how well he managed people, and the quality of his planning. Slowly he began winning the expedition members over.

Hillary wrote in his autobiography that when he first met Hunt in person, he was immediately impressed. On his views of Hunt after the expedition Hillary wrote:

> *"John Hunt displayed tremendous drive and energy…Nobody worked as hard as John, or was as ferociously determined that we would succeed…John's instant charm was a formidable weapon in his armory; it affected some of us more than others—but none doubted his unflagging devotion to our major objective."*

Band was also impressed with Hunt's leadership. He included in his list of reasons that the expedition succeeded:

> *"The meticulous preparations, planning, and inspired leadership of John Hunt in choosing a strong team of both climbers and Sherpas who worked superbly together and have remained good friends"*

DIFFERENCES IN ETHOS

The difference between Shipton and Hunt was their ethos—the spirit of who they were, and their attitudes and aspirations. Both men were highly capable and successful professionals, but their attitudes and aspirations were different. Shipton liked to climb for the enjoyment of it. Large expeditions, the organization of them, and the achievement of summits as national goals weren't of high interest to him.

Hunt, on the other hand, liked to organize things—and he was good at it. He was also passionate that Everest should be claimed by the British. The conquering of Everest in 1953 required that passion and those organizing skills. Hunt's values were more closely aligned to the ethos of the expedition's goals, and the ethos of the Himalayan committee than Shipton's were. A map of these relationships, and the leadership decision that the Himalayan Committee struggled with, is shown in Figure 12.1.

Good leadership fit is essential for the success of difficult projects. For good fit to occur, the ethos of the leader—their sense of spirit, their attitudes, and their aspirations—has to be consistent with the ethos of the project as a whole. If the style and experience of the leader is not aligned with

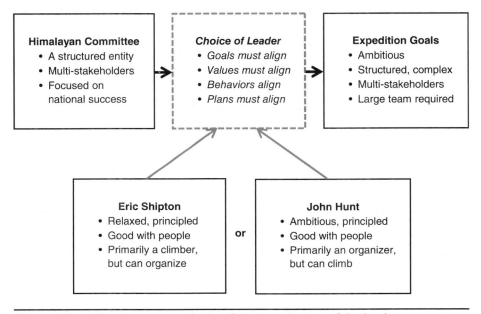

Figure 12.1   The importance of ethos fit in the selection of the leader

the purpose of the project, its goals and practices, the ethos of the system as a whole is disrupted, and significant problems can arise.

The Himalayan Committee got the decision right, but disruptions of ethos, within their own committee, came close to derailing it. Several of the committee members believed that Shipton's personality and climbing pedigree were more important than Hunt's organizing experience and passion for success. Fortunately, others on the committee could see that Hunts' experience and values were key.

BROKEN ETHOS IN MAJOR ICT-EB PROJECTS

It is important to recognize that subcultures, which are different from corporate cultures, exist in organizations, often as projects. If there is recognition of this there is less risk that a project's circle of ethos will be unconsciously squeezed to fit in with a higher-level corporate ethos which may not be the same. A project owner's comfort with different outcomes, and with different types of risk, is a good place to start a conversation on what a circle of ethos for a particular project should look like. If the conversation doesn't occur at all (as often they don't) risk increases.

The project management office (PMO) of a major organization (Y-Corp), which had just appointed a new CEO was in trouble. The CEO had come from an organization (X-Corp) with low portfolio, program, and project management (P3M) capability maturity but a strong compensating culture of individual heroism (people who made success happen despite the capability issues surrounding them). Both the ICT services side and the business side of the organization worked hard to ensure that failures didn't occur.

Security of information management was very important for the CEO's old organization X-Corp. The skilled ICT services group and the ever-watchful business groups collaborated closely to ensure security breaches didn't occur. It was X-Group's culture of heroism rather than their P3M maturity that kept them from failure. Many of their projects under-delivered, but as long as there were no major failures, especially no major information security failures, the organization's corporate leaders were happy. Also, although P3M maturity was low at X-Corp, the ICT services group itself had P3M maturity strengths which helped in their delivery of new ICT systems that were perceived as *safe* (if not always fully delivering on the business's needs).

Y-Corp, on the other hand, was an organization that was struggling with both its ICT service delivery and with P3M maturity. It also didn't have a culture of heroism to catch failures before they occurred. There were passionate heroes scattered across the different business groups at a senior level, but the absence of heroism as a culture intersected with the absence of P3M capability maturity in a high-risk combination. Y-Corp had recently experienced several brand-damaging project failures. One of the reasons the CEO from X-Corp had been brought in was to stop these failures.

When the CEO moved to Y-Corp, he couldn't understand why the organization was struggling with its projects. He was supportive of the people in Y-Corp, but although he wanted higher performance, he wasn't particularly passionate about project management frameworks or the concept of *P3M maturity* that he had been hearing about from some of Y-Corp's managers. He had seen P3M processes slowing up projects in his early days, and he believed they were too often processes for processes' sake. He told the head of Y-Corp's PMO that X-Corp never had a strong P3M framework and it had gotten by—and asked why Y-Corp was struggling so much? But without a culture of heroism to cover for low organizational P3M maturity, Y-Corp could never succeed.

The new CEO's approach was to increase the pressure on the sponsors of Y-Corp's transformation programs. But instead of things getting better, schedules started to slip, budgets started to overrun by more than usual, and the quality of services to customers dropped further. Then one day an electronic file containing critical client information was accidentally sent by Y-Corp to one of that client's competitors. Major damage to Y-Corp resulted.

A contributor to this failing was the lack of coherent project management ethos in Y-Corp's projects. The goals of the projects were to deliver major improvements in customer services, but the pressure on the projects' sponsors was to just get them done. The *make it happen or else* direction from above wasn't aligned with the *quality service* goals of the projects. There was no compensating culture of heroism in the ICT group, and no organizational foundation of P3M maturity to support the complex changes required.

To improve things, we recommended to the new CEO that he do three things. First, he had to make one of his deputies accountable for lifting the maturity of the organization's P3M capabilities. This person had to be a champion of capability improvement—a passionate believer in the value that mature processes and capable people can provide to complex projects. We impressed on the CEO that this person needed to have the CEO's visible support.

Second, an important component of the capability improvement program had to be the introduction of circles of project ethos and discussions of risk appetite—comfort with the risks posed to different outcomes.

Third, the CEO needed to find a solidly experienced professional to manage the organization's primary change program. The days when line managers can be delegated the management of a major change program, as a background role to be added to their existing 12-hour days, are gone. We impressed on the CEO the need to ensure that strong pedigrees of success with outcomes should under-pin Y-Corp's recruitments for project managers of all high-risk projects.

The organization's project issues—as measured by the number of project crises being discussed at senior leadership meetings—began to reduce. This happened from the top down through the creation of strong, engaged, and experienced project leadership, and from the bottom up with the introduction of new structures, processes, and training for project staff more suited to modern projects than the less formal approaches previously being used.

Y-Corp was on its way to becoming the high-performing projects organization that the new CEO had been tasked to create. Strong circles of project ethos and P3M capability-building underpinned the improvements.

CULTURAL CLASH OUTSIDE THE PROJECT

M-Corp had been experiencing problems with projects under-delivering benefits and overrunning budgets. M-Corp decided it needed to take action when a major corporate system replacement (CSR) project failed.

The CEO of M-Corp wanted action to ensure such a failure did not happen again. The CIO initiated a projects risk reduction (PRR) review to independently look at project risk levels, project management practices, and the organization's P3M capabilities. The PRR review struck trouble when the CFO, the sponsor of the failed corporate systems project, told the review team that he believed the CSR failure was a one-off, and that the PRR review was a waste of time.

The CFO had established a PMO 18 months earlier that was very popular with the project sponsors and managers who it served. It offered advice on project management practices, but the new P3M framework it specified wasn't mandatory. Some projects, mostly ones which were already struggling, declined to use the new framework because they believed it created extra work and the assurance reviews it specified were slowing them down.

The PRR review needed a close relationship with the PMO, but the PMO, sensing the CFO's lack of support for the review, and also that the review might be a threat to them directly, declined to provide it. The PMO's resistance was mostly passive, but the tension between the PMO and the PRR review team was causing issues. Some of the troubled projects, sensing the tension between the PMO and the review, were slow to provide information to the review team and declined to implement their preliminary risk reduction recommendations.

M-Corp was experiencing a clash of ethos. The direct approach of the PRR review was in conflict with the more relationship-oriented PMO. The CIO's strategy of initiating an independent review to advise on project risks was in conflict with the more flexible approach of the existing PMO and the beliefs of the CFO.

The review at M-Corp continued to struggle. It was a step-change attempt at reducing risk, but without senior support, and at odds with the existing culture of letting projects decide their own approach, the chances of it succeeding were limited. The review was completed but no major changes resulted from its recommendations.

Step-change improvements in risk culture can work in organizations and important relationships can be maintained in the process, even strengthened, but not if senior level support is missing.

When organizations are involved in high-risk projects or culture change initiatives (which are high-risk projects) the coherency of the project's circle of ethos should be discussed and tested by the project's steering committee, or in a separate process—a workshop attended by the project's sponsor. The project's risk appetite should be included in this process because it informs the discussion of the project's purpose—what is important and what isn't.

KEY LEARNINGS ON THE CIRCLE OF PROJECT MANAGEMENT ETHOS

1. In large, complex, or high-risk projects it is important that the project manager's and sponsor's sense of spirit, attitudes, and aspirations are consistent with the goals of the project and the ethos of the project's governing groups.

2. The purpose of a project, the values and behaviors of those managing it and those working on it, the actions the project takes, and the project's plans all need to reinforce each other. If any of these elements are out of step, project ethos can unwind and the project can become at greater risk of failure.

3. A project's *circle of project management ethos* should be the subject of regular discussion—typically occurring at reviews of risk appetite.
4. Failure to resolve misalignment of ethos between inter-dependent projects, or external business groups, creates risk.

13

Strong Humble Servants

"The fundamental 'Leadership for what?' question is the most important yet most difficult question for a leader to answer."

Brad Jackson, Ph.D., Professor, Head of School of Government,
Victoria University of Wellington, NZ

The four men looked over the lip of the crevasse at the two dogs standing on a narrow ledge 20 meters (65 feet) below. Captain Robert Scott and his sledge-mate Cecil Meares were lucky they weren't down there with them—or worse, dead in the infinite blackness beyond.

They had been traveling at a high speed with their team of 13 dogs when the snow surface they were crossing suddenly collapsed from beneath the leading dogs. Without realizing it, they had been traveling along the edge of a crevasse made invisible by a layer of fallen snow which had built up over a few weeks, but which wouldn't support their weight. All but one of the dogs had fallen into the crevasse. Meares, who had been riding the sledge and controlling the dogs at the time, had managed to jump onto the sledge's braking-board just in time to keep the sledge from following the dogs into the hole.

Ten of the dogs were saved by their harnesses. They were dangling over the edge of the crevasse and were relatively easy to pull back up. The job of rescuing the two dogs that had fallen out of their harnesses, but had been saved by the ledge further down, was more difficult. Scott and Meares were joined by Wilson and Cherry-Garrard, who had been traveling with a second dog team a short distance behind.

The four men discussed who should be the one to be lowered into the crevasse to rescue the dogs on the ledge. It would be painful, claustrophobia-inducing, and dangerous. It was February 1911—comfortable climbing harnesses had not yet been invented. Wilson and Cherry-Garrard both volunteered to go down. Meares declared that he had no interest. Scott replied that it was too dangerous for anyone to go, but that if anyone should go, it should be him. He then asked the other three to lower him over the edge.

This was the type of leader that the explorer Scott was. He wouldn't have any of his men do something he wasn't prepared to do himself. If there was a risk to be taken, and he could choose who should take it, he would choose himself. Scott was what is known today as a *servant leader*. It was a part of his leadership-DNA that he would place the needs and safety of his men ahead of his own. Servant leaders can manage much higher levels of complexity and risk than nonservant leaders.

The two dogs were rescued and a near-frozen Scott hauled back up to the surface.

Image 13.1   A vertical view from inside a crevasse. This is similar to what Scott would have seen from inside the crevasse as he rescued his dogs in 1911. The hole in the snow bridge at the top may have been slightly longer (Photo: Grant Avery).

SERVANT LEADERSHIP

Servant leadership emphasizes the needs of the leader's *followers*. These might be the members of the leader's team or of the broader organization, if the leader is a CEO. Servant leadership is beneficial to organizations because it engages and develops employees, through building trust, communication, and commitment.

The number six item on ESI International's (a global project training organization) annual assessment of the top 10 project management trends for 2014 was *Servant Leadership.* In their supporting text, ESI commented on the project management world's never-ending search for the right project-leadership model. The text suggested that servant leadership might be the answer to this search because of that style's focus on sharing power and serving others.

Servant leadership is known for its ability to increase performance and reduce risks in high-risk situations. As followers increase their trust in the leader, team engagement and commitment to the success of the mission also increases. The greater the risks of an initiative, the greater the value that servant leadership can provide.

In the Project Management Institute's (PMI's) March 2015 *Pulse* report "Capturing the Value of Project Management through Knowledge Transfer," PMI found that organizations which are most effective at knowledge transfer will improve project outcomes by nearly 35% over those that aren't. PMI wrote that organizations that are effective at knowledge transfer focus not just on culture, but on leadership and "*most importantly, on people, because knowledge lives in and is applied by them.*" The PMI report noted that a lack of trust within the organization, different business cultures, and intolerance of mistakes are key factors that inhibit effective knowledge transfer, and are likely to erode knowledge as it moves through the organization.

These are behavior areas that servant leadership directly addresses. The PMI finding suggests that servant leadership, with its focus on building trust, creating a unified culture, and encouraging tolerance of mistakes should be expected to boost organizational knowledge transfer and increase the significant benefits that knowledge transfer provides.

Many leaders fail to appreciate the high cost to a project of low engagement by team members—particularly when that cost is in increased risk. Intuitively, leaders know that committed team members are important, but the value of team-member engagement in a project is more than just *important*—it can *quadruple* the power of the team.

Metcalfe's Law states that the value of a communication network is proportional to the square of the number of users connected to it. The more people on the network, the more powerful and valuable the network is. The value of a team works the same way. The power of what the team can achieve climbs rapidly for each member of the team who is effectively engaged, and it drops proportionally for those who aren't. Figure 13.1 shows this square-law relationship at work.

This is how Scott was able to achieve the successes that he did in his 1902 and 1910 expeditions—through maintaining the trust and confidence of his men and the increase in the team's collective performance that this created.

Sir Ranulph Fiennes' 2003 biography, *Captain Scott*, references a number of comments made by Scott's men that reflect the high esteem in which he was held by those who worked for him. From Bill Burton (assistant stoker): "He (Scott) wouldn't ask you to do anything he wasn't prepared to do himself." From Edward Wilson: "He is thoughtful for each individual and does little kindnesses that show it." And from Tom Crean: "I loved every hair on his head. He was a born gentleman and I will never forget him."

WHAT IS SERVANT LEADERSHIP?

Servant leadership sits at the end of the service-leadership continuum; at the other end sit more self-serving leadership styles. Servant leadership

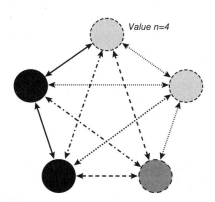

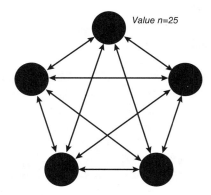

Team A – low engagement
- only two members fully committing
- communication between others is weak

Team B – high engagement
- all members fully committing
- communication between all is strong

Figure 13.1   The value of a fully engaged team

is service to others, and in particular, the leader's followers—while more
ego-oriented styles place the leader's interests first and may be narcissistically driven (see Chapter 7). This service-leadership continuum is shown in
Figure 13.2.

Daniel Goleman (best-selling author of *Emotional Intelligence*) in his 2002
book, *The New Leaders: Transforming the Art of Leadership into the Science
of Results*, estimated that how people feel about working for a company
(Goleman calls these feelings *climate*) can account for *20 to 30%* of business
performance, and that *50 to 70%* of climate can be traced to the actions of
the leader. The leader's power to influence the performance of his or her
team, to reduce the risks of project failure, is significant.

Servant leadership was coined as a leadership theory by Robert Greenleaf
in the 1970s. Greenleaf described servant leadership as a style of leadership where leaders have a genuine interest in serving their followers. Servant
leadership has been researched to varying degrees since then, attracting particular interest in the last 10 years. Prominent organizational authors have
noted its positive effects on profits and employee satisfaction, and over 20%
of *Fortune* magazine's top-100 companies are reported to have sought guidance from the center that Greenleaf established to promote servant leadership awareness and understanding.

The theory (and practice) of servant leadership is that because it has as
its focus the interests of the *followers* (those who work for the leader), it creates strong relationships within the organization or project, thus, increasing
performance.

In 2013, Denise Parris and Jon Peachey published a structured review
of 39 studies on servant leadership (starting with a wider group of 255)
that had been published in peer-reviewed journals between 2004 and 2011.
Parris and Peachey's goal was to assess and synthesize—in a disciplined way
not previously undertaken on this scale—the mechanisms, outcomes, and
impacts of servant leadership.

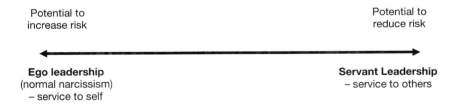

Figure 13.2   The leadership-service continuum

Parris and Peachey's conclusions included that servant leadership has the potential to provide the ethical grounding and leadership framework needed to help address the unique challenges of the twenty-first century—including technological advancements, the internet, increased communications, and economic globalization.

A concern from some about servant leadership is that, because it is focused on a style which has as its goal *serving its followers*, this might result in a loss of focus on the needs of the organization. Repeated studies tell us that the opposite is true. One of the reasons that servant leadership is being increasingly studied is because of the value that it can potentially provide the organizations that use it.

On the impact that servant leadership has on team-level effectiveness, Parris and Peachey found:

> "... a servant-led organization enhances leader trust and organizational trust, organizational citizenship behavior, procedural justice, team and leader effectiveness, and collaboration between team members."

A review and synthesis of servant leadership undertaken by Dirk van Dierendonck in 2011 published similar findings. Van Dierendonck wrote that servant leadership can be expected to influence followers on an individual level through self-actualization, positive job attitudes, and increased performance—and on a team level, through increased team effectiveness.

Combining the insights from a number of influential servant-leadership models created by a variety of research groups in recent years, Van Dierendonck presented a conceptual model of servant leadership that defines six key characteristics:

1. **Empowering and developing people:** Fostering a proactive, self-confident attitude among followers gives them a sense of personal power. Believing in the intrinsic value of each team member is key.
2. **Humility:** The extent to which a leader puts the interests of others first and keeps one's own accomplishments in proper perspective. Daring to admit one can learn from others and actively seeking the contributions of others, and retreating to the background when a task has been successfully completed.
3. **Authenticity:** Being true to oneself privately and publicly, being honest, and doing what is promised. Professional roles remain secondary to who the individual is as a person.
4. **Interpersonal acceptance:** Being able to understand and experience the feelings of others. Letting go of perceived wrong-doings, and cre-

ating an atmosphere of trust where people are allowed to make mistakes and can know that they will not be rejected as a result.

5. **Providing direction:** Making sure that people know what is expected of them (which is beneficial to them and the organization) and providing them with the right degree of accountability. Direction can include creating new ways to solve old problems.

6. **Stewardship:** This is the willingness to take responsibility for the larger organization, and to take a service focus rather than a control and self-interest focus. Leaders should also act not only as caretakers but as role models for others.

These six characteristics give a good overview of servant leadership behavior as it is experienced by the followers of the leader. Van Dierendonck's model also included two important motivations of servant leadership: (1) the leader's need to serve and (2) the leader's motivation to lead.

To be a servant leader, a leader must have as core motivations an interest in both serving and leading. Leaders who do not have a core interest in serving those who follow them, and *servers* who want to help others but who do not have an interest in leading, will struggle to deliver authentic servant leadership.

RELATED LEADERSHIP STYLES

Van Dierendonck's paper provided a useful comparison of servant leadership with other leadership styles. In his comparison of servant leadership with *transformational leadership* (another highly regarded style), he suggests that one of the problems with transformational leadership is its (sometimes) narrow focus on short-term profits, how this can increase narcissism (refer to Chapter 7), and how, in the long term, this could have disastrous consequences for the organization.

In his comparison of *servant leadership* with *authentic leadership* (also highly regarded in the literature), Van Dierendonck suggests that a strength of servant leadership over authentic leadership is that authentic leadership allows the leader to prioritize increasing shareholder value ahead of caring for the welfare of followers. This might occur, for example, when a manager believes it is his or her moral obligation to put shareholders first. An important element of servant leadership is that it takes into account all stakeholders, and it looks to achieve shareholder value through the empowerment and motivation of followers (team members).

This broader stakeholder focus may be more beneficial for shareholders in the long run because it maintains the engagement of the workers in the long term. A broader stakeholder focus could also be expected to mitigate the complex stakeholder environments from which so many of the risks suffered by complex projects and programs arise.

SERVANT LEADERSHIP AS A SUBCULTURE

Servant leadership is well suited for projects because it is relatively easily established as a *subculture* within culturally different, higher-level organizations. Examples of servant leadership as a subculture can be found in the military.

Military organizations are—by their nature—hierarchical, command and control organizations. They are characterized by high *power-distance* business cultures—cultures where authority levels are well-defined and differ greatly between levels. High power-distance cultures are not well-suited to servant leadership because followers are positioned by structural definition to have less importance than leaders. In the highest-performance, highest-risk operations of the military however, (for example, elite special service units such as the British SAS and the U.S. Navy SEALs) servant leadership subcultures are alive and well. Within these teams, the leader may be an officer, but it is understood by all within the team that the officer's job is to serve his or her team. That is to keep them alive and to achieve mission success, all in the highest possible risk contexts. During special service operations, power-distance between officers and men can drop to zero. Everyone contributes, frequently and equally, and trust is high.

Scott was a very successful Navy officer (a high power-distance occupation), but he ran his Antarctic research and exploration programs using a low power-distance approach. Scott retained certain structures and disciplines as a framework to manage his logistical challenges, but these frameworks did not define his leadership style, they helped reduce the complexity of his mission. Scott's servant-leadership style endeared his men to him in the highest risk of contexts and substantially underpinned the success of his missions.

JOHN HUNT, EVEREST 1953

Another man from a military background who managed high levels of complexity and risk in a civilian environment that was supported by a strong servant leadership style, was Colonel John Hunt, the leader of the 1953 expedition that conquered Everest.

No fewer than eleven major expeditions (nine of them British) in the 30 years prior to 1953 had failed to reach Everest's summit. Six climbers had made it to within 1,000 feet of the 29,000 foot summit, but none to the top. The distance was too far, the air too thin, the temperatures too cold, and the climbing too dangerous.

Hunt, recruited from the Army to lead the 1953 expedition, exhibited a number of strong servant leadership behaviors. Viewed through the lens of Van Dierendoncks' six key servant-leadership characteristics, a powerful servant-leadership picture can be seen.

Hunt Empowered Others

Hunt was a strong believer in the intrinsic value of every member of his team. He would regularly seek advice from the other climbers and told his top climbers that any one of them should be able to lead the expedition if the occasion arose. In his 1953 book on the expedition, Hunt wrote:

> *"It had seemed to me that it was unnecessary to set up a hierarchy of command and that there was always a danger of over-organizing. In any case, we always looked upon the leader's job as merely one among the many responsibilities which we shared out between us."*

Hunt Was Humble

Hunt was knighted for his role as leader of the expedition that conquered Everest, but he never lost sight of the positioning of the expedition's success as the success of a team, not of a leader. In fact, he went further in his public talks on this and couched the success of the 1953 expedition in the context of it being just one in a series of expeditions from different countries, each of which had built on the achievements of those that had gone earlier. He used the analogy of a relay race to describe this process in his book:

> *"... a relay race, in which each member of a team of runners hands the baton to the next at the end of his allotted span, until the race is finally run."*

Hunt Was Authentic

Throughout the expedition, Hunt was open about his decision-making processes and the importance of achieving the summit. No one's personal ambitions, neither his nor any of the climbers', should be allowed to take precedence over the team's collective goal. When the time came that his own ambition to be near the top of the mountain, at the 26,000 foot South Col when Hillary and Tenzing made their summit attempt, had to be put aside, Hunt didn't hesitate. It would have been a difficult decision for many leaders to make.

The problem was that Hunt had two roles to perform on the South Col on the day that Hillary and Tenzing were scheduled to attempt the summit. One was to oversee the launch of the Hillary and Tenzing summit assault itself, and the other was to provide logistical assistance to Bourdillon and Evans who were returning from their failed attempt the day before.

Consistent with Hunt's leadership philosophy that any of the summit climbers should be able to act as leader if the need arose, success didn't technically require Hunt to be on the South Col while Hillary and Tenzing were summiting. He did however want very much to be there, to be a part of that high-altitude team if it succeeded.

But the returning summit team of Bourdillon and Evans were in trouble. Bourdillon was ill and needed to descend quickly off the South Col before the rare air of the death zone killed him. Additional climbers were desperately needed to help Bourdillon descend from the South Col to a lower camp. Hunt could have selected a climber from Hillary and Tenzing's support team to do this, but that would break up a team that had been working together for some days and add risk to Hillary and Tenzing's attempt. If Hunt allocated no extra climber to the team helping Bourdillon down, Bourdillon's survival could be at risk.

Hunt did what he had to do. Their mission, and the safety of Bourdillon, must come before his own interest in being part of the excitement of the second assault. He descended with Bourdillon and monitored Hillary and Tenzing's assault by radio. This is classic servant leadership—service before self. Hillary and Tenzing successfully summited, and Bourdillon survived.

Hunt was being true to how he said things would work, sacrificing his interests for his team's interest. From the beginning, Hunt had said that anyone must be able to lead should the occasion arise, and nothing must stand in the way of the goal of the summit, or the safety of the climbers.

Hunt Was Interpersonally Accepting

The 1953 expedition was large and complex. New technologies, new environments, multiple ambiguities, multiple cultures, senior stakeholders, and a large team (12 European climbers and 28 Sherpa climbers on the mountain during the attempt itself) created an environment ripe for mistakes and failure. It was critical in the face of this that Hunt maintain an environment of support and trust in everyone's efforts. It was important that, should someone fail, they be supported to pick themselves up and continue on. If someone failed or slipped up, they needed to know that Hunt would continue to support them; that they would not be rejected.

During the expedition the climbers suffered multiple setbacks, but Hunt always assumed his men were doing their best. The first pair of the expedition's climbers to attempt the summit, Evans and Bourdillon, failed, in part, because of problems with their new closed-circuit oxygen sets. This was a huge disappointment for the two men, and a major risk for the expedition at the time—only one realistic summit opportunity (Hillary and Tenzing's) remained.

It would have been easy for Hunt to show disappointment at the failure of the first attempt but that was not Hunt's style. He had nothing but praise for Evans' and Bourdillon's efforts. He empathized strongly with them, writing:

> *"It was natural that disappointment should have been among their feelings, to get so near the ultimate goal—the fulfillment of a life's ambition—and then be denied it."*

And of the contribution that their summit attempt had made to the expedition's later success:

> *"They had (also) given us all, by their example, incalculable confidence in final victory."*

Hunt Provided Direction

The 1953 expedition's goal was the conquering of Everest. Hunt's focus was constantly on the goal: the amount of planning he put into it, the way he constantly tested his ideas with the other climbers, and the way he directed the different stages of the expedition; all of these ensured clarity of the expedition's goal and the way they were going to achieve it, throughout the five months they were away.

Eric Shipton, the leader of several Everest expeditions before Hunt, had been passed over as leader of the 1953 expedition, in part because the expedition's sponsoring committee (the Joint Himalayan Committee) felt he wasn't as passionate about the goal as the leader of such a major challenge should be. The committee felt Hunt had the passion for achieving the summit of Everest which Shipton lacked.

When Hunt was selecting climbers for the expedition he wanted his men to possess two qualities which, as he wrote, "do not easily coincide in any one mortal." Hunt needed (1) each and every climber chosen to "really want to get to the top" (and to each have) the 'Excelsior' spirit" (to push higher);

and, in contrast to this self-oriented drive to succeed, he needed (2) all climbers to possess a high degree of both selflessness and patience to ensure the unity of the team as a whole.

The climbers chosen needed to be selfless because, midway into the expedition, only four of them would be chosen (from a group of nearly 40) to make a final summit assault. The selection process would have to be utterly impersonal. It was important that all climbers understood this and supported Hunt's decisions whatever they were. This applied not only to the selection of the summit climbers, but also to the resourcing of the expedition's various interim stages—the construction of a complex logistics pyramid from the base of the mountain, all the way to its summit.

Hunt set these directions and made his choices consultatively and clearly, and as a consequence, enjoyed the full support of his team throughout the expedition.

Hunt Was a Steward

Perhaps the best evidence of Hunt as a *steward*—having as his focus the success of the mission on behalf of the greater organization (the Joint Himalayan Committee back in London) and on behalf of his men—was what his men said of him when success was achieved.

Hillary wrote of Hunt, indicating the expedition's spirit of cooperation and love they had for him:

> *"To see the unashamed joy spread over the tired, strained face of our gallant and determined leader was to me reward enough in itself."*

And later, on how Hillary felt as he greeted other expedition climbers further down the mountain:

> *"I felt more than ever before that very strong feeling of friendship and cooperation that had been the decisive factor throughout the expedition."*

Hunt's achievement in serving the needs of his men; building and maintaining their trust in such a high risk, complex undertaking; and in achieving the expedition's goal of conquering the mountain was significant—an example of the outcomes that a leadership style informed by a servant leadership approach can achieve.

Major and high-risk projects can benefit by looking for strong servant-leadership behaviors in the appointment of their senior leaders.

Image 13.2 Team photo of the 1953 Everest expedition after they had summited. Hillary is fifth from left at back, Hunt sixth from left, and Tenzing seventh from left. The photo has the feel of the strong team spirit that the expedition became known for (Photo courtesy of the Royal Geographical Society).

STRONG AND HUMBLE

Van Dierendonck's six servant-leadership characteristics show good alignment with the two differentiating characteristics of *Level-5* leaders identified by Jim Collins in his 2001 best-selling book, *Good to Great: Why Some Companies Make the Leap...and Others Don't.*

Level-5 in Collin's book refers to a five-level hierarchy of executive capabilities developed by Collins after a five-year research study looking at what it takes for good companies to become great. Level-5 leaders, sitting at the top of the hierarchy, are described as executives who *build enduring greatness.*

Collins' study started with 1,435 *good* companies and examined their performance over 40 years. From the group of good companies, Collins identified 11 that he classified as *great*. One of his selection criteria for *great* was that companies should have cumulative stock returns at least three times that of the market average over a period of 15 years (the cumulative stock returns of his final 11 companies averaged 6.9 times that of the general market).

Collins sought to understand what type of leadership it takes to turn a good company into a great company. Using the term *Level-5 Leader* to describe the leaders of his 11 good-to-great companies, Collins found they possessed two distinguishing traits. These were their (1) personal humility and (2) professional will.

The Level-5 leaders were also ambitious, but this ambition was first and foremost for the company, not for themselves. Collins also noted the importance of unselfish ambition. In an article on his website (www.jimcollins.com) Collins wrote: "we found that for leaders to make something great, their ambition has to be for the greatness of the work and the company, rather than themselves." In other words, service to others, not themselves.

Service to others ahead of one's self, humility, and will are all servant-leader behaviors. Collins' findings lend important support to the value of servant leadership.

NEUROLEADERSHIP AND COMPLEX PROJECTS

Servant-leader behaviors are of benefit to organizations, increasing team effectiveness and the ability of teams to perform difficult and complex tasks—abilities that are important in the world of modern project management. But what makes a leader a good manager of complexity? Powerful insights into the ability of individuals to manage complex situations are emerging from the field of neuroleadership.

Neuroleadership is a relatively new area of study enabled by the expanding field of neuroscience. Neuroscientific research, aided by the reducing cost of functional magnetic resonance imaging (fMRI) brain-scanning machines (the type of machine used for medical imaging of many types), has increased its focus in recent years on understanding how the human brain—the *healthy* human brain—works. Leadership researchers place people inside fMRI machines, ask them questions while they are lying down and relaxed, and take images of their brains to see which parts are working, stressed, or not working at all.

One of neuroscience's emergent findings is that our experiences of *social pain*—the feelings we experience when we feel a social disconnection with those around us (including our work places and or our bosses)—are processed by our brains in the same way as physical pain.

FIGHT OR FLIGHT

Naomi Eisenberger summarized some of the research in this area (including her own) in a 2012 paper entitled, *The Pain of Social Disconnection:*

Examining the Shared Neural Underpinnings of Physical and Social Pain. The origins of how the brain processes social pain go back to the earliest stages of our evolution. Infant mammals have always been dependent on their caregivers for nourishment, care, and protection. The social connection that infants have with their caregivers is important for their survival. As a consequence, humans have evolved such that threats to our social connections with others use the same pain signals in the brain that signify threats to the physical body—i.e., a social threat to a person is processed by the human brain as a survival threat—something to be escaped. It is felt in the same part of the brain that feels physical pain, because urgent action needs to be taken to address the threat.

Eisenberger notes that actual or even potential damage to our personal sense of social connection, or our sense of social value, can cause social pain. This can happen, for example, when we are devalued by someone, rejected, or negatively evaluated—events that are not uncommon in the workplace.

In a 2014 paper by Morelli, Torre, and Eisenberger entitled, *The Neural Bases of Feeling Understood and Not Understood*, the conclusions of the authors included that feelings of *not being understood* (associated with feelings of being socially distant from others) are also processed by the part of the brain related to social pain.

Social threats, because they are felt as pain, hold a significant potential to reduce our ability to manage complexity in the work environment—the work environment being a strongly social environment, and major projects more so. If we are in a fight-or-flight mode—in response to a physical or social threat—our cognitive and emotional functioning are not fully available to us. Valuable cognitive and emotional energy is diverted to the perceived threat. We become less able to evaluate and process the complex stakeholder and scoping problems that characterize large and high-risk projects. Our performance is reduced, and our risks, in an already high-risk context, go up.

Summarizing from the Eisenberger and Morelli et al. papers above, social pain, and the resulting reduced performance, can be caused by threats to our:

- Sense of social connection;
- Sense of social value; and
- Sense of being understood.

Leaders of teams need to be aware of how things they say or do affect the social needs of individuals within their teams. Social threats will trigger subconscious pain responses, which will reduce the ability of individuals to manage complexity.

A negative evaluation of a team member's performance, or perhaps an opportunity provided to one team member ahead of another, can quickly become social threats to those involved. Performance evaluations are a particularly high-risk area for triggering social pain-induced fight or flight responses. One high performer I spoke to summed this up as, "Tell me what I'm doing wrong, and I'm not listening. I'll try to make sure it's not noticeable, sure, but inside, I've turned your volume down."

Leaders, themselves, need to be aware of how their own social connections, sense of value, and feelings of being understood, can affect their own ability to manage complexity. These abilities are critical for the leaders of high-risk and complex projects. How do you as a leader feel, inside, when your social value is reduced?

Scott, Shackleton, and Hunt all worked hard to manage the social needs of individuals on their teams. They mostly did this without realizing they were doing it. They had partly learned these things from past leadership experiences, but it was also simply the type of leaders they were.

THINKING AND REFLECTING

Complex decision making works best when it is informed by our intuition.

Daniel Goleman summarized some of the neuroscience on this topic in his book, *The New Leaders: Transforming the Art of Leadership into the Science of Results*. Emotions associated with memories are stored deep down inside the brain in the amygdala. It is here that the brain continuously registers decision rules about what works and what doesn't. As Goleman put it, "It's not the verbal part of the brain that delivers the best course of action; it's the part that wields our feelings." And, "It takes the inner attunement of self-awareness to sense that message."

Our feeling for whether an action or situation is right or wrong, coming from a lifetime of experiences stored in the amygdala, can be tremendously valuable to complex decision making. The best leaders use it all the time. To effectively access this resource though, requires, as Goleman noted, an inner-attunement of self-awareness. Leaders who are able to think and reflect—developing their inner-attunement and self-awareness—are well-placed to access this resource.

In 2014 Paul McDonald and Yi-Yuan Tang published a paper entitled *Neuroscientific Insights into Management Development: Theoretical Propositions and Practical Implications*. McDonald and Tang's conclusions included that skill development in managers, including metacognition and mindfulness, based on an enhanced understanding of neurological structures and processes, has the potential to facilitate a new, more agile and adept, managerial generation. The type of generation needed to manage growing complexity in projects.

What Is Metacognition?

McDonald and Tang describe metacognition as the capacity to consciously think about what one is thinking. That is thinking not just about our thoughts in the moment, but about the factors that are driving our thoughts, including our assumptions and biases. Metacognition is a predictor of our capacity to learn from our experiences and the environments in which we find ourselves.

McDonald and Tang reference research that suggests that by learning selective attention (one of several metacognitive neural processes) managers can *better regulate their thinking in the face of overwhelming complexity*.

John Hunt's mission to conquer Everest, like many projects today, involved great complexity. Hunt's account of the expedition (published in his book *Ascent of Everest*) contains many technical descriptions of the expedition's activities, but also provides interesting insights into some of Hunt's thought processes. Regarding his use of metacognition, there is evidence that Hunt was someone who regularly reflected on his own thought processes.

As the expedition team began their trek through Nepal to Everest, Hunt reflected on his earlier worries about this phase of the trip—how it would be three weeks of *downtime* before they could begin the serious job of climbing the mountain. He wrote:

> *"In London I had fretted mentally at the prospect of having to spend nearly three weeks before we should be able to get to grips with the more serious part of the programme. Now, with seventeen days' journey ahead of us, the feeling of urgency was dispelled by the simple beauty of the countryside."*

And as they trekked toward the mountain:

> *"I think we were the more conscious of the happy present, in view of the more rugged prospect ahead of us; at least this was so in my case."*

When the expedition first sighted Everest, Hunt reflected on how their enjoyment of the sight of the mountain was greater as a group than it was for them individually. He wrote:

> *"The thrill was personal to each of us, but our joint excitement enhanced it."*

And then after spending a chapter describing the difficulties of the massive Khumbu icefall at the beginning of their climb, Hunt reflected on the amount of thinking and writing he had allocated to this challenge, first worrying that he had spent too much time on it, but then writing:

> *"If I have dwelt at some length on the Icefall, it is because it loomed so large in our activities on Everest and for so long a period…it would always be a source of anxiety."*

McDonald and Tang also concluded that the skill of *mindfulness* is important.

What Is Mindfulness?

Mindfulness is described as having a sense of self-awareness and self-observation. It can be developed by learning to focus one's attention, a common form of which is meditation. The ability of managers to *attend to the present* is a valuable skill for the managers of today's complex project environments. Our minds are constantly being bombarded by streams of thoughts, questions, tasks, issues, and risks. Focusing on one thing at a time—working on one thing at a time—is critical in this environment. *Multitasking* (or rapid serial tasking, as it is sometimes known) in a complex environment is not a good thing. It reduces the ability to picture complex information relationships and to manage ambiguities.

John Hunt regularly took time to step back and reflect on the environment around him, a useful, mindfulness skill. In the early stages of his team's acclimatization and familiarization training, on the lower slopes of Everest, Hunt had much to worry about. Still he found time to pause and reflect on the beauty of their location, writing (within a book filled with technical activity descriptions, and at a time when leaders were expected to be more staunch than sensitive):

> *"Around the blazing logs that night, with the stars winking and the air frosty, there was an atmosphere of relaxation and simple happiness…"*

Modern leaders and managers of business today are being encouraged by neuroscience researchers to pause during their working days (and before and after those working days) and to practice mindfulness exercises. These exercises are stated to improve our ability to break away from the chaos of information which bombards all of us in busy jobs.

Even a little practice of mindfulness can greatly improve a manager's ability to stay focused on tasks of importance as they arise, to discard distracting thoughts that are not important, and to be able to step back and observe patterns which might signal the nub of an issue; the same patterns that are built up from multiple life experiences stored in the amygdala, and which require an inner attunement of self-awareness for them to be accessed.

By developing our skills of mindfulness and metacognition, including selective attention, we enhance our ability to manage complexity further. We create space in our minds for clearer thinking and intuition to come together to more effectively solve the complex problems we daily face.

KEY LEARNINGS ON STRONG HUMBLE SERVANTS

1. Servant leadership is a style of leadership that emphasizes the needs of the leader's followers. It can add significant value to high-risk and complex projects.
2. Servant leadership, with its ability to build trust, unify culture, and encourage tolerance of mistakes, can boost organizational knowledge transfer—and lever the 35% improvement in project outcomes that effective knowledge transfer has been associated with.
3. Servant leadership is well suited for projects because it is relatively easily established as a subculture within culturally different, higher-level organizations.
4. Personal humility and professional will are leadership traits that have been correlated with Level-5 Leaders—leaders who have shifted companies from just being good, to being great. Humility and will are also servant leader behaviors.
5. Social pain is processed in the same part of the brain as physical pain. The fight-or-flight response that it triggers can reduce our ability to manage complexity. Social pain can be caused by threats to our:
   - Sense of social connection;
   - Sense of social value; and
   - Sense of being understood.
6. Leaders who inadvertently cause social pain for team members reduce team performance. Leaders who have social pain triggered in themselves have a reduced ability to manage complexity and risk in projects.
7. In combination with intelligence and planning, intuition—the wisdom of experience stored as emotions in the amygdala of the brain—is a powerful tool for managing complexity, but requires an

inner attunement of self-awareness for the best course of action to be sensed.

8. Metacognition is the capacity to think consciously about what one is thinking. Selective attention is one of several metacognitive neural processes. Practicing metacognition and selective attention specifically, can help managers better regulate thinking in the face of over-whelming complexity.

9. Mindfulness is the capacity to be self-aware and to self-observe. Practicing mindfulness (which includes meditation) can greatly increase the ability of leaders to focus on tasks of importance as they arise, to increase their capacity to observe patterns, and to access experience-based intuition.

THE IDEAL LEADER FOR A COMPLEX PROJECT?

This chapter, and several of the preceding chapters, have discussed leadership attributes which recent research strongly suggests are correlated with success in managing complex and high-risk projects. These attributes are also correlated with the leaders of complex and high-risk projects who have succeeded in some of the highest-risk contexts we know: *Heroic Age* Antarctica and 1950's Mount Everest. Modern managers of complexity can learn much from the stories and styles of leaders from those places and times.

Scott of the Antarctic and Hunt of Everest were ideally suited for the logistically challenging, large-scale, high-risk, high-profile, multi-ambiguity challenges with which they were tasked. They were both:

- Formally trained by the military at a senior level and experienced with the processes and structures required of large programs
- Leaders who had ambitions and ethos aligned with the ambitions and ethos of the steering-committees they served
- Heroic leaders who could make things happen, and could maintain support from stakeholders upward, as well as downward—in spite of the organizational and environmental constraints that surrounded them
- Servant leaders; it was in their DNA that they wanted to serve the men they worked with—they recognized it was their teams, not them, who were the reasons for their successes
- Thinkers and reflectors; they thought about how they thought, they tested ideas with others, and they took time to reflect on the beauty of the places they worked in

The following is a summary of the key leadership attributes covered in the last few chapters. Project owners and managers should consider the extent of these behaviors in their own high-risk projects, and in the recruitment of the senior managers who may be called upon to lead or participate in projects which are complex.

1. The manager is experienced with the processes and structures of high-risk projects
2. The manager has done this type of project before (or as close to this type of project as is possible with a project that hasn't been done before allows)
3. The manager's ambitions and ethos aligns with the ambitions and ethos of the project's steering committee
4. The manager demonstrates *heroic manager* attributes: the ability to manage multiple stakeholders, significant authority influences, ambiguities (scope, technology, and resourcing), and can succeed in spite of sometimes severe organizational constraints
5. The manager takes a servant leadership approach: they empower, they are humble, they are authentic, they are interpersonally accepting, they provide direction, and they are stewards
6. The manager's style is sensitive to, and mitigates, social-threat risks to team members
7. The manager practices (consciously or unconsciously) metacognition and mindfulness

Scoring these for high-risk projects is a subjective process. It's the process of reflecting on and discussing these behaviors, however, rather than the scores themselves, which provides value. Table 13.1 summarizes these behaviors, and provides a template for readers to use to explore the complexity leadership abilities of themselves and those around them.

The final chapter of this book summarizes the lessons of risk appetite, capabilities, and leadership that the earlier chapters have explored, then integrates them within a single model—a gestalt where the whole is much greater than the sum of the individual parts.

It is our failure to address these things *as a whole* which has created the global situation we currently have; one where galloping complexity and struggling capabilities result in nearly one in every three projects failing, and another one in three under-performing—a situation unchanged for 20 years, in-spite of massive investments in P3M capability building.

Table 13.1   Assessing leadership potential for complex projects

Leadership Match Assessment for Complex Projects			
Scores out of ten. Ten is high (an excellent performer), one is low (the attribute is not present in the leader)	**Scott**	**Hunt**	**Your Project**
Understands/experienced with big project processes and structures	8	8	
Has done this type of project before (or as close to context as possible)	6	6	
Ambitions and ethos align with the steering committee's	8	8	
Is a heroic manager	9	9	
Exhibits the characteristics of a servant leader	9	9	
Is sensitive to, and mitigates, social threats to team members	8	8	
Is a thinker and reflector	7	7	
TOTAL (out of 70)	**55**	**55**	

By using the tools this book provides, organizations will be able to sustainably strengthen project management performance—permanently reducing failure and increasing benefits delivery.

Web Added Value™

14

Epilogue

This book was written to solve a problem, the problem being that project failure rates, globally, are unchanged after 20 years of investment in project management capabilities.

Our projects are delivering more value today than they ever used to. We are more automated and more connected, and enjoy more wealth as a society than ever before—yet one in three of our projects fail, and another one in three struggle.

Can we have the greater connectedness and value that our projects provide us, and have lower failure rates at the same time? With the cash savings and faster business growth this would provide?—absolutely we can. By understanding and managing the risk appetite in our projects, increasing the maturity of our capabilities, and strengthening our leadership we can change our project management risk culture. Changing that culture is the key to our climbing higher *and* safer.

Figure 14.1 presents a schematic summary of the chapters that comprise *Project Management, Denial, and the Death Zone (PDDZ)*, the tools and learnings they contain, and the areas of risk culture they address.

The problem of the constancy of failure was described in the case examples provided in Chapters 1 and 2. Simply, when people are provided with new or strengthened capabilities, they don't climb safer, they climb higher.

Chapters 3 and 4 explained the cause of the problem. Risk homeostasis is the natural tendency for all people, and organizations, to operate with constant levels of risk, and to take action to return to those levels of risk if something happens that increases or decreases risk comfort. Risk appetite is the term used to describe the different levels of comfort that people

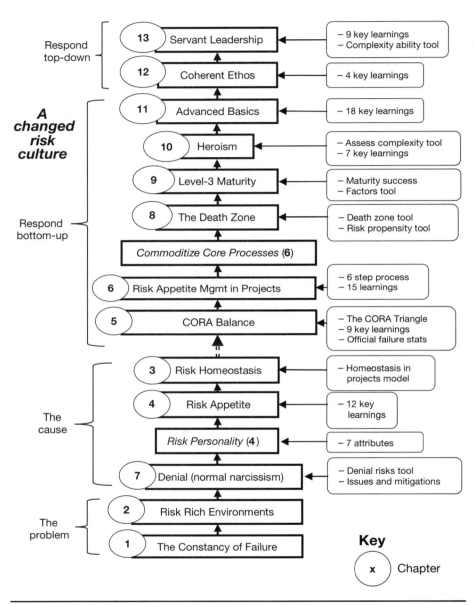

Figure 14.1   Schematic summary of chapters

have with different levels of risk in different situations. Not just people, but whole organizations. Importantly, risk appetite in organizations is not the same as risk appetite in projects.

Risk appetite, unless it is set using some kind of managed process first, is determined by our risk personalities. A number of factors determine our risk personalities. One of these is normal narcissism.

Chapter 7 looked at normal narcissism—what it is, the problems it causes, and what can be done to manage it. Normal narcissism (ego) is something we all have a little bit of, but the higher risk the project, the greater the risk that normal narcissism can create for it.

Critical to changing risk culture is understanding risk appetite's relationship to capability improvement, and its relationship to the scale and complexity of the outcomes we seek. These relationships were presented in Chapter 5 as the CORA triangle.

The CORA model (capabilities, outcomes, risk appetite) emphasized the importance of all three elements being managed together.

Chapter 6 addressed risk appetite in projects directly, and provided a risk appetite in-projects management process for readers to use. A minimum set of commoditized core processes was stressed as being an important first step in risk culture change.

Keeping projects out of the death zone was the subject of Chapter 8; a minimum level of capability maturity—Level-3—was stressed in Chapter 9; and the value of heroism to complex programs—on top of maturity, not instead of it—was stressed in Chapter 10.

Advanced basics, particularly new thinking around early stage business cases, and gated life cycle quality assurance reviews were covered in Chapter 11.

The last two chapters of the book provided a top-down response. Chapter 12 introduced the circle of project management ethos and its importance in reducing risk through strengthening team vision, performance, and leadership fit.

And Chapter 13, *Strong Humble Servants*, presented an overview of servant leadership and its ability to reduce risks and improve team effectiveness—and of neuroscientific insights into the importance of social threat management by leaders, and the power of metacognition and reflection to increase our personal abilities to manage complexity.

As was noted in the introduction, the book has taken an example and case-based approach because of the ability of this style of learning to provide insights into complex relationships.

Antarctica and Everest are risk-rich, leadership-rich, and lesson-rich environments. The Antarctic explorers of the *Heroic Age*, and the leaders and climbers of the 1922, 1924, and 1953 Everest expeditions, worked with levels of complexity and risk that would challenge most project managers today. Complexity and risk exist in the multiple ambiguities of scope, technology, stakeholders, and outcome expectations.

We can learn much from the leaders of those environments in high-risk situations, their behaviors, failures, and successes. What worked for them— and what didn't—correlates strongly with modern day academic research on leadership, risk taking, and project management.

The material discussed in these chapters covers areas that many owners and managers of high-risk projects will not be aware of. Readers are encouraged to use the references provided in the bibliography to explore these areas further. A number of these contain insights on leadership and complexity, leader-follower behaviors, and the human mind that was not possible to include in this book.

Image 14.1   Mount Everest today (Photo: Guy Cotter, Adventure Consultants).

When we know the drivers of failure in projects—the psychological drivers at the foundation level, not the mechanical things that people do wrong (there is no shortage of internet lists and books on these to be found)—we have the opportunity to address them.

Gerald Wilde, the father of modern day risk homeostasis theory, once wrote to me, "May the risks in your life be like the salt in your soup, not too much and not too little." May I say something similar of your projects—may they have enough risks to accelerate your business forward, but few enough that, using the right approaches, you still succeed.

And, last but not least, if you are ever given the opportunity to climb high on a mountain, do it safer first.

Appendix I: Glossary

CFIT: Controlled flight into terrain.

CORA: Capabilities, outcomes (size, risk, and complexity), and risk appetite.

Commodification: The transformation of something into a commercial commodity.

Death zone (Everest): The top part of the mountain—from 26,000 feet (8,000 meters) to 29,000 feet (8,848 meters)—where the air is so thin the human body begins to die.

Death zone (metaphor): A zone of risk-taking in project management where the outcomes sought exceed the organization's abilities to achieve them by a significant amount. Failure is common.

Denial (projects): A refusal to accept that the capabilities of an individual or organization are insufficient for the task or project at hand, or a refusal to accept that the risks of proceeding are dangerously high. Having (largely) as its origins the defense of the ego (*normal narcissism*).

Edema (oedema): A condition characterized by an excess of watery fluid collecting in the cavities or tissues of the body. At altitude, the brain and lungs are at particular risk, and the condition, unless quickly treated, can be fatal.

EPMO: Enterprise project management (or portfolio management) office.

Heaven and earther: An expression referring to something very important. Something that the people in control must *move heaven and earth* to ensure happens (or does not happen). For example, *"What are your project's heaven and earthers?"*

ICT-EB: Information and communications technology (ICT)-enabled business (EB). For example, "ICT-EB projects are particularly high risk." (Sometimes shortened to IT or ICT project.)

IQA: Independent quality assurance.

JASART: Joint Antarctic (USA-NZ) Search and Rescue Team.

KPI: Key performance indicator.

Loss zone (metaphor): A zone of risk taking in project management where the outcomes sought partly exceed the organization's abilities to achieve them—resulting in a level of failure.

MSP®: Managing Successful Programmes. Originally a British government methodology (the IP is now managed by Axelos) developed to support the scoping and delivery of complex change programs. It is sometimes called the program management version of PRINCE2®, but with a strong focus on business change and two levels of governance.

NPV: Net present value. The net financial value of a project over the life of its delivery and the life of the assets it delivers. The annual cash expenses are subtracted from the annual cash benefits for each year over the whole-of-life-cycle, with an annual risk-based discount rate applied.

OGC: Office of Government Commerce.

OPM3®: Organizational Project Management Maturity Model; a project management maturity model developed by PMI.

Outcome-maximize: People outcome-maximize when they attempt more with new capabilities, rather than reducing their risks. They climb higher, not safer.

P3M: Portfolio, program, and project management.

P3M3®: Portfolio, Programme, and Project Management Maturity Model; a project management maturity model developed by the British government (the IP is now managed by Axelos).

PDDZ: *Project Management, Denial, and the Death Zone.*

PMI®: Project Management Institute.

PMBOK® Guide: *Project Management Body of Knowledge* developed by PMI. Is also an American National Standard (ANSI).

PMO: Project management office or program management office.

PRINCE2®: PRojects IN Controlled Environments, version 2; a project management methodology developed by the British government, with IP now managed by Axelos.

Project (specific): A temporary endeavor undertaken to create a unique product, service, or result (PMI).

Project (general): Used to signify either a project or a program.

Program: A group of related projects managed in a coordinated way to obtain benefits and control not available when managing them individually (PMI).

Portfolio: A collection of programs, projects, and/or operations managed as a group. The components of a portfolio may not necessarily be interdependent or even related—but they are managed together as a group to achieve strategic objectives (PMI).

Project management maturity: The level or strength of an organization's project management capabilities.

Risk appetite: The amount and type of risk that a person or an organization is comfortable taking in different areas of their life or business. (*See also* risk homeostasis.)

Risk appetite rebalancing: The tendency for risk appetite to rebalance itself after a change in risk comfort levels within an organization (driven by risk homeostasis).

Risk envelope: The boundary that separates risks that are being managed largely in-control from risks that are being managed largely out-of-control.

Risk homeostasis: The tendency for people and organizations to reduce their risks when they are uncomfortable with the perceived risk levels they are experiencing—and conversely, to increase their risks when they are comfortable with the perceived risk levels that they are experiencing. (*See also* risk appetite.)

SAREX: Search and rescue exercise.

SMART: Simple, measurable, achievable, realistic, and time-bound.

Sponsor: The person directly accountable for the success of a project's business outcomes. For good governance to apply, the sponsor must have control of the project's resources, and an ownership stake in its benefits and risks. They should also be actively engaged in the project's leadership.

SRO: Senior responsible owner—a more specific term for sponsor.

Strategic misrepresentation: A significant exaggeration, or a direct lie, regarding a project's cost, schedule, scope, or risk status.

Sunk ego: The subconscious investment of one's ego, or personal reputation, in project decisions that one has made or has been involved in.

Appendix II: Bibliography

Allsop, Mike. *High Altitude*. Allen & Unwin, 2013.

Avery, Grant. Neuroscience and the Servant Leader: Reducing the Risks of Complex Projects. *PMI Global Congress North America*, October 2015.

Band, George. *Everest: 50 Years on Top of the World*. Harper Collins, 2003.

Barbuto, J. E., Jr., R. K. Gottfredson, and T. P. Searle. "An Examination of Emotional Intelligence as an Antecedent of Servant Leadership." *Journal of Leadership & Organizational Studies*, 2014.

Bourne, Lynda. "The Future of the Hero Project Manager." *PMI Global Conference EMEA*, May 2010. www.mosaicprojects.com.au.

Browne, Lord, of Madingley. Getting a Grip: How to Improve Major Project Execution and Control in Government, 2013. www.gov.uk.

Campbell, Andrew, and Sally Yeun. Creating a Sense of Mission. *Long Range Planning*, Vol 24, No 4, 1991.

Campbell, K.W., A. S. Goodie, and J. D Foster. Narcissism, Confidence, and Risk Attitude. *Journal of Behavioral Decision Making* (2004) 17.

Cherry-Garrard, Apsley. *The Worst Journey in the World*. Carroll & Graf edition 2nd printing, 1992.

Collins, Jim. *Good to Great: Why Some Companies Make the Leap...and Others Don't*. Harper Business, 2001.

Conefrey, Mick. *Everest 1953: The Epic Story of the First Ascent*. One World Publications, 2012.

Cummings, Stephen. *Recreating Strategy*. Sage, London, 2002.

Cummings, Stephen, and Duncan Angwin. *The Strategy Builder: How to Create and Communicate More Effective Strategies*. John Wiley & Sons, 2015.

Department of Treasury and Finance. Investment Management Standard. *Department of Treasury and Finance, Victoria, Australia*, 2014. www.dtf.vic.gov.au.

Department of Treasury and Finance. 16 Question Checklist. *Department of Treasury and Finance, Victoria, Australia*, 2014. www.dtf.vic.gov.au.

Elmes, Michael, and David Barry. "Deliverance, Denial, and the Death Zone: A Study of Narcissism and Regression in the May 1996 Everest Climbing Disaster." *Journal of Applied Behavioral Science* V35, No. 2. 1999.

Eisenberger, Naomi. "The pain of social disconnection: examining the shared neural underpinnings of physical and social pain." *Nature Reviews Neuroscience (online May 3, 2012)*, Macmillan Publishers Limited.

ESI. Top 10 Project Management Trends for 2014. www.esi-intl.com.

Fiennes, Ranulph. *Beyond the Limits: The Lessons Learned From a Lifetime's Adventures*. Little, Brown & Company, 2000, reprinted 2009.

———. *Captain Scott*. Hodder & Stoughton, 2003.

———. *Cold: Extreme Adventures at the Lowest Temperatures on Earth*. Simon & Schuster, 2013.

Foster, J. D., J. W. Shenesey, and J. S. Goff. "Why Do Narcissists Take More Risks? Testing the Roles of Perceived Risks and Benefits of Risky Behaviors." *Personality and Individual Differences* (2009) 47.

Gawande, Atul. *The Check List Manifesto: How to Get Things Right*. Profile Books Ltd., 2010.

Gauld, R. and S. Goldfinch. *Dangerous Enthusiasms: E-government, Computer Failure and Information System Development*. Otago University Press, 2006.

Gladwell, Malcolm. "Blowup." *The New Yorker*, (January 22, 1996) 32.

Goleman, Daniel. *The New Leaders: Transforming the Art of Leadership into the Science of Results*. Time Warner Books UK, 2002.

Greenleaf, Robert. *Servant Leadership: A Journey into the Nature of Legitimate Power and Greatness*. Paulist Press, 1977 (2002, 25th Anniversary Edition).

———. *The Power of Servant Leadership*. Berrett-Koehler Publishers, Inc., 1998.

Grijalva, Emily, and Peter D. Harms. *Narcissism: An Integrative Synthesis and Dominance Complementarity Model*. P.D. Harms Publications, 2014.

Hall, Lincoln. *Dead Lucky: Life after Death on Mount Everest*. Random House, 2007.

Heil, Nick. *Dark Summit: The True Story of Everest's Most Controversial Season*. Penguin Group, 2008.

Helmsman Institute. Why Project Complexity Matters, 2012. www.apmg-international.com.

———. Helmsman Guide to Complexity, 2009. www.helmsman-international.com.

Hemmleb, Jochen, Eric R. Simonson, and Larry A. Johnson. *Ghosts of Everest: The Search for Mallory and Irvine*. The Mountaineers Books, 1999.

Herman, Arthur. *To Rule the Waves: How the British Navy Shaped the Modern World*. Harper Collins, 2004.

Hillary, Edmund. *Nothing Venture, Nothing Win.* Hodder and Stoughton, 1975.

———. Wrong to let climber die, says Sir Edmund. *The New Zealand Herald,* 2006. http://www.nzherald.co.nz/nz/news/article.cfm?c_id=1&objectid=10383276.

Hillson, David and Ruth Murray-Webster. Shedding Light on Risk Appetite, 2011. www.risk-doctor.com.

———. *A Short Guide to Risk Appetite.* Aldershot, UK: Gower, 2012.

Howarth, David. British Sea Power: *How Britain Became Sovereign of the Seas.* Carroll & Graf, 2003.

Hoyland, Graham. *Last Hours on Everest.* Collins, 2013.

Hunt, John. *The Ascent of Everest.* Hodder and Stoughton, 1953.

Huntford, Roland. *Scott and Amundsen.* Hodder and Stoughton, 1979.

IBM. Capitalizing on Complexity: Insights from the Global Chief Executive Officer Study, 2010. www.ibm.com.

Inglis, Mark. *Legs on Everest.* Random House, 2006.

Institute of Risk Management. Risk Appetite & Tolerance Guidance Paper, 2011. www.theirm.org.

International Organization for Standardization. ISO 31000:2009, Risk Management—Principles and Guidelines, 2009. www.iso.org.

International Organization for Standardization. ISO Guide 73:2009 Risk Management—Vocabulary, 2009. www.iso.org.

International Organization for Standardization. (2009). ISO/IEC 31010:2009 Risk Management—Risk Assessment Techniques. www.iso.org.

Jarman, Rod. "Psychopathy as a Phenomenon of Interest in Information Systems Research." *Proceedings of the 21st European Conference on Information Systems,* 2013.

Kahneman, D. *Thinking, Fast and Slow.* Penguin Group, 2011.

Kets de Vries, Manfred F. R. 2003/92/ENT, Organizations on the Couch: A Clinical Perspective on Organizational Dynamics. www.insead.edu.

KPMG. Global IT Project Management Study: How Committed Are You? 2005. www.kpmg.com.

———. Confronting Complexity: How Business Globally Is Taking on the Challenges and Opportunities, 2011. www.kpmg.com.

Krakauer, Jon. *Into Thin Air.* Random House, 1997.

Larson, Edward J. *An Empire of Ice: Scott, Shackleton, and the Heroic Age of Antarctic Science.* Yale University Press, 2011.

Laub, J. A. "Assessing the Servant Organization; Development of the Organizational Leadership Assessment (OLA) Model." *Dissertation Abstracts International*, 60 (02): 308A, 1999.

Lessard, D., V. Sakhrani, and R. Miller. "House of Project Complexity—Understanding Complexity in Large Infrastructure Projects, Proceedings." *Engineering Project Organization Conference 2013*.

Lowe, George. *Letters from Everest*. HarperCollins NZ, 2013.

Major Projects Association. "Project Initiation—Making the Right Start." *Highlights from the Major Projects Association event held on February 25, 2014*. www.majorprojects.org.

McDonald, Paul and Yi-Yuan Tang. "Neuroscientific Insights Into Management Development: Theoretical Propositions and Practical Implications." *Group & Organization Management*, 2014.

Morelli, A., J. Torre, and N. Eisenberger. The Neural Bases of Feeling Understood and Not Understood. *Oxford University Press*, 2014. www.sanlab .psych.ucla.edu.

Morrell, Margot. *Shackleton's Way*. Nicholas Brealey, 2001.

Parris, D. L., and J. W. Peachey. A systematic literature review of servant leadership theory in organizational contexts. *Journal of Business Ethics*, (2013) 113, 377–393.

PricewaterhouseCoopers LLP (PwC). Insights and Trends: Current Portfolio, Programme, and Project Management Practices: The third global survey on the current state of project management, 2012. www.pwc.com.

Project Management Institute. *PMI's Pulse of the Profession®: PMO Frameworks*, 2013. www.pmi.org.

———. *PMI's Pulse of the Profession™: The High Cost of Low Performance*, 2013. www.pmi.org.

———. *Pulse of the Profession™: The High Cost of Low Performance*, 2014. www.pmi.org.

———. *Pulse of the Profession™: In-Depth Report: Navigating Complexity*, 2013. www.pmi.org.

———. *Pulse of the Profession™: Capturing the Value of Project Management*, 2015. www.pmi.org.

———. *Pulse of the Profession™: Capturing the Value of Project Management through Knowledge Transfer*, 2015. www.pmi.org.

Raskin, Robert and Howard Terry. "A principal-components analysis of the Narcissistic Personality Inventory and further evidence of its construct validity." *Journal of Personality and Social Psychology*, Vol 54(5), May 1988.

Ripley, Amanda. *The Unthinkable*, Random House Books, 2009.

Rose, Kenneth H. *Project Quality Management: Why, What and How*, Second Edition. J. Ross Publishing, 2014.

Rosenthal, S. A., and T. L. Pittinsky. Narcissistic Leadership. *Leadership Quarterly*. (2006) 17.

Royal Geographical Society, with Stephen Venables. *Everest Summit of Achievement*. Allen & Unwin, 2013.

Seaver, George. *Edward Wilson of the Antarctic*. John Murray, 1934.

Serrador, Pedro, and Rodney Turner. The Relationship Between Project Success and Project Efficiency. *Project Management Journal, Vol 46, No. 1*, 2015.

Scott, Robert Falcon. (1968 Twelfth printing). *Scott's Last Expedition—The Personal Journals of Captain R. F. Scott, C.V.O., R.N., on his Journey to the South Pole*. John Murray Ltd., 1913.

Sedikides, Constantine, et al. "Are normal narcissists psychologically healthy?: self-esteem matters." *Journal of Personality and Social Psychology, 2004, Vol. 87, No. 3*, 2005.

Solomon, Susan. *The Coldest March: Scott's fatal Antarctic expedition*. Yale University Press, 2001.

The Standish Group International. *The CHAOS Report*, 1994. www .standishgroup.com.

The Standish Group International. *The CHAOS Manifesto*, 2013. "Think Big, Act Small." www.standishgroup.com.

Thomas, Janice and Mark Mullaly. *Researching the Value of Project Management*. The Project Management Institute, 2008.

Van Dierendonck, D. Servant leadership: A Review and Synthesis. *Journal of Management*, (2011) 37, 1228–1261.

Wilde, Gerald J.S. *Target Risk 3: Risk Homeostasis in Everyday Life*, Digital Edition [Version 2014.03.20]. www.riskhomeostasis.org.

Index